WISDOM TRADITION

About the Editors

Prof. Sebastian Velassery is a professor of Philosophy in Panjab University, Chandigarh. Presently, he is a visiting professor at Jawaharlal Nehru University, New Delhi. He is awarded National Emeritus Professor by UGC in the subject of philosophy for the year 2017. He has published 10 books and more than six dozens of research articles in various national/international journal and anthologies. His latest book "Casteism and the Ideology of Exclusion: A Post-Script on the Humanization of Indian Societies" was released in April, 2016.

Dr. K. Gopathan Pillai is a Sr. Fellow in Santhigiri Institute of Culture & Human Development, Santhigiri Research Foundation, Santhigiri Ashram, Thiruvananthapuram, and Kerala. He has published several papers in research journals and authored two books and edited one.

WISDOM TRADITION

Cultural Creativity and Social Change

Edited by
Sebastian Velassery
K. Gopinathan Pillai

CONCEPT PUBLISHING COMPANY PVT. LTD.
NEW DELHI-110059

ISBN-13: 978-93-88937-36-8

First Published 2020

Published and Printed by

Concept Since 1974

Concept Publishing Company Pvt. Ltd.
A/15-16, Commercial Block, Mohan Garden,
New Delhi-110059 (INDIA)
T : 91 11 25351460, 91 11 25351794
E : publishing@conceptpub.com; *W* : www.conceptpub.com

Cataloging in Publication Data--Courtesy: D.K. Agencies (P) Ltd. <docinfo@dkagencies.com>

Wisdom tradition : cultural creativity and social change / editors, Sebastian Velassery, K. Gopinathan Pillai. Vadackumchery, James, author.

pages cm

"The present volume has evolved out of the papers presented in seminars sponsored by the Indian Council of Philosophical Research (ICPR) and Ministry of Culture, New Delhi at different parts of India"—Acknowledgements.

Includes bibliographical references and index.

ISBN 9789388937368

1. India—Civilization—Congresses. 2. Social change —India—Congresses. 3. Hinduism and social problems—India—Congresses. 4. Self-knowledge, Theory of—Congresses. 5. Spiritual life—Hinduism—Congresses. I. Velasery, Sebastian, 1953- editor. II. Gopinathan Pillai, K. (Krishna Kurup), 1955- editor. III. Indian Council of Philosophical Research, sponsoring body. IV. India. Ministry of Culture, sponsoring body.

LCC DS423.W57 2019 | DDC 954 23

Preface

The sustainability of India as a country, in spite of the amazing cultural diversity, social complexity and successive onslaughts and encroachments into the cultural fabric and economy, has been a puzzle to the world. Sanathana dharma which drew its sustenance from atmajnana tradition or wisdom tradition was universalistic and inclusive. It was beyond religion, caste, race and gender and sought to unify people around One Supreme truth.

The eclipse of Sanathana dharma at a particular phase in India's spiritual history seems to have arrested spiritual progression and social evolution of India. The gradual emergence of belief systems and practices contrary to dharma of the concerned Yugas landed India into the vicious cycle of caste system giving way to social disintegration, cultural decay and disunity. The long narratives of relentless sacrifice and efforts of myriad of seers to rectify the deviations and distortions in the Hindu religion and to restore dharma bespeak another story of their unfulfilled missions. The present work is an effort to bring into limelight the relevance and importance of wisdom tradition of India to raise people beyond caste, religion and gender and to achieve unity and righteousness.

In the present volume an attempt is made to revisit and rediscover the core teaching, practices and transforming presence of great seers in the intervening intervals in India's turbulent social and cultural history who sought to restore socio-cultural momentum by defossilising tradition and activating social change. From Adi Sankara to Narayana Guru, one could discerns how the successive Guru Paramparas strived to bring about an egalitarian social order by eliminating dehumanizing social evils, superstitious belief systems and practices. It was an irony to find that despite the periodic awakening and dynamism their mission had created, human life and social fabric could not be cleansed of the inherited impurities and social evils. However, the revelatory spirituality of Navajyothisree Karunakara Guru and a way of life founded by him in accordance with the dharma of the present Yuga seems to have marked a fundamental shift from the existing paradigm of spirituality and haves opened up space for fresh and fruitful dialogue on spirituality, religion, culture and society. We do believe the present volume which is the first in the series on Guru Tradition of India that we propose to bring out will generate fresh thinking and initiative in ushering in cultural renaissance in India.

Sebastian Velassery
K. Gopinathan Pillai

Acknowledgements

The present volume has evolved out of the papers presented in seminars sponsored by the Indian Council of Philosophical Research (ICPR) and Ministry of Culture, New Delhi at different parts of India. We express our gratitude to ICPR and Ministry of Culture as well as different contributors to this volume. We would like to express our gratitude especially to Prof. Mrinal Miri and Prof. S.R. Bhatt as they have been instrumental in allocating funds for these seminars as Chairpersons of ICPR. Let us express our immense gratitude to all the Sanyasis in Santhigiri Ashram, Prof. Rajasekharan Nayar and Janardhana Menon and many others who have been working towards the noble cause of finding out Indian spirituality as Dharma which goes beyond the confines of religions.

Sebastian Velassery
K. Gopinathan Pillai

Contents

The Contributors

Prof. C.D. Sebastian is a professor of Philosophy in IIT Mumbai. He has done commendable research work in Buddhism. He has published several books and contributed research articles in various journals.

Dr. C.V. Babu is Asst. Professor in the Zakir Husain College, Delhi University. He has completed an international project and published several research papers in journals. He has published two books.

Dr. K. Gopathan Pillai is a Sr. Fellow in Santhigiri Institute of Culture & Human Development, Santhigiri Research Foundation, Santhigiri Ashram, Thiruvananthapuram, and Kerala. He has published several papers in research journals and authored two books and edited one.

Prof. Mrinal Miri, Former Nominated Member of the Rajya Sabha, Ex-Vice Chancellor of North Eastern Hill University, Ex-Director of Indian Institute of Advanced Study and Ex-Chairman of Indian Council of Philosophical Research, is a philosopher at the core. He has been awarded a Padma Bhushan for his contribution in the field of education and literature. He was a member of the National Advisory Council established by the Manmohan Singh UPA I government. He was also a member of the council set up for the implementation of RTE Act also called as NAC. He has published many articles in various national and international journals. Miri's original thoughts on moral philosophy and tribal philosophy is widely acclaimed in Indian and western philosophical circles. His latest books are *Identity and Moral Life*, *Philosophy and Education*; both published by Oxford University Press, India.

Mr. P. Chandramohan was Curator in the Nehru Memorial Museum, New Delhi. His strong grounding in history, especially in the social and intellectual history of India is evident from his several writings. He has published several research articles and three books.

Prof. P.I. Devarajan is professor in the Payyanuur Centere of the Sri Sankara University of Sanskrit, Kalady. He was awarded ICPR Sr. Fellowship and he has contributed chapters to several books in philosophy. He has published many papers in research journals and authored two books.

Prof. Panneer Selvam was a professor in Madras University. He was a National Fellow of ICPR and was visitng professor in a couple of foreign universities. He has contributed several articles in national and International research journals and authored a few books in philosophy.

Dr. Reena Thakur Patra is a Research Associate in the Philosophy Department in Panjab University, She has published many papers in national and international journals.

Dr. Saji Varghese is an Associate Professor in the Lady Keynes College, Shillong. He is currently engaged in an international project and has published several papers in research journals. There are three books to his credit.

Prof. Sebastian Velassery is a professor of Philosophy in Panjab University, Chandigarh. Presently, he is a visiting professor at Jawaharlal Nehru University, New Delhi. He is awarded National Emeritus Professor by UGC in the subject of philosophy for the year 2017. He has published 10 books and more than six dozens of research articles in various national/ international journal and anthologies. His latest book "Casteism and the Ideology of Exclusion: A Post-Script on the Humanization of Indian Societies" was released in April, 2016.

Swami Navanavma Jnana Thapaswi, a member of Santhigiri Sannyasa Sangh and member of Director Board has published several spiritually and philosophically illuminating articles in Santhigiri Publications. He has represented Santhigiri in many International Conferences.

Introduction

Indian Cultural Traditions

Santhigiri Research Foundation has initiated for quite sometime a dialogue on the Wisdom Tradition of India and it has gathered momentum over the years by giving rise to serious debates on the basic premises of Indian spirituality and the historical factors that have contributed to the gradual shrinkage and its impact on socio-cultural life leading to social disintegration, cultural decay and caste induced disunity among the people as well as the ways and means to get over this undesirable occurrences. This volume is the outcome of our efforts in this direction.

The subject matter of this book is not purely based on Indian philosophy as understood by many of the Indian philosophy scholars. Indian philosophy is usually divided into systems—orthodox and heterodox—and its philosophy, history and culture have never been made accessible and interesting except by rhetoric.

The intent of this volume is particularly concerned about the culture of India which is rooted in a tradition usually known as *Guru* Tradition. Thus, this book is based on the general philosophy and world-view that the cultural tradition and the philosophy of India are based on *Gurus*, *Bhaktas* and their paths.

However, the devoted work of a generation of scholars has thrown a flood of new light upon the subject. But the results of their investigations have been chiefly intended for the specialists and many are still singularly blind to India's spiritual and cultural values and her contribution to world culture. Historians and scholars have agreed upon the fact that India has made rich contributions to the development of world civilization. Today, the world finds itself in urgent need of the very insights of Indian philosophical thought, which is not conveyed to the common folk in its authentic form and content. India's insight of the spiritual nature of man and the oneness of human existence and her insight of the underlying unity of the different systems of thought provide the world today with that firm foundation on which alone a stable commonwealth of nations can be built.

The Vedic Age and India's Cultural History

It is commonly pronounced by the scholars that the Vedic age of the Aryans had reached the stage of excellence of Indian Civilization and culture. They had attained a high stage in knowledge, power and social organization. In the periods that followed all those assets that were valuable in man's life—philosophy, religion, sciences and even codes of conduct—were traced back to the Vedas. In fact, the Vedas have left abiding monuments in all facets of life. It is not an exaggerated statement that many of the later intellectual activities of Indian thinkers, to a great extent, have been but a renewable attempts to present some aspect or the other of the Vedic thought. All philosophical systems of Indian Philosophy, whether heterodox or orthodox, are more or less representations of the Vedic conceptions of reality. The entire mythology of the later periods was based on the Vedic traditions. Even ordinary sciences like astronomy and medicine were associated with the Vedas. The entire Sanskrit literature of the later ages records the attempts of ancient Indians to understand the Vedic civilization to revive the Vedic culture and to approximate their lives to the ideals of the Vedic understanding of life and civilization.

The organization of Hinduism as a religion is said to be one of the principal achievements of the later Vedic period. The doctrines about soul (*jiva*) the Absolute (*Brahman*), relation between man and cosmos, between man and the Absolute, the principles of *Karma*, *mukti*, *maya*, transmigration of the soul etc. were evolved and stated in the Vedic literature and also in the Upanishads. It was not only the doctrinal basis of Hinduism that was established in the later Vedic times, but the social basis of Hindu life was also firmly and solidly laid in this period. The *Grihya Sutras* prescribed in the minutest details the duties of man from birth to cremation laying down the ceremonies for each occasion, so to say, ceremonies at birth, naming, initiation, education, marriage, etc. If the *Grihya Sutras* created Hindu community, the *Dharma Sutras* have organized the Hindu society on a conscious foundation by laying down social customs, usages, codes and laws.

In addition to *Grihya Sutras* and *Dharma Sutras*, equally important is the social doctrine of *Varnashrama Dharma*. It was a social conception by virtue of which one's life was divided into four periods—*Brahmacharya*, *Grhasta*, *Vanaprastha*, and *Sannyasa*. Every Hindu householder was supposed to follow this ideal.

Another development of the later Vedic period was the development of the *Chaturvarnya* system, later metamorphosed into caste system. It was a system that divided the society into four classes—*Brahmins*, *Kshatriyas*, *Vaishyas*, and *Sudras*. It was also an attempt to relate the conscious organization of the Hindu society and also of the maintenance of the supremacy of the priestly class.

Indian Culture and the Message of Spiritual Unity

Today, when India is once more emerging from eclipse, it is more than ever incumbent to explain to the world of her glories of the past achievements in the domain of philosophy, religion, art, and even political philosophy. The message of spiritual unity has been India's life-long contribution to the world. This message is based upon her perception, realization and practical application of the eternal truth of the spiritual nature of man and the spiritual unity and solidarity of humankind and civilization. This is fully borne out by the historical evolution of her spiritual course of life throughout the centuries. It is criminal to belittle or ignore a culture which could give birth philosophers like Sankara, Ramanuja, Kapila, and grammarians like Panini, the great philosophical wisdom which is exhibited in Upanishads, religious teachers and reformers like Buddha and Vardhamana Mahavira, rulers like Asoka and Akbar, Krishnadevaraya and Shivaji, saints like Ramakrishna Paramahamsa, Vivekananda, Aurobindo and Ramana Maharshi, saint and politicians like Mahatma Gandhi, Poet like Kalidas and Tagore. It is equally noteworthy to state that India has produced great epics like *Mahabharata* and *Ramayana*, and treatises like *Thirukkural*.

The magic wand of India's life is religion. Religion, in essence, is the unfoldment of man's real nature, which is pure consciousness. This universal consciousness is the very soul of the human being and as all life is the evolution of that which is within, the universal spirit necessarily expresses itself through various peoples and nations in different circumstances and with widely different customs and methods of life. This is said to be the basic philosophy that was inherent in all Indian philosophical systems.

Caste System and the Culture of Exclusion

One of the bitterest results of India's unconsciousness of her spiritual and ethical unity is casteism. The caste system in India's cultural and social life in its present form developed in the later Vedic age and the Epic periods and therefore it is more than 2000 years old. It is complicated and has split up Hindu society into more than 3000 watertight compartments. It has not only been the strongest impediment in the way of the solidarity of the Hindus but has created social inequality among them. It was against this system that Buddha and Mahavira, Nanak and Kabir raised their revolt, but it has been surviving all these onslaughts.

Caste system in its early stages was not practiced the way it evolved to be. In the Rig Vedic age, there were only two classes of people in the society—the Aryans and the non-Aryans, or the fair-skinned Aryans and dark coloured aborigines. The old pride of a conqueror was retained by the Aryans because of manifold reasons. It made them unwilling to allow the fusion of their race with that of the conquered *Dasyus*. Further grouping of the Aryan society into *Brahmins*, *Kshatriyas*, and *Vaishyas* took place centuries after and the process developed much on the lines of evolution. The fourth class of the people who formed the bulk of the society was called *Sudras* whose duty was to serve the other three classes. They were the menial and servile workers.

This may be said to be the origin of caste system in Indian societies. In its original form, it was a class system. A man's class was decided by his profession and conduct and not by his birth as it is evolved to be and practiced today. Dronacharya, the famous military instructor of the Pandava brothers of *Mahabharata* was a *Brahmin* by birth; the great sage Vasishta was born of a prostitute; Parashuram, a *Brahmin*, became *Kshatriya*; Vyas was of a fisher woman; Vidura, who was the guide, philosopher and friend of king Dhritarashtra was a *Dasiputra*.

It has been sufficiently argued by historians and scholars that formation of caste system was engineered and patterned by the considerations such as racial factors, the philosophy of action, political domination and occupational bias. The class-divisions eventually had become hereditary due to the selfishness of the priestly class who gave a theological and supernatural explanation of their origin and accordingly they interpreted *Sastric* injunctions to perpetuate the hereditary superiority of their class as the superior caste.

Even after seventy years of independence from Great Britain, Indian people continue to be in the grip of caste consciousness. Historically, India has been surviving as a nation for millennia with closed groups divided by caste, creed and language. It was a group of people, which have been bound down by the authority of *Smriti*, *Achara*, *Dharma Sastras*, and *Dharma sutras* that enabled the Hindu society to develop a philosophy of exclusion and made a section of people as untouchables and deny them the rights as persons and very often their existence as individuals. The traditional social value of *Varnasrama dharma*, which has been operating the social consciousness of this country, resulted to a segregation of the majority people in the hierarchic pattern of social arrangement, which restricted the interaction between individuals belonging to various groups. Since the status and opportunities of the individual are coupled with the *Jati* (caste) that he/she belongs to by birth and one's birth itself is theologically conditioned by the past *karmas* that one performed in the previous births, oppression towards these groups were made easy and theologically found correct. The age-old Indian concept of *Dharma* which was interpreted in terms of *varnashramadharma* by Manu, Prasasthapada and Kautilya seldom provided a place for the majority group of people, who were called *Sudras* and later metamorphosed as *Dalits*. In terms of consciousness, this has been reflected in the various Hindu literatures which were in Sanskrit language. Unfortunately, a predominant section of Indian people were denied access to this language and literature. The effect was a reduction of *anvikshaki* (philosophy) to the higher castes or the *Brahmins* who have been able to systematically reject reason that is philosophy including any deeper and authentic sense of human freedom. Resultantly, the Indian concept of *Dharma* underwent a series of interpretations and conveniently used as a theological weapon for the suppression of the human spirit. Down the centuries these broken ones (*Dalits*) were imposed enslavement by the powerful interpretations of the apparently harmless exegesis and footnotes of the doctrines like *Dharma, Karma, Svadharma, Niskama karma* and *Mahayoga*.

Such an outlook and world-view engineered to look upon women as inferior to man in intelligence. In *Anusasana Parva*, Yudhishtira asks Bhishma why this is so. He replies that a woman is naturally a temptress and a lurer; she is not endowed with the strength of will to resist temptation, and therefore always stands in need of protection by man. (43.19) A menstruating woman and a woman who has delivered a child were equated with a corpse and an outcaste by this oppressing philosophy, which has not generated an outlook for equality, freedom and social justice. Even in this modern age, this particular attitude towards women conditions the mental framework of people in some parts of India. Although women were accorded great esteem in Vedic times, yet were condemned to a most humiliating position in the age of the *Smritikars*.

Creativity and Social Change

The present Indian society is moving from its closed systems towards a state of change and progression marked by the assertion of the human spirit irrespective of innumerable castes and their consequent creeds. The philosophical requirement at present is a re-understanding and a re-creating of the metaphysical notions like *Dharma*, *Rta*, *Yajna*, *Tapas* and *Nyasa* which have their *Vedic* past and which was used conveniently and very often theologically by the upper castes in order to subvert and suppress the identities of a huge section of people. Rather than the caste-duty, which was regarded as *Dharma* from time immemorial, we need to reinterpret these concepts as these were instrumental in patterning and structuring the basic thrust of Indian world-view so that we may be able to appropriate the real meaning and content of Indian culture. In other words, the meaning of these concepts and especially the concept of *Dharma* has to be understood in terms of human dignity and worth irrespective of caste and creed, which is the ethics of the 21st century.

Here we face certain important challenges of enormous importance; two important constants that accompany man in his life and society in its marching towards progress are creativity and social change: creativity as the basic faculty of the human spirit and social change that he causes permanently by his creativity. In other words, creativity and social change are concomitantly interrelated in every culture and specifically in the transformation of a culture and its civilization. Where there is creativity, there is social change. In man's case, being creative as he is, as the existence of man necessarily implies it, there ought to be creative capacities of man, which he articulates in his life situations in the society. Thus, it implies that as long as man is as he is, he initiates social changes because the power of the human development lays just in the mutual dialectical interaction of these factors, the former representing a human constant and the latter a necessary social motion in which and through which this human constant gets developed and applied itself.

It follows then that man is basically a creative being and his creativity distinguishes him in the phylogenetic sense from all other species. It is the basic content of man as well as his joy, which he expresses in his art, philosophy, in lifestyles, and also in his social life. Thus, creativity in human life leads to his fulfillment as human, which he realizes in the course of his history and the evolving civilization. What we mean by creativity needs an explanation: it is the faculty that results in transforming in some way of the existing reality, be it natural, social, material or spiritual, and in introducing new elements given by personal specificity and thus paving to the creation of a new reality and new starting point for new transformations.

Reforming Movements and Transformations

This process of a continuous creativity draws upon not only individual experiences but also upon the activities of small and large societies. In the Indian historical and cultural life, these processes of creating new realities and transformations are evident in the various faces of her sojourn. The consequences of this accelerating process in the history of Indian societies have generated different philosophies, which in turn, were conducive in promoting and initiating social and political changes. We may call it as revolt, but such revolts on the existing social conditions have marked the beginnings of human creativity and thus of social changes. As for instance, in the Greek Islands of Ionia, Heraclitus preached his new doctrines; in Iran Zoroaster launched his protest against the prevailing religious superstitions; in China people welcomed the philosophic teachings of Confucius who gave them a higher conception of duties of life. In India people were disgusted with old philosophical dogmas and were striving for simple methods of worship and easier means of liberation from the ills of the mundane existence. Consequently, new leaders of thought and religion sprang into vigorous activities and gave a new direction to life in India. They revolted against the old order of things such as the existing social patterns, the ritualistic form of religion, the absolute power of the priest-craft etc. They discarded the principle of social immobility, inequality and injustice; these philosophies of revolt were anti-social and anti-caste in spirit. It upheld the sanctity of human spirit and its freedom irrespective of the caste and creed. These reforming movements—humanitarian and theistic—have eventually gathered force and momentum in the socio-cultural life of common people. They were ascetics and wandering teachers and some of them rejected the authority of Vedas and Vedic priests and denounced blood sacrifices, which constituted a large part of the *Brahminic* rituals and even denied the very existence of God. Right conduct, they declared, was the only way of getting out of the existing meshes of doctrines like *karma* and *Samskara*. The greatest of these existing teachers who were wanderers were Vardhamana Mahavira and Gautam Buddha. The philosophy of the former took the shape of a reforming movement known as Jainism while those of the latter led to another movement in India's cultural history called and formed as Buddhism. They were not initially a creed but 'an appeal for holier living in the bosom of the existing Hindu religion and society'. In other words, these movements revolted against the burdens of ritualism, belief in *Mantras*, extreme form of sacrifices, supremacy of *Brahmins*, caste system in the society and the like.

Social Change and Reformation: The Non-Elites

There were other sects who revolted and taught variations of doctrines and practices in the upward march of Indian social and cultural life. The *Ajivikas*, for instance, were said to be the *Sudra Sannyasis* whose leader was Makkali Gosala. Born a slave himself, Makkali was a radical teacher who denied even the basic doctrine of Hindu thought, so to say, the theory of *Karma*. He argued that 'man is subject to the laws of nature. Action, therefore, cannot lead man out of the inevitable and so a quietist view of life is desirable'. Gosala's followers centred on Sravasti, the capital of Kosala, where Gosala preached and died sixteen years before Vardhamana Mahavira. Ajivikism altogether disappeared from India in the 14th century A.D. after being shifted from province to province.

There were other sects like Ajita Kesakambaten and Purana Kassapo who were popular teachers and taught different ideologies and doctrines that were questioning the existing theories of Hinduism. Besides these sects, there were developed within the fold of orthodox Hinduism some other sects, which did not distinctly repudiate the Vedas. The features of these sects 'were the worship of one particular

God as the supreme deity. He was conceived as Vishnu, Siva, Sakti or some other form. Salvation could be achieved through His grace and one has to follow the path of *Bhakti* for this. The devotees of Vishnu called *Vaishnavas* or *Bhagavatas* developed a sect called *Bhagavatism*, while those of Rudra developed a sect called *Saivism*.

Apart from other cults and philosophies like *Vaishnavism* and *Saivism*, there were other philosophies and reformations that took place in the cultural and social development of India, notably the *Bhakti* cult, the *Sakta* cult, and the *Tantrism*. India has produced great philosophers like Sankara, Ramanuja, Madhva, Vallabha, and Nimbarka who interpreted the philosophical contents of the Upanishads in different perspectives. The history and cultural development of India cannot be completed without the name of Guru Nanak, the founder of Sikh religion. Though he was married and had children, he renounced the world, wandered over many lands, visited all holy places and gathered spiritual experience. His mission was to bring to an end the conflict of religions. He was the reviver of the pure monotheistic doctrine of the Upanishads. His followers came to be known as Sikhs who were hammered into a military nation by the successors of Nanak who were known as the *Gurus* of Sikhs.

Indian Tradition and Ontology

The fact that every access to 'Culturality' is made possible through a specific ontology should give us pause before generalizing the insights of one's tradition. Our truths, despite its universal claims, are valid only within the parameters of the ontological tradition of a people and their country. In the case of Western ontologies, the world of history is so serious that its approach to reality and truth are wholly determined by it. Indeed, here only the historical is true and therefore the historical is real. For what is not historical is illusory and therefore not true in the Western tradition. Hence, in the Western world-view all things begin not only in time, they also develop in time and the concept of history is of paramount importance for the Western mind.

In the Indian tradition, however, there is no such once for all beginning or end of all creation. Hindu metaphysics and world-view consider that all things are potentially embedded in an inexhaustible ultimate Reality, which periodically manifests itself in multiplicity and eventually takes that back into its unmanifested Being. But this taking back or destruction means not total annihilation of being but its transformation into another shape and another name; the new that is beginning now being organically related to the old which has come to an end. This is true of human beings as well; the law of *Karma* and rebirth ensuring that each new generation being born is a remodeling of the old that has died (except for the liberated few). It amounts to saying that Indian ontologies are built on the reasoning of 'faith' rather than in abstract reason itself.

Vision of the Universe

The famous and most significant hymn of *Purusha sukta* (*RgVeda* X.90) says, "With sacrifice the gods sacrificed to the sacrifice". This hymn in the *Purusha sukta* projects the vision of a universe wherein everything is connected to everything. Individual things do not exist. The full identity of any thing is to be found only in its relationships to the total whole. Herein lays the ontological rootedness of the interrelationship between individual and society, ethics and religion, spirituality and mysticism in the Hindu/Indian cultural tradition. Professor McLean has underlined this basic philosophy in a different context in the following words: "It elaborates the distinction of the composite and differentiated from the incomposite and undifferentiated being, but avoids duality inasmuch as the very being or existing of the composite beings of the differentiated universe is nothing other than the participating—the sharing and manifesting—of That One. Further, it enters into the Absolute in order to learn more of that Wisdom and Love which is the Plenitude of perfection, unsublatable and creative." (McLean, George F., *Plenitude and Participation*: Sri L.D. Swamikannu Pillai Endowment Lectures, 1977-78, Univ. of Madras, India. Also refer McLean, George, F., *Reconstruction of the Person: Culture and Metaphysics*, Lectures delivered in Panjab University, Chandigarh through an invitation by the Indian Council of Philosophical Research, as the *Philosopher of the Year* in January, 2004.)

Concept of *Dharma* and Harmony

If the concept of *Yajna* in Indian cultural tradition is the world-process and *Rta* the principle that ensures harmony and order in that process, then *Dharma* is the unique ontological relationship that a thing has to the rest of the world of relationships in the world process. The harmony of the world-process is preserved when each thing remains true to its *Dharma* and when we respect the *Dharma* of every being. We might call the *Dharma* of a thing its very nature. On such a background, one needs to respect the *Dharma* of a particular thing because of its deeply *Dharmic* (religious) act. Accordingly, the practice of *Dharma* consists in the awareness of the *Dharma* of the universe and in a life that lives in consonance with this awareness. These contentions obviate the necessity to appreciate and appropriate *Dharma* with its two aspects: the cosmic connections and the sacrificial effects. Integration into the cosmic sacrificial process demands that one respects the *Dharmic* relationships that are operative in the universe. And to respect the complex *Dharma* of the universe is to respect the law of cosmic harmony and to become part of the cosmic sacrificial process. It also presupposes the idea that one discovers oneself only by discovering one's relationship with the universe. And the more one discovers the universe the more one discovers oneself.

Want of philosophical reflection and critical attitude that engineered the Hindu society owing to its political, religious and cultural factors made the Indian society hierarchical in character and confused two different conceptions of *dharma*, one corresponding to the nature of a thing as it is, relevant to the idea of physical laws, and the other—the norm things are required to achieve,—relevant to the idea of social, political and religious laws. *Dharma* when it functions as a natural or descriptive concept (the way things are) is quite different from *dharma* when it functions as a moral or prescriptive concept (the way things ought to be). But both may be referred to as the nature of things particularly when it means the essential nature, not accidental properties, so that the distinction between nature and norm disappears. Accordingly, there was a calculated and intentional confusion between the two uses of this term *dharma* and took the purely descriptive as the prescriptive, that believes that something is *dharma* (morally commendable) because it is *dharma* (happens to be the way and hence its nature in the sense of what it is). It paved way for the justification of caste system and untouchability on the ground that it is part of *dharma*, the implication being that the irregularities of the system ought to be there as lawful, right and virtuous, because it is the nature of it. Since a religious and lawful sanction has been volitionally attached to it, the initial ideal was lost sight and the system developed fissiparous tendencies and evolved the code of inequities, which have given it a bad name outside as well as inside India. Unfortunately, the cultural and religious supremacy of the *Brahmins* who were supposed to uphold the meaning and worth of the doctrine of *dharma* could not do the same and identified it with *Varna* and *Jati* with privileges based on birth and which prevented the concepts of rights and freedom in this country. The essential basis of the *Varna* system metamorphosed later as the caste system was the development of groups of individuals in consonance with their qualifications in virtue and justice; the keystone of the structure was not detachment but union. The element of exclusiveness and untouchability was otherwise repugnant to the social philosophy and tradition of not only the Aryan race but also of their philosophy, which was rooted in the doctrine of *dharma*.

Kautilya's *Arthasasthra* and the Political Tradition

The Indian political tradition as articulated in its most important text on politics—Kautilya's *Arthasasthra*—facilitated the inner strength and growth of groups of People. Although the Kautilyan tradition of theory and political practice conceptualized a notion of society in which individual rights was not given adequate emphasis, yet participatory rights were accorded adequate weight and emphasis as it accommodated all *Varna* and *Asrama* in the system. In the political tradition of Kautilya, there can be no such theory that can be theoretically constructed by a God. The theory is subject to and implicated in practice through the mediation of *Smrti* and *Sadacara*. In other words, the Indian classical political tradition conceptualized the relation between theory and practice in such a way that neither theory nor practice exist and function independent of some less time-bound, if not time-less category. One may then ask the question: under what structural conditions can such a theory of theory function? The answer is that this is possible only in highly integrated communitarian societies in which the elite and the ordinary folks (*Brahmin* and *Sudra*) accept unquestioningly the authority, content and message of *Smrti* and where the *Sadacari* (exemplar) can be located and recognized without any conflict of interpretation and evaluation. The society in this political tradition was a society that internalized through disciplining one's disposition to perform his function and duties and the sum total of performances by all members of society lead to orderly community existence. In short, the classical Indian political tradition was society centred as it subordinated state and government to the societal mandates. This is the idea of the active involvement and participation of a group of people as a community in the conduct of various institutions and organizations they belong to in their day-to-day living and this may exist in a system where the government at the centre is paternalistic.

The picture of the Indian society that one gets from the political treatises and the law books is that of a full-fledged caste society where all kinds of functions—intellectual, religious, political, military, commercial and manual—were being carried on by hereditary groups each functioning according to the traditional rights as laws, according to rights/laws specially made by the group itself, such as a guild, or according to local customs and organizations such as caste and village councils in interdependence with one another but without much interference from outside agencies including the political authority itself. The various groups of the society thus enjoyed a large measure of internal autonomy, within of course of their own limitations, and the main functions of the society were carried on in a decentralized manner according to the customary laws of caste over which the king had no authority.

Such an idea of unity and plurality-relativity implied in India's social philosophy viewed the society as an organism. Accordingly, the Indian conception of a society was not a collection of individuals loosely joined by self-interest but an integral unit like an organism made up of many different but interrelated and mutually dependent parts. Thus if *Sudras* were required by 'sacred law' to be the servants of higher castes, the higher castes were ordained by the same law to look after *Sudras* and their families as a matter of duty, infringement of which according to Kautilya, was a punishable offense. The interests of different groups were ameliorative and not antagonistic because they have basic needs and goals in common interdependence and harmony were therefore natural. Each part or group contributed to and received from the whole. The good of an individual was tied up with the good of all.

Such a social and political tradition in India accorded more importance to the state of existence in society than the individual existences. Thus the relations among groups and men were a moral problem rather than a legal one in India's intellectual tradition. Added to this understanding was the concept of man that this tradition upheld. According to the Vedas, man is an integrated whole made up of the physical body (*Sarira*), sensitive mind (*Manas*) rational intellect (*Buddhi*) and enduring soul or self (*Atman*). Indian philosophy is unique in declaring 'Yatha Pinde Tatha Brahmande', i.e. microcosm is macrocosm. Such an outlook and conception when combined with its idea of society as an organism paved way for a conception of unity at the cost of individual rights and freedom. Consequently, if *Brahman* is the Transcendent, the individual self (*Jiva*) too is considered as Transcendent in this tradition. In other words, individual consciousness is not enclosed in itself but constantly and progressively opens to the Reality, which is transcendent in nature.

Four-Fold Nature of the Human Self

Indian Philosophy and world-view advances a four-fold nature to the human self that corresponds to *Brahman*, the absolute reality. Human's soul or self is the infinite ground of his being. His intellectual/rational aspect is the cause of his personal being. However, in the case of man, body, mind and intellect are limited by time, space and causality. The human subject is not free at all these levels although he is endowed with the power of choice, freedom and volition. The integration, according to Indian ethics, goes a step further and is consummated when body, mind and intellect are centralized, harmonized and organized by the unitive *atman* and thereby bringing about a unity in diversity and harmony in discord. Generally, this is said to be an actual human existence in the various philosophies of India.

The above considerations of the concept of man *vis-à-vis* the supreme Person points to the fact that Indian philosophical thought is devoid of all absolute distinctions. Accordingly, Indian Philosophy generally maintained that all realms of existence are continuous, the physical, the vital, the mental and the spiritual. Thus, there is no absolute barrier between the natural and the super-natural, the sentient and the insentient, the physical and the psychic, the sexual and the spiritual and indeed between God and man. In sum, these are some of the dimensions that we meant in the Indian cultural tradition.

Individual Human Rights: The Indian World-view

This tantalizing experiential metaphysics of the 'Indian' is the philosophy and world-view within which this culture thrived and progressed. Such an understanding and world-view of India's

Philosophy has hardly ever taken any interest in individual existences but instead on the socio-community existences. Accordingly, unlike the Western tradition, this tradition to a certain extent could not develop the concept of social justice based on the concept of social equality of man. Rather, this tradition emphasized on the concept of compassion and was sensitive enough to the distress and pain of the people one personally has to deal with. Justice compared to compassion is an abstract virtue and it is less dependent on personal involvement. Compassion is best exercised in one's immediate circle while justice refers to society at large. The traditional Hindu culture fosters a good deal of concern and affection to one's relations, dependents and friends and even those who personally seek help but was not concerned with social justice.

These reflections suggest that we need to thematize the issue of individual Rights, or what is known in today's world as human rights, which is predominantly a Western concept, from a different perspective in this culture. An issue becomes a problem only when it is present in our awareness as a privation. The issue of individual rights had never been a problem for the Indian masses, as they were leading an individual existence with the support, concern and care of their social existence. In view of the predominance of social existence over individual existence, conceptually and ontologically, the essential being of man was looked at as a part of the whole, the whole being the society or even the cosmos. Accordingly, it generated a sense of compassion rather than social justice in man toward all beings.

Universal Unity and Harmony of Beings

The world-view, which this culture fostered and developed, was the universal unity and harmony of all beings. Resultantly, the issue of individual rights among men or *Varna* or *Jati* did not take the shape of a problem, nor did any form of struggling for individual rights become recognized as a legitimate moral activity. The philosophy of ideal unity, which this culture fostered, has its beginnings from *Rgveda*'s *Purusasukta* onwards and generated the desire for cooperation rather than rebellion and the desire for individual rights has never been a problem. Even the philosophical trend did not encourage struggling for power, dominance or self-advancement. Given the philosophical background and the conception of man as a part of the cosmic *Purusha* and also because of the ideal of harmony and unity, the issue of rights could not detain the status of a genuine and independent problem. The individual grievances as well as the group grievances were sacrificed in relation to the value of universal unity. Hence, conceptually, not only were the actual experiences of human relations ignored but also the issue of rights never aroused as a problem. As for example, the idea of justice had never been regarded in this culture as the central idea while dealing with human relations. The harmony and the consequent equality of men were to be arrived at through compassion and the mutual conscious striving for harmony.

Such a line of thinking and philosophy in this culture sprouted the distinctive idea of social harmony and social democracy, which is rooted in the concepts of *Dharma*, *Yajna*, *Rta* and Varnashrama. They were meant to realize the individual that the performance of one's own good leads to the good of the society. Such a societal order, along with its required social, economic and political aspects, has to follow from *dharma* itself. Thus, the presence of *dharma* in the universe, underpinning the right functioning of things, sometimes thought of as their norm and sometimes simply as their nature, was taken for granted in India, not only by the Hindus but even by the Jains and Buddhists too. Hence, the Indian social and religious philosophy recognized an organic vision of society where all functions were recognized as essential parts of one order.

The unity, which this tradition talked about, is openly acknowledged to transcend reason. To say in this scheme that the doctrine of the unity of all existence is not rational is to utter a tautology, since it amounts to saying that unity cannot be comprehended by means of the use of a device which works through mutual exclusion of polarized oppositions, a device which reason inevitably uses for doing the kind of job it is supposed to do, discrimination of differences. In this tradition and culture, hence the idea of the oneness of reality helped to develop characteristic attitudes in the phenomenal sphere too. It has made Hindu phenomenal ontology pluralistic and led to the acceptance of a variety of conceptual schemas for phenomenal classification and explanation. The effect is that this tradition does not demand that all beings should be capable of being packed into one beautifully coherent system. It has also led to a relativistic epistemology, the doctrine that no one conceptual schema can claim to constitute the truth absolutely; its truth being relative to its proper framework of reference, so to say, it has led to a pluralistic methodology: 1. Empirical, based on perception and inference, as used by *Nyaya*, 2. Discriminative, based on conceptual or rational clarification as is used by *Samkhya* (*Samkhya* means discrimination) and 3. Intuitive, as is used by Vedanta (and others in different measures).

Unfortunately, this cultural tradition, which is rooted in *Yajna*, *Rta* and *dharma* is in danger now because Indian society in general and civil society in particular as the arena of *Guru* consciousness, which guarantees democratic dialogue and contestation has not been appropriated by certain political ideologues. The ontological principles of *Rta* and *Dharma* as organizing principles can become a means of bringing social groups together in the Indian context and serve as criteria for evaluating specific practices. If civil society has to be appropriated properly in the Indian socio-political and cultural arena, then the ontological principles of *Yajna*, *Rta* and *Dharma* as organizational principles can provide thematic coherence in the sphere of civil society. The concept of *Yajna* in the Indian tradition is to be understood as a re-membering of the dismembered *Purusha* whose sacrifice is meant for not only the re-integration and inter-dependent nature of reality but also for the interconnectedness of everything because *Yajna* is meant as sacrifice wherefrom beings achieve their unmistakable identity and difference. The emphasis upon diversity and the privileging of differences can adequately legitimize and bring forward new forms of power and thereby levels down the existing norms of globalization with its peculiar ways of not tolerating any difference or variety. What we should look forward is not a uniformity of sameness, but a cosmic garden of unity and variety, identity and difference. Towards that end, the principles of *Yajna*, *Rta* and *Dharma* harmonize and regulate our interconnectedness which otherwise defines the fundamental inviolability of persons in a civil society.

An Initial Conclusion

Let us recapitulate the essentials of the historical and cultural factors, which stimulated the rise of the issue of individual rights and freedom in this culture. In the earliest period of Indian culture, there was idealism for the universal unity so to say an organic world-view, which predominated the social, political and philosophical scene of Indian Life. Accordingly, man was said to have an ontological connection with the universal substance and the attempts to actualize the natural state of harmony with all beings were expressed in the formulation of moral codes for both the ruler and the ruled. The idea of four ends of life developed by this culture and philosophy may be said to be a more religious kind than philosophical and political, yet it under girded the development of a cultural continuum based on the doctrine of *dharma*. In accordance with the organic view which the Indian tradition developed and fostered always upheld that not only that all differences participate in a unity but also that in their own ways each reflects the totality of existence. The pursuit of four ends by men through four stages of life is indeed the pursuit of every kind of possibility that is open to man, righteousness, material well-being, pleasure and liberation or spiritual well-being and freedom and achievement of all these by a man would mean that he would have realized in his life the totality and unity of existence. Thus, the relations among men were a moral problem rather than a legal one. Accordingly, to be a sage or a gentleman who wishes to perfect and transform himself was to pattern himself after the ideal of the compassionate man. This kind of a life perspective could not allow the struggle for personal freedom, at the expense of other people's happiness, to be a genuine goal of morality. In other words, the general view of life, for an Indian, was to submerge his/her ego, to disappear, and to be absorbed into the universal harmony. Even during the period of rationalistic school of Indian Philosophy—*Navya-Nyaya*—and the reformation movement by many leaders—Dayananda to Gandhi—moral philosophies had assumed a predominant role in the creation of an ideal society. This ideal of harmony had persisted for a long time because there was no clear consciousness of the meaning of a person independent of the family and the society, where the individual freedom as understood in Western Philosophies was disvalued Although there were many changes in the various communities and groups that held political power the people maintained the mentality of 'accepting' whatever living conditions were thrust upon them.

We have been arguing that the core of traditional Indian philosophy is rooted in the metaphysic of the experience of *Dharma*, *Rta* and *Yajna*, which I would like to call as the cultural ontology of India that had been deduced from its mythological thinking and expressed a philosophical content. From this tantalizing metaphysic of experience, Indian philosophy could generate a special realm of unity that binds not only the sentient but also the insentient beings. Thus, the Indian by its generic sense was not underlined a notion of separation as expressed in the Western metaphysics but have highlighted the concept of unity. Accordingly, in its understanding of "being" Indian philosophy is radically different from Western conception of being. In the Western concept of being what we see is the necessary emphasis on the separation guaranteed by the necessity of opposition; In the Indian thought, the necessary opposition is not centred on the universals of philosophy but on the persons of their origin in terms of their caste and class, which is again a contestable issue.

In its understanding of being, the concept of *Yajna* is predominant in Indian thought, which necessitates the possibility of meeting the other as a necessary part of oneself which is not emphasized in Western thought. In the Western conception, the difficulty is centred on the understanding of the internal multiplicity of man. But in India's philosophy and world-view, the emphasis is on the understanding of man's unity. There is an inherent rationality that manifests in all creation in Indian thought. It can be a potential resource and source for a new meaning of rationality. There is a specific Indian ontology whose understanding of being corresponds to a specific way of thinking too. The crux of this specific way of thinking is given by different understanding of time. If Greeks conceived of time as the life of being, classical India perceived time as the life breath of reality. Hence, Classical Indian philosophers contended that it is time that 'matures beings and encompasses things'. According to them, time is the 'Lord who works change in beings; time created earth; in time is consciousness' and in a more explicit way, 'in time is life' (*prana*) In the earliest experience of the Vedic Indians, time was described as the actual existence of beings. Resultantly, the word *Kala* which designates time appears (only once) in the *Rig Veda* that speaks of *ayu* or *ayus* which means the vital force, the time of life, the long life, the existential span or duration of every being. Moreover, according to the Vedic Seers, time is born with sacrifice and it is by sacrifice that it is once again destroyed. This concept is rooted but on the intimate relation between worship and time and provide us with a key to the understandings of the central place of sacrifice and man's participation in the unfolding of time. It amounts to saying that time and reality belong together and the experience of time amounts to the experience of reality.

Structure of the Volume

Articles in this volume contribute to the debates on the issues of religion, culture, caste, sociality and cultural identities by examining the underlying issues of culture, spirituality and identities from sociological, historical, religious and philosophical perspectives. This project is the partial fulfillment of a philosophical praxis undertaken by different philosophers and social thinkers. Generally, the articles in this volume are concerned about multifarious aspects of spirituality and its different proclivities. The ideal of emancipation which was supposed to be the primordial 'discovery' of spirituality is getting lost its discovered truth. Thinking about all these truths are our ambiguities, anxieties, self-reflections and therefore criticalities too.

When we look into the general current of thought that reflects in this volume, one is reminded of Indian spirituality which entails the existence of two kinds of ontology. The first one we may call as the ontology of permanence and the second may be called the ontology of impermanence. Accordingly, we may say that there are two conceptions of reality in this culture and therefore the philosophies and world-view in this tradition may be categorized in terms of these two categories of ontology.

When we turn our attention to the former level of ontology which adheres to the meaningfulness of a static being, we are destined to start with *Vedanta* wherein the concepts of *Maya* and *Atman* are predominant. According to this philosophy, the ostensible and tangible world cannot be regarded as absolute reality but as a veil that hides the Supreme Self. What the *Vedantin* asserts is that deliverance from the cosmos is the primary concern of human existence. *Maya* cannot be considered merely as an illusion or as the play of the cosmic *Purusa* but may be considered as the activity of the Divine Spirit through which the Divine Spirit manifests in its manifold and diverse ways. Therefore, the underlying point is the positive characteristic of *Maya* which is the divinely created energies that is manifested in the diverse activities of the Divine. The philosophical significance is the fact that the cosmos in this philosophy is a prison for the knowledgeable and the sagacious.

1. The first chapter of this book by **Prof. Mrinal Miri** can be categorized from the perspective of Socrates whose cherished aim was to establish universal definitions for ethical conduct of individuals through his midwifery. Socrates proclaimed that the virtuous man is the one who knows moral goodness, namely the man of wisdom. This insight of Socrates could be expressed in the questions, "How do persons come to know what is good for them? Indeed, can they enjoy the good without knowing it? If they enjoy the good after knowing it, how do they know it, more clearly what determines or informs one's value system? The basic premise of Miri is that spirituality is an epistemic notion, a notion about knowledge—quite specifically—knowledge of the self or self-knowledge. Accordingly, Miri argues that achieving knowledge should be regarded as highest attainment of a human subject who requires efforts of a very special kind. Distancing oneself from attachment is a moral value in the Indian spiritual tradition. In that case, Miri questions whether the disengaged self must also be disengaged from the life of morality because the arena of the moral life is the mundane world of *Samsara* and its human relationships. According to him, the spiritual "'discovery" of the self can be given an intelligible, significant content only if it is seen as the overcoming of the ego that leads to a knowledge of the true springs of our actions of historically and contingently constituted being. Miri compares such a state of mind by invoking Gandhi and his concept of Swaraj. To achieve such self-knowledge and awareness is also to attain true freedom, say, *Swaraj*. Miri concludes his chapter by stating that the episteme of the tribal vision is similarly continuous between the natural, the moral and the spiritual. To dismiss this epistemic dimension as either irretrievably erroneous or lacking in autonomy is a moral lapse of an intellectual one.

2. The chapter entitled **Reviving the Wisdom Tradition by *Navananma Swami*** is noteworthy in the sense that it expounds the basic premises of the teachings of Navajyothisree Karunakara *Guru*, who has gifted to humanity a distinctive teaching and path to practice spirituality in accordance with *Yugadharma*. He argues that the wisdom tradition of India was originated from the Adi *Guru*, Manu and Manu lineage. The incessant stream of *atmajnana marga* grounded on *Guru*-disciple order, which was beyond religion and any form of segregation, marked the highest stage of Indian spirituality, the Swamy observes. The disappearance of this *Jnana marga* at a particular point of time due to an error occurred to a great Rishi in the Manu lineage invoked a curse from *Brahman* whereby *dharma* was erred and the spiritual path towards Supreme Light was eclipsed and the memory of Manu and Manu *dharma* was vanished from human heart. This revelatory narrative received from *Brahma* *prakasham* to the founder *Guru* of Santhigiri Ashram, Navajyothisreee Karunakara *Guru* and the restoration of lost *Yugadharma* by the *Guru* has fulfilled the unfulfilled mission of the past messengers of God, Swami observes based on the *Guru*'s teaching.

3. Sebastian Velassery in his chapter entitled '*Guru* Tradition, Cultural Creativity and Social Change: The Onto-Genesis of Indian Cultural Tradition' attempts to examine the foundations of the cultural heritage of India which is rooted in a tradition which he calls as *Guru* Tradition. According to Velassery, it is this tradition—*Guru* Tradition—which drew upon its resources from the past that have prepared its people to shape a conscious existence and formed the foundations of a qualitative life. An understanding of such a tradition in India as *Guru* Tradition means that the deepest identity of a person as *Guru* is found precisely in transcending oneself and reaching out to others; that *Gurus* are situated in communities and cultures and these are the grounds upon which Indians have developed their identities as a people. Accordingly, Velassery suggests that the foundations of the meaning and quality of life of the Indians have centred on *Gurus* who were considered as the embodiment of the Absolute or Transcendent. This positive notion of the *Guru* has always had an identical or unchanging meaning in both the Indian Philosophical tradition as well as culture. More than by mere accretion, the notion has managed to incorporate the great achievements of human self-discovery for which, in turn, it has been both the stimulus and the goal. The author examines the nature of the *Guru* through reflection on a series of paired and progressively deeper dimensions: first, as a role, and as the one who lives out this role; second, as free self-consciousness that realizes itself as the Identity and as the subject of that freedom; and third, as moral agent who fulfils the plenitude of consciousness. This is an affirmation of existence as sharing in *Sat*, *Cit* and *Ananda* and reflects the meaning of the transcendent for man and of man in the Transcendent.

4. Another important chapter in this collection is written by **C.D. Sebastian.** Sebastian's chapter is an in-depth search for bringing out the hermeneutics of the Buddhist preceptor legacy in relation to social change and cultural creativity. Toward this purpose, Sebastian firstly outlines what is meant by *the hermeneutics of a historical legacy*, as it has been mentioned in the title of the chapter. The Hermeneutics of a historical Legacy is an imperative to spell out the historical events such as the transition from Siddhartha Gautama to Gautama Buddha or the inception of Buddhism and the successive contributions (moments) by the Buddhist *Acharya*s. In order to look into these historical events in the Buddhist preceptor tradition and interpret it, we take recourse to the theories of 'historicism' and 'hermeneutics', which are interrelated in its approach and goal. Subsequently, the author takes up two most important facets of Buddhist preceptor tradition for social transformation, namely, the *Bodhisattva ideal* and the *egalitarian principle*. In this sense, the social concern and transformation was the primary motif for the development of the Bodhisattva ideal. Sebastian argues in the course of his chapter that these two facets ought to be seen in Buddhism as catalysts for social transformation and repudiation of caste-hegemony and subjugation. According to him, these two facets catalysts in the Buddhist preceptor tradition has much to do with the contemporary discourse on 'engaged Buddhism.' Toward this end, C.D. Sebastian makes use of some of the Buddha's discourses, later texts and treatises to hypothesize speculate and then deduce conclusions from the analysis of such texts.

5. Panneer Selvem in his chapter on Spiritual Evolution of Life with Reference to Sri Aurobindo has made an earnest attempt to examine, analyse and evaluate the concept of Aurobindho's Gnostic humans through whom Aurobindho envisions a fundamental cultural and civilizational transformation. Prof. Selvam notes that the scientific theory of evolution is itself an argument in favour of the spiritual evolution of man that Aurobindo forsees. Man's future evolution has its roots in his own type, since the impulse towards self-exceeding is also his fundamental principle. To be a man fully, he should be a gnostic being, a Superman. The author emphasizes the position of Aurobindo that spiritual human society will realize the three essential truths of existence—God, Freedom and Unity, which are the three aspects of one and same truth. None of the three can be realized without the realization of the other two. Sri Aurobindo says: "When man is able to see God and to possess him, then he will know real freedom and arrive at real unity, never otherwise." The spiritual society will live as collective soul and not as a collective ego. It will be the outcome of the realization of God within and on this earth. To find the Divine self in the individual and collectivity and to realize spiritually, mentally, vitally, materially its greatest, largest and deepest possibilities in the inner life of all and their outer action and nature. Since the inner divine compulsion grows in the individuals, society will lift the outer compulsions. In a perfect spiritual society, all will be perfectly free. The author seeks to raise the hope of better social and global order grounding on the exposition of Aurobindo about the future of humanity.

6. P.I. Devaraj in his chapter invites our attention to the social dimension of religion apart from its transcendent aspect. According to him, it is this social dimension of religion which can augment social transformation in a given society. Toward this purpose, Devaraj analyzes the social philosophies of certain religious revolutionaries of Kerala like Sri Chattambi Swamikal and Sree Narayana Guru in Travancore and Brahmanada Sivayogi, Vagbhatanada and Ananda Thirtha in Malabar and recently the awakening task is taken by Navajyothisree Karunakara Guru. They revolted against the existing social evils in which *Brahmins* enjoyed a monopolistic position and eventually helped in ushering a new social order in which the non-*Brahmin* communities came to have their legitimate place. The socio-religious movements under the leadership of these visionaries were revolutionary in their practical plane. The social reformers before the advent of these thinkers regarded the situation of lower caste with 'sympathy' but did not tried to liberate them from the centuries old social tyranny. There was very little or no stress on economic inequality and exploitation. But the above said thinkers have all fundamentally subscribed to the humanist philosophy and they recognized the dignity of man. They thought that the spread of secularism is necessary to bring about a unity in a multi-religious country like India which is said to be the basic tenets of the *Guru* tradition in Kerala and Karunakara *Guru* was no exception.

7. P. Chandramohan's chapter entitled 'The Religious Thoughts of Narayana *Guru*: Tradition Modernity Dualism' is a critical-creative attempt toward discussing in detail the religious ideas of Narayana *Guru* in the context of concepts like modernity and tradition which is conceived as binary opposites. What the author intends to do is to transcend these boundaries (of tradition and modernity) by relocating Sree Narayana *Guru* as a synthesizer of such a dualism, which the intellectuals could not transcend and may be regarded as the reasons of their failure to fathom the entrenched ills of Kerala society. According to him, rationalism and religious universalism, the two important intellectual and ideological strands of the nineteenth century, were the binding principles of Narayana *Guru*'s socio-religious reform activities. Chandramohan further argues that the socio-cultural ideas of Narayana *Guru* were occasioned by the missionary presence but not created by missionaries. A historical re-look at the Kerala society amply illustrates the point that the religious beliefs and practices were a mixture of magic, sorcery, witchcraft, divination and several other forms of popular religion; the forms differed slightly between the *avarnas* and *savarnas*. The most distressing factor, however, was caste. The practice of untouchability, inapproachability and unseeability affronted human dignity. It is often said that such practices had led to the 'decadence' of the society; it is at such sites that we find tradition becoming antithetical to modernity. Having realized the interconnection between religious beliefs and social practices, Narayana *Guru* started his activities by making reform resonant with religious idioms in order to legitimize the need to reform oneself and others. According to Chandramohan, the objective of Narayana *Guru*'s religious reform efforts does not merely seem to enable the low castes to have access to the Brahminical gods, but to create a system of worship of their own.

8. K. Gopinathan Pillai in his chapter on **Navajyothisree Karunakara *Guru*: Continuity and Change in the Wisdom Tradition of India** has made an endeavour to bring into the mainstream of philosophicl discourse the life and teaching of Navajyothisree Karunakara *Guru* which the author argues marked a fundamental shift from the past spiritual discourse on *dharma* and religious faiths and practices. The author observes that *Guru* did not subscribe to any of the existing spiritual philosophies and religious practices. In 1973 during the occasion of the spiritual fulfilment of the *Guru*, the author states, everything on the vision and mission of *Guru* were revelaed from *Parabrahma prakasham* and thereafter *Guru*'s activities were on the guidance of the revelatory words and visions received from the Supreme Light. According to the author the mission of the *Guru* was to restore *Yugadharma* by rectifying an error that occurred to a Kalanthara *Guru* in spiritual vision in the 3rd *Chaturyuga* of the 7th Manwantara. The revelatory spirituality of the *Guru* and the way of life the *Guru* has nurtured and nourished in the Santhigiri *Guru parampara* offers promise and hope for the evolution of a new generation devoid of inherited impurities in soul and genetic order by giving way to a humane social and world order, notes the author.

9. C.V. Babu in his chapter entitled "Navajyothisree Karunakara *Guru*: The Source of Revelation to Social Evolution" attempts to look into the First Error that happened in Manu tradition as revealed to Navajyothisree Karunakara *Guru* and the Curse from *Brahman* as consequence of this error that lead to the downfall of Manu lineage. According to Babu, the entire teachings of Karunakara *Guru* are anchored on this point of revelation identifying the two elements of Error and Curse which worked as undercurrents of socio-cultural manifestation of Indian spirituality and philosophy. Satyatranan's error is primarily concerned with his notion of *Brahman* that *Guru* is *Brahman*. The error pervaded to the entire world by human *karmic* intervention through centuries and centuries with least possibility of rectifying it due to the total ignorance of such an error as ever had happened. It all shows that Manu tradition had been such an all-flourished tradition but met with a collapse falling out of divine grace due to this error that has been pervading as erroneous influence to the entire humanity. As an answer to this error, Navajyothisree Karunakara *Guru* shows that it is the way that *Guru* becomes *Brahman* as the state of being authorized as the nucleus of the merging point. *Guru* is a medium to Brahman. It is the creative source of the will of *Brahman* that authorizes *Guru* to be the centre of dissolution into Brahmn. The discernible point is that the will power is emerged from *Brahman* and not from Manu. According to Navajyothisree Karunakara *Guru*, in Indian tradition it is only Buddha who could save himself from this mistake to a great extent. The error of declaration of oneself as *Brahman* evolved to the extent that the leftovers of that tradition has paved way for a group of people who as *Brahmins* have eventually proclaimed to become embodiment of *Brahman*.

10. The chapter "A Gandhian Imagery of the 'Civilisation of the World—A Legacy rooted in Guru tradition", by **Saji Varghese** is an attempt to relocate Gandhi in the lineage of India's wisdom Tradition and to examine his contribution to the civilizational growth of humanity. He argues that Gandhi's basic concepts of truth, non-violence and *satyagraha* were rooted in India's *sanatana dharma*. Gandhi was a resurrection of the collective consciousness of India that had always stood by the dictum of *Loka samgraha*.

11. Reena Thakur Patra's chapter is a serious philosophical journey toward understanding the genealogies of the concept of sustainable development in philosophy *per se* and comparing those genealogies with two important conceptions of rationality, i.e.; metaphysical rationality and instrumental rationality. Reena Thakur argues that the quality of human life includes two aspects: its spiritual character and the ability to know and to act. The former consists of ideals which include values, moral consciousness and creativity. The latter consists in knowing ways and means of shaping nature and the capacity to organize and administer socio-economic and cultural development. Reena argues that the results and consequences of the transformation of the instrumentalization of reason have resulted to the loss of spiritual roots in human understanding on freedom, justice, equality, happiness, development, tolerance etc. Consequently, we have lost the 'human' in human settlements, in family relations, in neighbourhood, religion, economy, ecology and polity. Sustainable living in Indian tradition, she argues, may be best described as the concomitant relation between reason and being, so to say, a philosophy and a world-view that emphasizes the metaphysical dimension of human existence. Such a life when lived may be called as the sustainable living; like all other Oriental traditions, Hinduism emphasizes on the deliverance from the cosmos which is *Maya*. *Maya* is not mere illusion, nor it is an epistemological category of nescience; rather it is the divine play or art. It is not only capable of concealing the Divine Self, but also gifted to reveal the same Self.

In brief, this volume does not claim that it is an outline of Indian cultural heritage or philosophical creativity. Rather, this volume points to the fact that from time immemorial, *Gurus* and *Guru paramparas* have played decisive role in determining the course of socio-cultural and spiritual development of India. As far as India is concerned, it is evident that the comprehensive life vision and philosophical insights of these masters have contributed to the cultural creativity and unity of the country; in fact it is the *Guru* tradition and its legacy transmitted down the tradition that was instrumental in preserving and sustaining the Cultural legacy of India and its values and ethos at both the individual and community levels. An understanding of Indian tradition as *Guru* Tradition means that the deepest identity of a person as *Guru* is found precisely in transcending oneself and reaching out to others; that *Gurus* are situated in communities and cultures and these are the grounds upon which Indians have developed their identities as a people. Accordingly, this volume overtly suggests that the quality of life of the Indians have centred on *Gurus* and their *Parampara* who were considered as the embodiment of the Absolute or Transcendent.

It was India's *Guru paramparas* which preserved this nation against the onslaught of series of foreign aggressions and encroachments. The spiritual wisdom, the crafts, art and culture that

India sustained through her religious order and socio-economic structure bespeak the unique contribution of India's *Guru parampara*. In the civilizational evolution of humanity, the contribution of India's Guru parampara is to be objectively analyzed and evaluated. More significant is to examine the contributions of Guru parampara in bringing in social unity by eliminating the social evils that segregates man from man and deprives man in the name of caste and religion of his right to live a dignified life.

Santhigiri Ashram
Thiruvananthapuram

Sebastian Velassery
K. Gopinathan Pillai

1

Spirituality as a Form of Knowledge[1]

Mrinal Miri

There are many received views about spirituality or, simply, the spiritual. Here in this very brief talk I shall consider only one such view and this is the view that spirituality is an epistemic notion, a notion about knowledge—quite specifically—knowledge of the self or self-knowledge. Achieving such knowledge, according to this view, counts among human being's highest attainments, and it requires efforts of a very special kind.

The view that self-knowledge requires efforts of a special kind, that it is a matter of achievement, implies that the self is not transparently, self-evidently, available to us. Within many religious traditions, the assumption is that the original, unknown or epistemically beclouded self is *given* and stands apart from the physical world with which we human beings are willy-nilly engaged. It is, however, precisely this engagement with the physical world that is the stumbling block to achieving authentic self-knowledge. There are many traditionally prescribed practices aimed at removing this stumbling block: some kinds of meditations, yogic exercises, the idea of a spiritual retreat away from the entanglements of everyday life, performance of various kinds and degrees of austerities and so on.

One of the traditional Christian conceptions of "the spiritual life" that still enjoys great respectability and reverence is as follows: "For each of us, no doubt, a vision is conjured up by the phrase, 'spiritual life' and for most in our personal lives at least this is an eschatological vision—something to be piously hoped for in the future, but far from our daily lives where, spiritually, we just 'bump along". In its Catholic Christian form, it might involve long periods of quiet, focused reflections, dark churches and dignified liturgies.

In its higher reaches it involves time spent in contemplative prayer, guided or solitary retreats, and sometimes the painful wrestlings with God so beautifully portrayed by the Metaphysical Poets. Above all it involves solitude and collectedness. It does not involve looking after small children."[2] Or take the great Sufi tradition. True self-knowledge which is also necessarily knowledge of God involves deliberate "uprooting of what we call sensory knowledge and complete rejection of knowledge based on argumentation, scholarship and study. In the Sufi tradition this is called *fana*—annihilation. And it is *fana* that finally leads to *baqua*—permanence in God." The role of music in the movement from *fana* to *baqua* is absolutely crucial (at least in the Chisti tradition). A verse extolling the two is introduced by a *quwwal* (musical performer), then it is highlighted by a prominent master or senior devotee, then it becomes the focus of constant repetition to the point of transforming both consciousness and physical existence, and then in some cases the result is a shift from ritual engagement to mortal disengagement. The verse, the music, the mood render the listener/devotee blank to any mood save that of the calling, and the call, once heeded, leads to death. To outsiders, it appears as suicide, but to insiders it is surrender to love. Within the high Hindu Brahminical tradition too the spiritual life is frequently seen as demanding complete "detachment" from the life of the world—*Samsara*—and being firmly established in this detached consciousness—*sthitaprajna.* Sometimes, the original, detached self, which the life of spirituality endeavours to "recover", is also called the "witness" consciousness or self—the self as the disengaged witness to *samsaric* life. One difficulty with such views of the original self and self-knowledge is that if life begins with complete ignorance of this self, then how do we know that the spiritual practices that we devise will lead to its knowledge?

But a more serious difficulty for me with this view of spirituality is that the disengaged self must also be disengaged from the life of morality, because the arena of the moral life is the mundane world of *samsaric* human relationships. The original self is as disengaged from the life of the virtues and vices as it is from all other aspects of the ordinary world of sense perception, of desires and emotions. My present self is shaped by the contingencies of my engagement with the world around me—my specific location in it, the language that I learn to wield which I cannot do except in and through relationships with the other, my memories and the human practices in which I willy-nilly get caught up, e.g. the games that I play, the books that I read, the conversations I have, the life within and outside my family, my professional commitments, my friendships and so on. It is in this arena of the contingencies that the so-called virtues and vices—qualities of character such as—honesty, courage, justice, love, generosity, jealousy, greed, cowardice, deceitfulness etc.—come necessarily into play; these qualities of character are the very stuff of the moral life—without them the moral/immoral distinction disappears; and therefore morality itself disappears.

Self-knowledge is crucial to the life of morality. Is my honesty genuine? Is my courage not really a cover for my deep-seated cowardice? Is my generosity not really self-seeking by other means? To seek and find authentic answers to questions such as these is an integral part of the life of morality. Self-deceit and self-ignorance are, as it were, constituent hurdles to the life of the virtues, and the ego is their impeccable ally—the "big fat ego", as someone calls it. The overcoming of the ego is a necessary step in the battle against the "cunning" of self-deceit. The spiritual "discovery" of the self can be given an intelligible, significant content at all only if it is seen as the overcoming of the ego that leads to a knowledge of the true springs of our actions of our historically and contingently constituted being. Overcoming of the ego also must mean moral transformation, and it is my contention that moral transformation and spiritual self-discovery are of a piece.

One may approach the problem by asking the question, why should one be moral? The question arises against the background of the fact that one of the most profound predicaments of human life is the difficulty of cultivating the moral motive. The difficulty springs from the fact that to be established in the moral form of life requires what Kierkegaard calls the "transformation of our whole subjectivity". To be morally motivated is not just to do the right thing in a given situation, but to be settled in a state of mind such that the right conduct simply flows from it. One of Wittgenstein's aphorisms in *Culture and Value* runs as follows: "No one can speak the truth, if he has still not mastered himself. He *cannot speak* it—not because he is not clever enough yet. The truth can be spoken only by someone who is clearly *at home in* it". One can achieve such a settled state of mind or a state of being at home only by undertaking an arduous internal journey into the "springs of action, to root attitudes, thence to their expression in conduct". Such a journey frequently involves the dismantling of whole forms of life before a settled state of moral "purity" is achieved. This is primarily an epistemic journey—a journey of self-discovery overcoming self-deception, self-knowledge overcoming self-ignorance. The assumption is that the possibility of the moral motive is conditional upon the possibility of achieving lucidity, utter clarity about oneself. Self-discovery is a matter of self-education.

The aim of moral self-education is to overcome the powerful impulses towards self-deception and self-ignorance, which tend always to entrench us in forms of life which are devoid of the moral motive. These impulses are powerful because they emanate from the ego. The first step towards overcoming the ego is to develop a form of attention, a concentration of epistemic energy, which will enable us to counter the benighting force of the ego, and, as it wore, afford a glimpse beyond the ego into the self. Such attention and concentration of energy produces insights into moral truths: "true *ahimsa* (love) drives out all fear", "the power of *ahimsa* is incomparably superior to that of violence", "true humility is the other side of true dignity". An important aspect of such insight, such quickening of awareness, is that it bears upon one's experience of the world and thence on one's conduct, so that one acts differently from how one would have done otherwise.

To my mind, spirituality is another name for this kind of attentiveness or sensibility, and the concentration and gathering of energy that is associated with it. I would also like to think that at least part of the aim of spiritual practices, e.g. meditation is to achieve the stability of such attentiveness. I take here the example of Gandhi.

The truth that Gandhi was concerned with was the truth (the real as opposed to the Illusory) of the moral life. He believed that there is an "interior route" to moral truths just as there is an exterior route to the truths of the natural sciences. His experiments consisted in traversing this interior route until the possibility of the moral life is established. They were, as it were, purificatory exercises, which took him to the roots of the matter to what I have called "springs of action" resulting in "transformation of subjectivity", and subsequent pulling down of a form of life and founding another. Gandhi's fasts were an instrument of this experimentation; and there were several occasions in his life—in the early years, while in London, in South Africa and back in India—when dismantling of a form of life and establishing another took place. The journey is far from easy. As Gandhi puts it: "it may entail continuous suffering and the cultivating of endless patience. Thus step by step we learn to make friends with the entire world: we realize the greatness of God or Truth. Our peace of mind increases in spite of suffering, we become braver and more enterprising... our pride melts away, and we become humble...the evil within us diminish [es] from day to day."

The use of the word "experiment" is also suggestive of the fact that the moral quest—the traversing of the interior route—is not just a psychological journey, but an epistemic one—a journey which yields at once self-knowledge, and a knowledge of moral truths, such as the ones I mentioned a little earlier on. To achieve such self-knowledge, such quickening of awareness, is also to attain true freedom, *Swaraj*—a state where one's actions flow with utter spontaneity from one's knowledge. Freedom is not the capacity to choose at random between alternative courses of action, but to act from an integral moral-epistemic stance.

For Gandhi, as for many others, the religious vision is inseparable from spiritual experience and the authenticity of the latter is guaranteed by the moral transformation that ensues. Morality, religion and mysticism are of a piece. The crucial difference between the Gandhian vision of spiritual life and some of what I have called the "received" versions of such a life is that for Gandhi, an active, total (that is, with one's entire being) engagement with ordinary life—being 'fully there', imaginatively present to that which concerns us—can be informed by the most profound spirituality; spiritual pursuit does not require disengagement from *samsaric* life. To be spiritual and to be moral is to respond with utter *ahimsa* to what requires our response: "My countrymen are my nearest neighbours. They have become so helpless, so resourceless, and so inert that I must concentrate myself on serving them. If I could persuade myself that I should find Him in a Himalayan cave, I would proceed there immediately. But I know that I cannot find Him apart from humanity." "I do not believe that the spiritual law works on a field of its own. On the contrary, it expresses itself only through the ordinary activities of life." Working on the spinning wheel, looking after an injured calf, being engaged in *Satyagraha* for a particular end, keeping one's own home clean and tidy—each one of these activities can be touched by a joyous spirituality, a sense of being in touch with the real order of things.

It would be interesting to compare the account of spirituality as knowledge of the self that is rooted in historical contingencies with the modern—rather post-modem—discourse of the politics and knowledge of "identity", the anti-colonial nationalist discourse of Indian identity, the black movement, feminism, ethnicity, subalternity, the *Dalit* movement in India and many others. Self-knowledge is the central concern of these discourses and the aim of such self-knowledge, as in the case of spirituality, is freedom. But one crucial difference between the idea of freedom that is part of the concept of spirituality and the notion of freedom that is embedded in the various discourses of identity is that while the latter is also seen as freedom from deception, here the deception has not so much to do with the self-aggrandizing strategies of the ego as with the relationships of power between the dominating other and the dominated self. These discourses are, therefore, necessarily also political discourses.

But, of course, the two discourses are importantly connected. Take, for example, the discourse of feminism. The politics of self-knowledge here can lead, and frequently has led, to a deepening perceptiveness and sensibility within an area of moral darkness created and sustained for centuries by the visible and invisible strategies of the "will to power". And it is in such unsuspected corners of darkness that the ego thrives and exercises its powers of self-deception. A community's will to power provides a fertile ground for the cunning of the ego to devise its own schemes of self-deception. In the domain of politics, the feminist discourse, with all its internal differences and occasionally serious self-questionings, has been a formidable weapon in the "game" of power; in the moral domain, it can be a source of spiritual renewal of the kind that I have talked about. And, of course, for someone like Gandhi, politics *is* the proper arena of moral agency.

Connected with the politics of self-knowledge that I have just talked about is the question of diversity of cultures and civilizations in the world and the possibility or otherwise of intercultural understanding and knowledge. One way of making clear the idea of modernity is to see it as centrally motivated by the idea epistemological unity as embodied in the natural sciences. If cultural diversity is a fact of life, then modernity's definition of culture must desist from any reference to the unitary idea of knowledge and truth. Universal, overarching epistemology must not be seen as overriding cultural diversity. Diversity of epistemic visions is an inalienable part of the diversity of cultures.

What, then, about self-knowledge which we have claimed to be embedded in the idea of spirituality. I do not here wish to go into questions of incommensurability of visions and relativism that have been raised in the recent debate in the West about the issues of diversity. I shall limit myself to making just the following point: Although the view that a language embodies a form of life or culture is misleading in many ways, there is an element of truth in it. It is misleading because there are many identifiable cultures in the world, which are naturally multilingual. Take, for instance, the culture of the part of India that I come from: Assam. There are many native languages spoken here—with varying degrees of differences between them. While some of them might, linguistically speaking, be members of a *family* of languages, others may belong to different "families" altogether. However, it will be a grave mistake to split the culture of Assam up into different cultures along linguistic lines. Multilingualism is a part of this culture: people move from one language to another or from one "dialect" of a particular language to another with a natural ease that is hardly like a schizophrenic jump from one world to another, or from one vision to another. The culture, as it were, includes difference or multiplicity within itself. The element of truth in the idea that language is constitutive of a form of life can be stated as follows: Language is a *gift* that, as St Augustine might have said lights up the world for us. It is a *gift* because of its *givenness.* We cannot set out to invent language, because in order to invent language we must already have a language to invent it in. But every language is a distinct way of lighting up the world. Self-knowledge of the kind that we have talked about is necessarily articulated in language and every language has built into it the possibility of an articulation specific to it. In a multilingual culture such articulation might take an interestingly variegated form. But even if articulation of self-knowledge is presumed to require singularity of language—it will be wildly false to think that this will rule out the possibility of conversations between different articulations and transformations as a result of such conversations. There are traditions of spirituality which are distinct, but which can yet talk meaningfully with each other. A most powerful validation of the truth of this is the utter authenticity of the life and thought of Gandhi.

I would like to add here a word about tribal cultures, particularly about the tribal cultures of India. Of course, we have used all kinds of unfortunate adjectives in describing our tribes, e.g. "primitive", "prehistoric", "savage", "and uncivilized" and so on. In this, the 19th and early 20th century nationalist anticolonial discourse in India is not much different from the European discourse of the non-European other in the era of European expansion into the so-called "new" and the "old" worlds. The central European preoccupation with reference to the possible other in the age of colonial expansion was whether he was within the threshold of salvation, conversion, or whether he was irretrievably established in the domain of the Devil. If the former, then, in essence, he is the same as the European although the road to realizing this essence could indeed be hard and arduous; if the latter, then he was beyond hope just like his counterpart in Europe. The anticolonial, nationalist history and anthropology of colonial India substantially retained this distinction between the self and the other—the self in this case being the self of the great Indian civilization. It will be an extremely interesting and instructive exercise to locate the place of tribal India in the intellectual history of 19th and early 20th century India. This will, however, take me too far a field in the context of the present chapter.

All I wish to say here is that the world that the tribes inhabit are as real and as capable of transformation from within, as the world constituted by the language of modernity. One thing that can certainly be said in favour of the tribal vision is that the disjunction between the disengaged original self and the *samsaric* world of the received view of spirituality that we discussed at the beginning of the chapter does not exist in this vision. The world of the tribesman is seamlessly continuous between the inanimate, the animate and the human; she/he is ensconced in the contingencies of time and space as anything else in the world. Self-knowledge for the tribesman, therefore, must be bound by these contingencies. The epistemies of the tribal vision is similarly continuous between the natural, the moral and the spiritual. To dismiss this epistemies as either irretrievably erroneous or lacking in autonomy is, to my mind, as much of a moral lapse as an intellectual one.

Notes

1. Ideas similar to the ones expressed here have appeared in one or two other publications of mine.
2. Soskice, Janet Martin (1992). "Love and attention", In: Michael McGhee, *Philosophy, Religion and the Spiritual Life,* Cambridge University Press, pp. 61-62.

2

Reviving the Wisdom Tradition

Sanatana Dharma and Hinduism

Swami Navananma Jnana Thapaswi

Swami Navananma Jnana Tapaswi

Indian culture represents a unique all-embracing worldview and a vibrant way of life. The cultural stream of India is very extensive and comes down from eternity. It had never been just a philosophical conception cut-off from practicality. India's spiritual vision leads our awareness to eternity through the rise and fall of civilizations, as revealed by the sages through the concept of *Manu* cycles or the Manvantara order, which is spanning billions and billions of years, measuring the age and rhythmic movement of the universe. In spiritual terms, the continuity of this cosmic vision functioned through an all-inclusive spiritual concept known as *Sanatana Dharma*, which meant an eternal system of *dharma* in relation to creation, life and existence. This spiritual culture was shared and perpetuated through a line of spiritual masters and their disciples and came to be known as *Guru-Sishya Parampara* or the Wisdom Tradition—the *jnana marga*.

We can see that the source of everything related to Indian culture and heritage has been derived from this wisdom path handed down through the *Guru-sishya* tradition. It had existed as a righteous and sublime way of life inspiring and touching all aspects of life. It nourished *Dharma*, i.e. the right knowledge and right conduct that enriches and expands the horizon of life. This spiritual vision of India had existed as a life-vision related to the inner transformation of life-force or *jeeva*, which can be seen as the practical expression of spirituality. The wisdom path of India aims to lift man from his bare emotional existence to the highest pedestal of consciousness and human values through a process of transformation, which ends with *mukthi*, i.e. liberation from the cycles of births and deaths. This vision of the Indian sages is constituted by the ancient *Manu*-centric *Sanatana Dharma*, from which this spiritual culture originated.

When we deliberate on this subject, we have to highlight certain fundamental truths. We can understand it in depth only through a review of Indian culture, which flows in two distinct socio-spiritual streams, i.e. the *Sanatana* culture and *Haindava* culture (ritualistic Hinduism), as distinct from each other. We know that the ancient-most culture of India is known as *Arsha Bharata Samskara* or *Sanatana Dharma*, which is the *rishi* culture.

***Manu*: The Nucleus of Creation**

We have to re-examine the eventful history of how *Sanatana Dharma* could not elevate itself to its desired status and how it has got degenerated into the present day *Haindava* culture, through its long course over the ages. We cannot understand this history without mentioning about the *kaala ganana* or cosmic age calculation.

Indian Cosmic Time Calculation
1 Kalpa = 14 Manvantaras
71 Age Quartets = 1 Manvantara
1 Age Quartet = Satya, Treta, Dwapara and Kali
= 43,20,000 years

The wheel of time called as *Kalpa*, *Manvantara*, *Chaturyuga* etc. is related to the *parinaama* or evolution of an atomic life-form into the absolute status of *Brahman* through the ebb and flow of *srishti*, *sthithi*, *samhara* and *moksha* i.e., creation, sustenance, dissolution and ultimate liberation. In the duration of a *Kalpa*, the creation completely merges with *Brahman*, the Supreme Light. This system of time is determined and ordered for the time-bound evolution of *karma* and *dharma* of all life-forms beginning from the microbial life-forms. The history of man's spiritual quest reveals two types of realities. One is his subjective individuality and the second is its cosmic identity linking him organically to the Cosmic Truth in a parental relationship, God being the Cosmic Father or Creator.

The *rishis* measured every episode of creation in terms of *Manvantara* equivalent to the age of a *Manu*. Every solar system and life cyfles originates from the *sankalpam* (conception) of *Manus*. In the endless march of time, uncountable *Kalpas* and *Manu* cycles have gone by, which would explain the reason behind a vast and expanding universe. For the same reason, the Indian *rishis* named God as *Brahman*, its meaning being 'That which Expands'.

The cosmic phenomenon has got a nucleus, a functional centre from which everything manifests. That nucleus is the *Manu*, the Absolute in the form of the Archetypal Preceptor God, the instrumentality through whom the Will of the Absolute is carried out, controlling the temporal dimension including *karma* and *dharma*. Every *yuga* in a *Manvantara* fulfills the law of evolution in a structured way. The wisdom tradition envisions a gradual evolution through various time segments known as *satya*, *treta*, *dwapara* and *kali yuga* within the time period of a *Manu*, consisting of seventy one age quartets or *chatur yugas*. There are fourteen such *Manu* cycles in a single episode of creation known as *kalpa*. We can guess the depth of Indian spirituality when we know that the length of a *chaturyuga* itself has a duration of 43,20,000 years. We are in the seventh cycle of such an episode of creation, initiated by Vaivaswata *Manu*, the seventh *Manu*. In the present *Manu* cycle, this is the *Kali yuga* of the twenty eighth *chaturyuga*. There are forty three *chaturyugas* (28+43=71) yet to pass to complete the present *Manu* cycle.

The History of Spiritual Deviation

When this *Manu*-centric age calculation was distorted, the *karma* and *dharma* to be followed according to each age went wrong. Twenty five *chaturyugas* have passed in this manner. It would be difficult for us to grasp its magnitude in one word. In the *Manu*-centric *Sanatana*

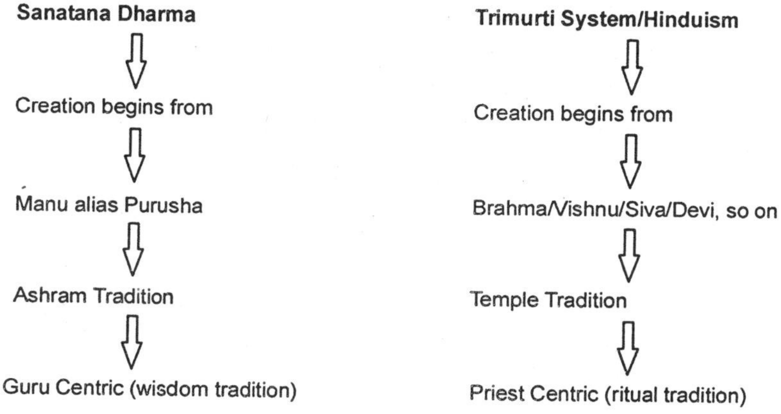

Dharma, *Manu* alias the Cosmic Purusha is the Creator, not the *Trimurti* gods—*Brahma*, *Vishnu* and *Maheshwara*. From the time the puranas began to explain creation in terms of *trimurty* gods, changing the time order of *Manu* as beginning from Brahma, the ancient Sanatana stream of spiritual culture took a diversion and began to flow through a diversified path, fragmenting Indian spirituality into three broad sects, *Saiva*, *Vaishnava* and *Saktheya* with hundreds of sub-sects.

Navajyotisree Karunakara Guru explains the history of this spiritual diversion in the following words:

'What we are going through is the time-order of *Manvantaras*. That is our perspective or cognition of the world. In the *Manu*-tradition a great spiritual evolute fell from grace (in the third *chaturyuga* of the present seventh *Manvantara*). As a result the *Brahman* initiated a corrective in the seventh *chaturyuga* (by evolving the *Trimurty* system) which was brought to a completion in the eleventh *chaturyuga*. Thereafter astral matters related to *mukti* were revealed which got codified as Vedas, Sastras and the Upanishads, without changing the old *Manvantara* order (to reaffirm that order). Since the sages could not transcend those who received these astral matters did not enquire into the reason why they had received such knowledge, and they used their intellect in understanding the path shown by the Almighty and charted their version of the *Manvantara* time-order *chaturyugas*, *manvantaras* and *kalpas* as subservient to *Brahma*. Thus they could not invoke *Manu*, the First *Guru* and grasp the Error and correct it. This is a peril that has befallen us.

'The Error was repeated again and again as the evolutes, who were the spiritual authorities of revealed knowledge, could not discover the mystery and unravel it in full before us.... The feeling of 'I' (*Aham Brahmasmi*) developed in the line of *Manus*. In the higher planes of knowing it was seen that all the wisdom and knowledge attained so far have come through it (the *Manu* tradition). This 'I-ness' can be seen in any of the books of Vedanta. You talk to any common person—this bloated notion of a free 'I' (ego) can be seen. When this comes up in the circle of ascetics (*brahmacharis*), then such notions come forth through the master-disciple lineage. In the tradition of deity-worship (*devaparampara*), the 'deva' (god) I am devoted to or the 'devi' (goddess) I am devoted to is the greatest and most glorious (is observed). Because of such possessiveness in individuals, all kinds of deities, *chamundi*, *yakshi*, *pey*, *maruta*, *matan*, *mantramurthi* (dark, evil spirits such as succubi, ghosts, ghouls etc.) became the 'Lords'. This has happened because of people's selfishness and egoism.

'Due to the emergence of *Varnasrama*, castes and castes upon castes, those who worshipped according to the *Trimurti* tradition could not function in accordance with the goodness of the Age. Earlier to this, tales were created using the medium of *Srutis* and *Smritis* and they were presented as authentic. Before that, as there appeared the creed of 'materializations' (*siddhi*), some *sannyasis* themselves handled the traditions of *siddhi*. As it all came up to this, the tradition of *Manu* faded away even from memory. This degradation of the times is due to the refusal to modify the customs that required a change according to the age and the falsification of the ideology that the abode of *Brahman* should all the time be with the celestials (*devas*) and *Brahmins*'.

Sanatana Dharma and Hinduism

The *Manvantara* time-reckoning was thus re-charted bringing it under the *trimurti* tradition, giving it a new definition. It distorted the *Sanatana* spiritual culture that followed the *Guru*-centric *jnana* path respecting the age-specific *dharma* and *karma*. Moreover, the status of Guruhood was substituted by the temple tradition involving priest-craft and worship of *devi-devas*. Guru-hood in the *Sanatana* culture transcends the statuses of all spiritual entities including the *trimurti* gods, *devi-devas* as well as the planes of *rishi*, *sannyasi*, etc. above the *trimurtis*. This deviation fragmented the Indian society spiritually as well as socially.

As already mentioned, this mistake gave India two contradictory spiritual characteristics. We can identify these two spiritual characteristics in terms of the *Arsha Bharata Samskara* guided by the *guru* tradition, and the *Haindava* culture, which has grown through the popular temple tradition with all sorts of superstitions, caste restrictions, untouchability and so on. The *Haindava* culture was strongly established here in which different spiritual entities with different identity, *naama-rupa*—names and forms and rituals were installed in temples and worshipped in order to appease them through tantric and mantric rituals with the intermediacy of priests. Along with this, the practices of blessings, performance of *siddhi*, miracles and exorcism also emerged.

The *jnana* path tried to nourish the qualities of truth, love, compassion and humility through right thoughts and deeds and strived to earn *punya*—virtue through the ways of *karma* and *dharma* and *bhakti* for attaining spiritual sublimity. In contrast, for the fulfillment of desires and other objectives, when people began to adopt a faith system based on the worship of spiritual entities beginning from *trimurtis*, demigods, *yaksha*, *gandharva*, *kinnara*, *bhuta ganas* and other angelic beings as well as all types of demonic and disturbed spirits roaming the earth's atmosphere, these meritless spiritual practices resulted in the physical deformity as well as mental degradation of the populace. They were further made to suffer confined in the ghettos of caste, religion, clan, tribe, with each caste, clan and tribe owing allegiance to different gods, occupation, customs, rituals, etc.

Such a degrading and retrogressive culture was perpetuated in the society through mythology, language, arts and literature, religious edicts, etc. as well as through the wondrous tales of *siddhi* and through the scholarly discourses about *maya*, *dvaita* and *advaita*. This spiritual diversion has been the root cause for the subsequent spiritual fall and cultural degradation of Indian society. The concept of age-specific spiritual reformation is resisted by the orthodoxy substantiating the *chaturvakyas* (four great enunciations) in the Vedas, all of which try to imagine the individual soul as equal to *Brahman*, the Supreme. 'Aham Brahmasmi', one of the *chaturvakyas* means that 'I am *Brahman*'. The individual soul is only part of *Brahman*, not *Brahman* itself, said Navajyotisree Karunakara Guru.

Vedas are bound to *Yuga Dharma*, i.e. they are age-specific. The sages in every age receive the revealed 'word' from *Brahman*, which becomes the Vedas. The wisdom tradition worked through the *Guru-sishya* order. *Guru* is the highest symbol of perfection, the connecting link to the Absolute Truth. Such a *Guru* would be the spiritual authority of the age, of *karma*, *dharma*, *jnana* and *mukthi*. The wisdom tradition is a knowledge related to life and its fulfillment. With the advent of Vedic ritualism, this pure life-culture became defunct. The graceful *Guru* fathoms the threefold time and the cause-effect background of life-experiences. This inner fathoming or mental absorption of an omniscient *Guru* is to be known as *Smriti*. The word *Smriti* means *Guru*'s perception of those karmic entanglements, which are behind the emotional swings in life, in the form of sorrows and happiness, and the advice *Guru* gives to the disciple for overcoming such hurdles is to be considered as the *Veda* or *Sruti*.

When one approaches a *Guru* in order to liberate the soul from its emotional and karmic entanglements, such process of learning sitting beside the *Guru* is Upanishad. Such a culture of learning from the Master and living by his guiding words was the essence of the Wisdom Tradition of Indian spirituality. When the spiritual guidance of such a *Guru* embodiment was unavailable, people began to lead life unaware of the evolving course of *dharma*, accepting the Vedas and Upanishads—the pre-historic catalogues of *dharma*, as the inviolable source of wisdom.

Reviving the Wisdom Tradition

The saying that '*Guru* Sakala Dharmata' is based on this exalted vision of the absolute truth of God. The absolute truth of God self-manifests and gets activated through *Guru* and his Word, which is to be followed by the family—the mother, father, children and others. The divine Word revealed through the *Guru* becomes the guiding force behind the institution of family—the *Grihasthashram* and *Grihasthashrama Dharma*, orienting life and culture to a pedestal of absolute purity and sublime truth. It is this lost *guru*-disciple *ashram* culture which we have to re-establish as the highest aspect of Indian culture and spirituality. Today, unfortunately, the householders are totally cut-off from this *ashram*-centric spiritual culture.

The individual as well as family life is affected by the good and bad deeds of ancestral souls. There are also the negative influences because of the distorted worship of maligned spiritual entities, followed by the families as mentioned earlier. The *Guru parampara* of Navajyotisree Karunakara *Guru* strives to unburden the individuals, families and *gotras* from the negative *karmagati* and spiritual influences, through a way of life that follows the word of *Guru* vigilantly by mind, word and deed, keeping only the *Atmajnani Guru* in the heart. Only the realized and divinely authoritative *Guru* can perceive the *karmagati* of a person and guide one to the Absolute Truth through ultimate *bhakti*, the surrender in devotion, realizing that 'Guru Saakshaat Parabrahm', i.e. *Guru* is the very embodiment of *Brahman*.

We can thus see that this *guru-sishya* tradition is the essence of the spiritual soul of India, which strives to evolve the human spirit from the status of a human to the many dimensions of the divine such as *deva*, *rishi*, *sannyasi*, *jnani*, *bhakta* and *muktha* leading to ultimate liberation. These spiritual embodiments are related to expanding levels of human consciousness related to spiritual evolution. *Guru Margam* or the wisdom path combines *jnana, karma, yoga* and *bhakti* in order to nourish *dharma* and through that one's success in life by way of enhanced *punya* and through that, fortune and wealth. Navajyotisree Karunakara *Guru* reminds us that we have lost this wisdom tradition. The history of the degeneration of this wisdom path is very old as it began twenty five *chaturyugas* ago in the present *Manu* cycle.

The spiritual view of India is a path that strives to fulfill *dharma*, i.e. the duties and purpose of life, *artha*, the earning of wealth etc. required for attaining material and spiritual well being, *kama*, exhausting or fulfilling all desires and finally, earning *mukthi*, getting release from the cycles of births and deaths. It is essential that we realize when and why this wisdom tradition was lost to India. The backbone of *Sanatana* culture was to realize the path of evolution in a natural and rational way and moreover, in accordance with the will of God. It was intended to actualize this knowledge in life and evolve oneself to the path of *jnana*.

We should be able to understand that the prayer 'Loka Samastha Sukhino Bhavantu' as the essence of this spiritual culture. The Indian spiritual concept is the path of fulfilling the purpose of life through *karma* according to *dharma* and the concept of *parinama* or evolution through the wheel of time. It is a complete life-vision in which from an atom to the Absolute attains perfection undergoing transformation. It is in this manner that the Indian spiritual concept had existed as the richest spiritual path in the world. We have to realize that our present spiritual, cultural and social situation is very pathetic. The spiritual guidance of Navajyotisree Karunakara *Guru* sheds light on the cause-effects of this spiritual degradation, which is both ironic and distressing.

The *Guru*'s is a path of spiritual renaissance to redeem the society from this spiritual degradation and value erosion. *Guru* brings to our focus the deviation occurred in the transformational path of spirituality relevant to the age and to *dharma* and *karma*. It is an indisputable fact that *Guru*'s movement of spiritual renaissance, as a correction to this situation, is able to impart to the modern world a new light and inspiration, brilliance and strength. *Guru* presents before us a new path of *karma* and *dharma* respecting the yuga *dharma* in order to rectify the situation taking into consideration the spiritual as well as material aspects. In *Santhigiri*, *Guru* has begun to develop it as a liberating culture without the restrictions of caste, religion, class, gender etc. to fulfill the dictum 'One Caste, One Religion and One God for Humanity'.

3

Guru Tradition, Cultural Creativity and Social Change

The Onto-Genesis of Indian Cultural Tradition

Sebastian Velassery

The present chapter is attempted to examine the foundations of the cultural heritage of India, which is rooted in a tradition, which I would like to call as *Guru* Tradition. It is my endeavour to reaffirm that, this tradition drew upon its resources from the past, that have prepared its people to shape a conscious existence, and, formed the foundations of a qualitative life. What I intend to emphasize here is that, there was a concerted effort in our tradition, to answer to the question of human experience, which, was guided and anchored by a heritage, that, allowed room for personal creativity. An understanding of such a tradition in India as *Guru* Tradition means that, the deepest identity of a person as *Guru* is found precisely in transcending oneself, and reaching out to others; that *Gurus* are situated in communities and cultures, and these are the grounds, upon which, Indians have developed their identities as a people. Accordingly, it is suggested that, the foundations of the meaning and quality of life of the Indians have centred on *Gurus*, who were considered as, the embodiment of the Absolute, or Transcendent.

The *Guru* Tradition in India is based on a sound heritage, stemming from its ancient civilization. It is the ancient and unbroken teaching system, by which, Self Knowledge is transmitted from the one enlightened of it, to the one aspiring for it. What does the Indian psyche[1] innately know about *Gurus* and the *guru* tradition? What information has it inherited, throughout generations of spiritual transmission, about how the *Guru* has been the vital force of the Indian Philosophic and cultural traditions; how he ensures a fresh and ongoing contribution to it; how he disseminates its ideas; and how he is himself the living embodiment of the philosophical ideas that he teaches? This chapter addresses these and other similar questions by documenting and analysing the *Guru* and the *Guru* Tradition, as it is reflected in, the Upanishads and other scriptures. We shall focus particularly, on three crucial questions on *Guru*, as the subject of a moral consciousness, and thus of a cultural tradition.

1. Is the *Guru* only a set of roles constituted entirely in function of a structure or system, in which, one plays a particular part? Or is the *Guru* a subject in his or her own right, with one's proper dignity, heritage, goals and standards?
2. Is the *Guru* merely a stream of consciousness, who achieves a certain level of self-transcendence? Or is the *Guru* an essentially free and responsible psychophysical subject?
3. Does the *Guru* as a free subject is a creative centre, whose basic dynamism, consists in realizing a unique inner harmony within himself/herself and thus paving a harmonious life to the outer community?

The word "*Guru*", a Sanskrit term specifically describes the most elevated spiritual teacher, means "heavy, weighty"[2] with spiritual authority; its esoteric definition is derived from the Sanskrit roots *Gu*, "darkness", and Ru "dispeller of."[3] *Guru*, therefore, means the one who dispels the darkness and brings forth the light; he is the one who, by the weight of his own enlightenment, enlightens. The word "darkness" specifically refers to the ignorance of the Self, *Brahman*, the ultimate Reality, the one source and essence of all existence. Under the influence of the ignorance of the Self, a person mistakes the body and mind to be his true reality. *Guru* is the one who assists in removing the ignorance of the Self, by introducing Self Knowledge, or the knowledge that one is the indivisible whole.

I
GURU TRADITION: THE VEDIC PRIESTS AS *GURU*

Ancient India presents an interesting series of parallels and differences with other south-eastern societies. While ancient China, benefited by a cultural continuity between the ancient civic society and its feudal period, India's cultural history was marked by major mutations.

Historians suggest that, there are no continuities between the early city literary groups and Vedic priests. The high development of writing testifies to the conclusion that, India had a schooled class of priest-scribes. The lack of logical evidence of royal or princely treasures, does not suggest any differentiation in the Indus valley civilization between, a secular and a priestly class. The point is that the Vedic priests were very different from literarily trained priest-scribes who were *Gurus* in their vicinity and for the common man.

According to the historians and scholars, a hereditary priesthood did not exist in the Vedic period.[4] The apparent conflicts, over whether the Vedic prototype of the later *Brahmins*, was priests or magicians, and, whether the office was hereditary, are issues under contentions and, debate among historians. But it may be noted here that, religion of the Indo-Europeans in the Vedic period was, a matter of household observance. According to Deshmukh, "the word Brahmin which is considered by Schrader to have originally meant a magician in the Rig Veda, denotes at first a "poet", "sage", and then "officiating priest" or still later "a special class of priests" and this is not questioned by Sanskrit scholars. The authors of the Vedic Index think that the word does not mean merely "poet' or "sage". But can in the Rig Veda it is almost always seen to be translated by the word "priest", 'since the priest was of course the singer'; but they do not say that the original meaning was a priest, and that it came to mean a "poet" or "sage" later on. Thus, the meaning of the word undoubtedly shows that, the Brahmin was originally, a singer of the hymns and probably also a composer, who was revered for, these admirable virtues of his...Very soon, after the community of these singers came to have a sort of vested interest in maintaining the hold of sacrifice on the popular mind, and also they believed in the increased efficacy of the rites when performed by them.[5] In the estimation of the composers of the Vedic hymns, the position of *Purohita* or domestic priest was the height of ambition. As Keith indicates, the Vedic *Purohita* was the forerunner of the Brahmin statesman.[6] He accompanied the king in battles, for his prayers and spells were thought to be essential for victory. In reward for his services, he received generous gifts, at times a portion of the king's revenues. The sacrificial fee (*dakshina*) was originally a cow placed at the right hand of a singer.[7] In Vedic times, education tended to glide into the hands of *Brahmins*. The student (*Brahmacharin*) underwent a three-day initiation ceremony, during which, he worshipped the fire, and wore a *munja* girdle as a sign that, he was twice-born boy. Initiation incorporated him into a teacher's family, the *guru* who stood in *loco parentis*. There were a number of types of teachers. The *Achara* and *Kulaguru* were in charge of a number of pupils; *strotriyas* were teachers in whom the basic passions had been subdued by Vedic study; *Tapas* practiced austerity. *Vatarasanas* were ascetics; a pupil was required to service, menial and otherwise, such as begging for alms, tending the teacher's household chores and affairs. Studentship lasted from twelve to thirty-two years.[8] *Brahmins* began their studies between eight and sixteen; Kshatriyas eleven to twenty-two; *Vaishyas* twelve to twenty-four.[9] When the studentship was over, a ceremonial bath was taken, the vows taken as *Brahmacharin* were terminated, and the teacher was given a substantial present. At the birth of his grandson, the *Brahmin* was expected to retire from the household and become a forest dweller.

Guru as the Intellectual

The role of the priest-intellectuals had to change with the transformation of northern India, from a land of semi-feudal manorial communities, to one of patrimonial kingdoms. The conflict between semi-feudal nobles and their priests, on the one hand, and the kings and their priests on the other, was a major factor in the crystallization into endogamous groups, by the *Kshatriyas* and *Brahmins*. However, the rise of the kingdoms, had far more extensive bearing on the role of the intellectual, than forcing of traditional-priest intellectuals toward endogamous closure. Among the classes of teachers were the *Achara* (spiritual teacher of the highest grade who accepted no fees), the *Guru* (who also taught gratis, particularly in moral matters), the *Upadhya* (who demanded pay, and gave instruction in some particular subject), the *Sikshaka* (who gave instruction in arts, such as dancing). Teachers who had given up the world also included the Buddhist *Bhikkus*, Jain *Nirgranthas* and the *Ajivikas*.[10] The school was usually in teacher's home. According to great Indian grammarian, Panini, the various classes of subject matter included the Vedic texts, works of original thinkers and system-makers and ancient tales or works of fiction dealing with mythological subjects.

During the patrimonial and civic period, many forces were at work toward the separation of education from the household of the *Guru* and the formation of specialized schools. Accordingly, the Indian social system was getting transformed from one of semi-feudal manorial communities to loosely knit kingdoms comprising a series of forms varying from peasant villages to thriving cities. This is the time, according to the historians, that the *Brahmins* got a strategic position to monopolize their intellectual roles as *Gurus*. As Weber observed, the *Brahmins* infiltrated the learned occupations, particularly administrative posts, which demanded writing skill and education, as did the clerics of the middle-ages.[11]

Guru as the Enlightened

The historical and cultural development of *Guru* as the living force has been evolved and present in Indian tradition, culture and life for thousands of years. Though scriptures such as the *Rig Veda*, the Upanishads, the *Bhagwad Gita*, and the *Ramayana* have the worship, devotion and respect of the people, from all strata of Indian Society, throughout the ages, the presence of the *Guru*—the one who is enlightened as to the truth of the scriptures, and who is, thus the living scripture—continues to be the central force in Indian Philosophy, Spirituality, and culture. The *Guru* is the spirit of Indian Philosophy and culture, which has as its basis and goal, the consciousness that has directly realized the essence of the scriptures—the *Guru* Consciousness. The dynamic sacred centre of Hinduism is, in fact, the enlightened *guru*, whose charismatic leadership creates the institution for philosophical, religious, and social change. From ancient to modern times, the *Guru* has continued to be the Indian philosophical tradition's very source, and the insurance of its vital maintenance and growth.[12]

Guru as the Vision of Oneness

Guru Consciousness, expressed through the vehicle of an enlightened human being, is the unchanging state of Oneness (*ekatva*), whose nature is indivisibility. The *Chandogya Upanishad* propounds Pure Existence or Being as one without a second—*ekam evadvitiyam.*[13] There exists no other, no *dvitiya* all the appellations of the *Guru* Consciousness are synonymous with Oneness and the vision of that *ekatva*. The vision of the Self, or *atma-darshana*, is attained upon the successful removal of *avidya*, ignorance of the Self. The nature of *avidya* is dualistic consciousness or vision (bheda-darshana). The *Guru*, having permanently annihilated the very seed of duality from the *hrdaya-guhya*, has opened the scope of his vision to the vista of the Self. The term *hrdaya-guhya*, translated, as the "cave of the heart" is an expression adopted throughout the Upanishads to represent the innermost centre of the individual person, or *jivatman*. When a person has attained the state of de-identification from the ego-consciousness at this deepest place, then, the Upanishads explain, liberation has been attained.

Guru as the Delivering Self

The Upanishads resound with descriptions of the ultimate reality, *Brahman*. Each passage or narration intends only to lead the *Sisya* to an understanding of the unchanging, immortal substance that is *Brahman*. The significance of this is the context of a definition of *Guru* is that the Upanishads reiterate that the one who undertakes spiritual practices and identifies with *Brahman* will transform into that ultimate Reality, the source of all existence. The one who completes the spiritual path of transformation into the ultimate Reality becomes the embodiment of that Reality. Such a one becomes the *Guru*—the enlightened one, the liberated one—gifted with the eponymous power; to dispel darkness. By virtue of having conquered *avidya*, the *Guru*—who has become the absolute light of consciousness—is empowered to remove *avidya* from the vision of the devotees by shedding the light of knowledge. The *Guru*'s role is to exhibit freedom, and affect freedom in those souls aspiring to perfect freedom. The aspirant has reached a point of disillusionment with what he or she perceives as his or her world and him—or herself and initiates a spiritual search. The emancipated being, the *Guru*, is the only one who can guide the soul to its own perfection, for the *Guru* is the one who has travelled the path and reached the destination. Thus, *Guru* is the only one who can create *Guru*. The *Sastras*, or scriptures may describe the ultimate Reality, and inspire or teach the students about that Reality, but they cannot serve as living teachers to guide the soul through the unexpected obstacles or doubts, which arise in the life of the person undergoing the process of transformation.

Having attained the height of Self Knowledge, the enlightened being is no longer engaged in actions to become free. Freedom is the nature of the *Guru*. Thought and activity is known as the knowingness of the Self. Relaxed in the knowledge of the all-permeating nature of the *Atman*, the *Guru* is not a vehicle for revealing self-knowledge.

Though ignorance does not exist as a reality for the enlightened one, still the *Guru* acts for the liberation of all, removing the darkness of ignorance by shedding the continuous light of the Self. In the *Yoga-tattva Upanishad* it is concisely expressed thus: At an unprohibited, far off, place. Calm and quiet, undisturbed, The Yogin guarantees protection to all beings, as to his own self.[14]

Guru Consciousness as *Brahma-Cetana*

The term "*Guru*" represents not only the enlightened teacher but also the state of *Guru* Consciousness. *Guru* Consciousness is synonymous with *Brahman*, a term first used in the Upanishads to represent the Self, the one essential Reality.[15] That person who transforms his or her dualistic consciousness, by which he or she sees him or herself as a subject to an object and realizes the one indivisible reality of *Brahman*, becomes the embodiment of *Guru* Consciousness. In this respect, the state and the person who has attained the state are one and the same. Although *Brahman*'s nature is essentially ineffable (*anirvacaniya*) it is realizable through direct experience (*atma-saksatkara*). And the one who realizes it, is *Brahman* himself. Thus, as *Brahman* is defined by such epithets as immortality (*amrta*), freedom (*svatantra*), perfection (*purna*), infinity (*ananta*), eternal existence (*sat*), pure consciousness (*cit*), indivisible bliss (*Ananda*), so also the *Guru*, who has realized *Brahman*, can be defined by the very same epithets. It is on this premise that, the *Guru* is qualified as fearless (*abhaya*), free (*mukta*), fulfilled (*trista*), the knower (*jnata*) of the unchanging knowledge (*Jnana*), encompassing all those attributes, which reflects the height of spiritual attainment. The *Guru* is the one who is fully united with the *Guru* Consciousness and never turned away from it. As a result, he is noble in his very presence; his very knowledge and power to transmit this consciousness remove the darkness for those aspiring to live the state of Oneness. By association with the *Guru*, who is the living embodiment of *Brahman*, as well as by the *Guru*'s teachings about *Brahman*, the student is able to reunite himself with his or her true Self—the *Guru* Consciousness, the state of Oneness.[16]

Guru as the Deified Person

In attaining the perfection of enlightenment, the *Guru* has attained the state of immortality (*amrta*), and is thus said to be, unborn (*ajara*) and undying (*amara*): "Knowing that immortal *Brahman* I am immortal (*vidvan brahma 'mrto' mrtam*)."[17] The sublime meaning of this teaching is that the realized one is no longer subject to the changes caused by birth and death. He has crossed the threshold of human consciousness where birth and death are fixed realities. Now, birth and death are but motions occurring to the body and not to the *Guru* Consciousness. Though such a declaration seems unimaginable, to the realized one it is the truth: "The knowing Self is never born: nor does he die at any time. He sprang from nothing and nothing sprang from him. He is unborn, eternal, abiding and primeval. He is not slain when the body is slain."[18] The enlightened author of the *Brihadaranyaka Upanishad* has attempted to define this state thus: "When all the desire that dwell in the heart are cast away, then does the mortal become immortal, then he attains *Brahman* here (in this very body)." Just as the slough of a snake lies on an anthill, dead, cast off, even so lays this body. But this disembodied immortal life is *Brahman* only, is light indeed, Your Majesty.[19] The above verse clears any misconception about death not occurring to the body of the realized one. His body, like any other, undergoes death, and his body also experiences pain as any other body would; however, the consciousness of the *Guru* is absorbed in the state of deathlessness and painlessness. Hearing the claims about deathlessness, bodilessness, and painlessness, someone who does not understand these states might interpret them literally, and think that the *Guru* would not experience death, if killed, or pain, if tortured. The voluntary self-mortification to authenticate the experience of bodilessness and painlessness advocated and practised by some pseudo-enlightened teachers and sects, is not the intended meaning of this Upanishadic definition. The Upanishadic *Guru* did not subject themselves to unnecessary physical tests to substantiate the claim to bodilessness nor did they commit suicide to prove their deathlessness; their concern was to attain the state of immortal consciousness. The Upanishadic *Guru* understood the value of the body as the instrument for the attainment of the realized state. Therefore, they advocated proper treatment and conditions for the vehicle that enabled one to conduct practices for the attainment of 'Brahma-Vidya, the very knowledge which liberates one from the sense of death. [By knowing] that which is inaudible, intangible, invisible and changeless.'

[That which is] unperceivable by the sense of taste, and of smell

[That which is] indestructible and perennial beginningless, endless, greater than the great, remaining eternal,

He, who knows it, becomes free from the jaws of death.[20]

Upanishads as the Source of *Guru* Tradition

Though Indian legend claims the existence of *Gurus* for thousands of years, the first scriptural evidence for the *Guru* Tradition is the Upanishads.[21] Accordingly, for this reason, Upanishads are regarded as the primary source material for the research on the ancient *Guru* Tradition. In this scripture, which contains the metaphysical knowledge of India, there are countless instances of the *guru-sisya-parampara*, so to say, the *Guru* Disciple tradition. There are examples of disciple seeking a *Guru* for instruction in Self Knowledge, instances of aspirants engaging in years of preparation for receiving Self Knowledge from an enlightened being, and countless examples of *guru-sisya-samvada*, or dialogues between *Guru* and disciple in which the *Guru* unfolds in the aspiring disciple the knowledge of the Self or *Brahman*.[22]

Self-Knowledge and *Guru* Tradition

The subject of Self Knowledge is the central theme of the Upanishads and of the *Guru* Tradition, both ancient and modern. Self Knowledge is the state or condition of awareness attained by one who has become enlightened or liberated. Self Knowledge is the original consciousness, prior to any state of consciousness that is affected by duality or ignorance. The nature of Self Knowledge is Oneness; hence, it is the pure or unadulterated knowledge of Oneness. When the subject of Self Knowledge is introduced in the Upanishads, it is termed as *Brahma-vidya*—literally, *Brahma*, "Self" and *Vidya*, "Knowledge"—and is presented as both the original and the final knowledge, the realized Knowledge, which is not subject to change or improvement. It is the unchanging Knowledge because it uninterruptedly knows the unchanging, unmodifiable reality, the Self or *Brahman*. Hence, in the *Guru* Tradition, whether ancient, medieval, or modern, the subject and nature of Self Knowledge, or *Brahma-Vidya*, remains unchanged because Self Knowledge is not a kind of knowledge, which is dependent on time; it is said to be eternal. Therefore, the *Guru* tradition is not a tradition of accumulative knowledge but of realized knowledge, which is both timeless and universal. Self Knowledge, or *Brahma-Vidya*, is expounded in the Upanishads with the sole purpose of engaging the aspirant in a process of learning through which he or she will evolve into the consciousness of *Brahma-Vidya* and, thus become liberated from the dualistic nature of the mind. Therefore, where the central purpose—*Moksa or liberation*—is repeatedly described by the Upanishads is *Gurus*; it is meant to explain that when the very root of the ignorance of the Self is dissolved, the person has become liberated from ignorance. Liberation precipitates a unique state of consciousness in which only Self Knowledge shines. All notion of duality or of anything existing as, separate from the Self, is transformed into the knowledge of Self-alone. The unfoldment of this transformation from the state of *Avidya*—which is literally translated as "nescience" with a meaning "not" and Vidya meaning "knowledge"—to the state of enlightenment is the teleos of the *Guru* tradition, both ancient and modern. With this ultimate purpose fulfilled, the *Guru* tradition is perpetuated as a living embodiment of cultural creativity, and not simply as a scriptural tradition that speaks only of enlightenment.

However, in the Upanishads, which are the scriptures referred to as *Vedanta* (literally, "the end of the Vedas"), the *Guru* is repeatedly defined as that being that has dissolved or transformed the divided human consciousness back into its originality, *Brahman*. Here, *Guru* is presented neither as deity, priest, poet, nor teacher, but as a consciousness, *Guru-Cetana*—a transcendent consciousness identical with the ultimate reality—*Brahman* or *Brahma-Cetana*. The one who has transformed his human nature as a result of directly realizing this *Brahma-Cetana* becomes its embodiment and is, therefore entitled to be called *Guru* and enact the role of the liberated teacher.

According to the Upanishadic *Gurus*, *Brahman* is indefinable. Though indefinable, they attempted to describe its characteristics, in order to offer a glimpse into the nature of the Absolute Reality. However, to limit *Brahman* certain characteristics would be to define the indefinable. The descriptions of these characteristics are simply an attempt by the Upanishadic *Gurus* to make the nature of *Brahman* understandable to the elevated souls, which are seeking to attain the emancipated state of consciousness.

Brahman is described as the original light (*Jyoti*), the original creation (*Hiranyagarbha*), immortal (*amrta*), indestructible (*aksara*), truth (*satya*), Pure knowledge (*jnana*), infinite (*ananta*), bliss (*ananda*), fearlessness (*abhaya*), freedom (*mukti*), pure substance, the very Self (*atman*). The *Guru*, having realized *Brahman* Consciousness, exhibits these qualities. *Guru* Consciousness is birthless (*ajara*) deathless (*amara*), pure (*nirmala*), and true (*sat*), and so forth. The *Maitri Upanishad* describes these conditions of the Self in the following ways. He is the Self, which is free from evil (*papa*), ageless (*ajara*), deathless (*amrtyu*), sorrow less (*Asoka*), and free from uncertainty, free from fetters, whose conception is the real, whose desire is the real. He is the supreme Lord, he is the ruler of beings, and he is the protector of beings.[23]

Guru Consciousness is said to be *Nirdvandva*, or uninfluenced by the pair of opposites. This implies that anger or joy, or hatred or love or heat or cold, or goodness or evil, or birth or death, etc. does not affect the *Guru* Consciousness; it remains unmoved because, it is permanently established in its original, unchanging state. It is free from all conditions because, it is its own condition, Self-luminous (*Brahma-Jyoti*). *Guru* consciousness, *Brahman* Consciousness, remains ever full (*Purna*). In discussing *Brahman* Consciousness, the language of contradiction is inevitably encountered, yet in the *Guru* Consciousness no contradiction exists because, all elements are included in it. The *Kathopanishad* describes these apparent contradictions in the following way: Sitting, he moves far; lying he goes everywhere who, save myself, is fit to know that god who rejoices and rejoices not? Knowing the Self who is bodiless among bodies, the stable among the unstable, the great, the all-pervading, and the wise man does not grieve.[24]

The *Brahmavid*, who has attained the state of liberation, lives these qualities continuously. The possibility of descending into the state of darkness, death, destructibility, untruth, ignorance, limitation, suffering, fear, and bondage is finished. Reaching the height of *Guru* Consciousness, there is no return to the realm of duality. The transformation from *Avidya* (ignorance) to *Vidya* (knowledge) has materialized in the being of the *Guru*. Thus, the *Guru* Consciousness is permanently one with *Brahman*.

It is this leap from the human to the ultimate consciousness that evokes the sense of mysterium in the unenlightened mind as it attempts with a sense of fascination, to comprehend as to how the enlightened mind perceives consciousness (*Cetana*), or infinity (*ananta*), or bliss (*ananda*), or even from the undivided state, form (*rupa*). This fascination with the enlightened consciousness encourages an ontological, epistemological and soteriological investigation into the ultimate Reality. This is that and thus they recognise the ineffable Supreme bliss. How then come to know this? Does it shine (of itself) or does it shine (in reflection)? The sun shines not there, nor the moon and the stars, these lightning shine not, where then could this fire be? Everything shines only after that shining light. His shining illumines this entire world.[25]

The Upanishadic description of the embodiment of *Guru* Consciousness is twofold. The first aspect discusses the human characteristics that the *Guru* has transformed through *Sadhana*, which has resulted in his attainment of the undivided state of consciousness. These human characteristics are desire, fear, sorrow, anger, happiness, worry, possessiveness, envy, jealousy, ambition, and so forth. Having transformed these characteristics, how does the *Guru* communicate through the *Guru* mind and *Guru* ego? And if the *Guru* has transcended human emotions and qualities, how does he operate through the human vehicle? How does he relate to the environment, to society, and to the world at large? The second part of the discussion investigates the relationship that the *Guru* as the embodiment of *Guru* Consciousness, has with human existence. Clarifying the link between the *Guru* Consciousness, and the human manifestation of this consciousness, will dispel the mass mysteries and misconceptions held about the nature and manifestation of the authentic *Guru,* and will offer an understanding of the *Guru* and the *Guru* tradition, that will be comprehensible to the developed intelligence of our time.

Characteristic Features of *Guru*

The one who embodies *Guru* Consciousness is considered to be unique, not only because, this attainment is so rare among the multitudes of unrealised beings, but also because *Brahman* is the source of all originality and genius; thus the *Guru* emanates special qualities. The Upanishads teach that, the attainment of this consciousness and the qualities associated with it, is feasible only when the *tattvas* have been mastered in the mental and physical bodies of the enlightened one. "The *tattvas*—the elements of earth, water, fire, air and other—are described in *Taittiriya Upanishad* as the fundamental elements comprising the entire creation. From this Self, verily, ether arose; from ether air; from air fire; from fire water; from water the earth."[26] Mastery over the *tattvas* is accomplished at the different levels of mind and body, referred to in the *Taittriya Upanishad* as sheaths.[27] The first sheath is the *Anna-rasa-maya*[28], the self which consists of the essence of food; within the first sheath is found the second, the atma-pranamaya,[29] or the self which consists of the life-force; the third sheath, existing within the second, is the *atma-manomaya*[30], or the self which consists of mind; within that lies the fourth sheath, the *atma-vijnanamaya*[31] or the self consisting of intellect; and within that lies the fifth, the *atma-anandamaya.*[32] The self-consisting of bliss. This mastery of the *tattvas* at the level of the sheaths, is the foundation for a host of special qualities for which the authentic *Guru* is recognized:

He attains self-rule. He attains to the lord of Manas, the lord of speech, the lord of sight, the lord of hearing, the lord of intelligence—this and more he becomes, even *Brahman* whose body is space, whose Self is the real, whose delight is life, whose mind is bliss, who abounds in tranquillity, who is immortal.[33] Having become the master of mind, intelligence, sight, sound, smell and so on, the *Guru* is no longer the victim of the weaknesses of any of those faculties. Thus, the *Svetasvatara Upanishad* exclaims: When the fivefold quality of *Yoga* is produced, as earth, water, fire, air and ether arise, and then there is no longer sickness, no old age, and no death to him who has obtained a body made of the fire of *Yoga.*[34] Acquiring "a body made of the fire of Yoga", the *Guru* achieves the capacity to tolerate physical discomfort, and still remains at ease. The pairs of opposites have been conquered, thus the *Guru* has surmounted heat, cold, hunger, loneliness, fear, anger, lust, and pain. If a teacher of *Brahma-Vidya* has not transcended any of these emotions, then the title of *Guru* is not merited.

With the removal of the cumbersome barrier of duality, the *Guru* is no longer bound by the confines of time and space. Consequently, many powers are said to be at his command. Because he is the very Self, he can see clearly the nature of all manifestation and into the heart of matter: "But he, ever blissful, with all penetrating power, omnipresent, glows through his own light as pure, enlightened, eternal, spotless and calm."[35]

Is the person of the *Guru* truly omniscient? The disciples surrounding many powerful *Gurus* have often claimed that their preceptor had the power of omniscience. This conviction has led some devotees to perceive their *Guru* as a god, but to some non-devotees, this power has seemed like that of an outstanding magician. Though such powers, or *Siddhis*, are conceivable (and guaranteed by the scriptures[36] in the enlightened one, it is not this meaning of omniscience that is intended by the words. "Through the eye of knowledge the *Brahman* as (knower of *Brahman*) see the one alone extending throughout, from *Brahman* down to the world of plants."[37] By omniscience is meant perceiving *Brahman* in all existence as all existence. The *Katha Upanishad* states about this vision of the Self and about the one perceiving it in the following way:

> In all beings, dwells this (*Purusa*)
> As *Atman*, invisible, concealed from view,
> He is only seen by the keenest thought,
> By the subtlest (intelligence) of those thinkers

Who see into the subtle?[38]

The one who sees into the subtlest of realities (*suksmati-suksma*) actually sees that which is inherent in the being and not separate from one's Self. The ultimate Reality is the source of all manifestation, the quintessence in all creation, the originality here defined as *Atman* or *Brahman*. As the above verse also indicates that which separates the realized from the non-realized consciousness is the power of vision. This vision is not simply the outer faculty of sight, but relates to the root power of seeing, which is attached to the power of thought: the person who has developed his or her thought has, at the same time, developed the inner vision, where the source of the gross, material world is perceived. That *Brahmavid* who has cultivated and developed the spiritual thought has at the same time opened the spiritual vision and sees the *Atman*, the subtlest of all realities, the source of all. Thus, it is said that the *Guru* has opened the third eye (*dyoya-drsti*) and is, therefore, a Seer. It is in this sense that the *Guru* is said to be omniscient: he sees all because he is all.

The realized being has often been referred to as a *Siddha*, a perfected master, because all the elements are at his command. But the purpose and role of the *Guru* is simply to eliminate darkness by bringing the light of *brahma-vidya*. Any master who sees powers or *Siddhis* for any purpose other than illumination of the Self is not living the realized state such a person is not perfected, for he hasn't conquered greed, the need for personal power or the desire for fame. The archetypal *Guru* has no need for ego-gratification, or for a large following. The only refuge and shelter for the *Guru* is the Self. The *Tejobindu Upanishad* describes this condition in the following way:

> Essentially associating with the lonely-
> He who is God, sure knows the highest-
> Greed, delusion, fear, pride,
> Anger, love, sin renouncing,
> Cold and warm, hunger and thirst,
> And intentions, whichever change,
> Not proud of the *Brahmana* descent,
> Not have the rubbish of liberation texts,
> Knowing no fear, nor lust, nor pain
> Nor respect, nor disrespect anymore-
> Because from all these is free
> *Brahman*, the highest goal of all endeavours
> *Brahman*, the highest goal of all endeavours.[39]

The nature of the *Guru* is replete with the power of attraction. Because of his vision of Oneness, all life is attracted to the warmth of this person. Oneness attracts and creates Oneness. Exuding the qualities of "lightness, healthiness, steadiness, clearness of complexion, pleasantness of voice, and sweetness of odour."[40] The enlightened being is always sought out. In the *Chandogya Upanishad* it is stated: "One who knows this becomes one beautiful to see and heart of in renowned, yes, one who knows this."[41]

Caste System and *Guru*

The bloody persecution of Buddhists under the Sunga dynasty, which followed the Maurya, has signalled the beginning of a counter-attack on the heterodoxies and also the rise of the caste system and the attendant close of India's most creative period. With the rise and hardening of the caste system, the place of the intellectual came to be epitomized by the *guru*.[42] As established during the Brahminical restoration, the position of the *Guru* was modelled after the relation of the Vedic teacher to the student of the Vedas. In early times, the kings and nobles as house Chaplin's and tutors employed experts in Vedic lore. However, in the course of the restoration of Hinduism, plebeian mystagogues and soul-helpers that were often interpenetrated their ranks.[43] They were instrumental in helping the restoration of

Hinduism. They established religious orders and achieved spiritual domination over the masses. The majority of the mendicant *gurus* were *Brahmins*. They were not the bearers of a new religious interpretation, but of a new kind of religious authority. The apotheosis of the *guru* is dramatically illustrated by the fact that even religious reformers who turned every effort toward the destruction of idolatry were deified in their turn. Weber observes the following: "The leading *guru* in a territory is similar to a Bishop of a Western church, visiting his diocese accompanied by his following. He had power to excommunicate individuals in the case of grosser sins. He bestowed absolution for penitence, placed a tax on believers".[44] As a living saviour, the *guru* replaced all transcendent objects of worship. Hence Weber insists that adoration of the living saviour was the final stage in Hindu religious development. Accordingly, they were accorded great esteem by their followers or a sect of people who followed them as *Sishyas*. In the period of the orthodox restoration, Hinduism itself was transformed from an aristocratic and intellectual religion to a religion adapted for the salvation needs of the Indian masses. The key intellectuals of the Neo-Hindu restoration were no longer the Chaplin's of royal and noble households but apotheosised leaders of mass salvation cults, so to say, the *GURUS*.

II
GURU: A POST-UPANISHADIC EXAMINATION

The metaphysical culture of the Upanishads is the fertile ground from which other cultural traditions have arisen in India. Thus the descriptions of the person of the *Guru* in the *Kularnava Tantra*, the *Guru* Gita from the *Skanda Purana*, *Astavakra Gita*, *Tripura Rahasya*, *Uddhava Gita*, *Avadhuta Gita* and many other scriptures, are extensions of the Upanishadic archetype. It is essential for this examination of the *Guru* to refer though briefly, to other scriptures within the philosophical and spiritual tradition of the Upanishads, for these reveal the impact of the Upanishadic *Guru* Tradition in Post-Upanishadic times. The two representative scriptures to be examined here are the *Kularnava Tantra* and the *Guru Gita*.

One of the most thorough descriptions of the nature, role and qualities of the *Guru* is located in the *Kularnava Tantra*.[45] This scripture describe the rarity of the enlightened being by the example of light, stating that many are those teachers who radiate light equivalent to lamps, but rare is the one who reflects the comparable to the sun (XIII, 104).[46] According to the *Kularnava Tantra*, the *Guru* has the following qualities: He is charming *(manohara):* endowed with all attributes (*sarvalaksana-sampanna*): is a knower of all the agamas (*sarvagamartha-tattvajna*): knows the application of all the mantras (*mantra-vidhanavid*): bewitches the world *(loka-sammohanakara*): is of happy countenance (*sumukha);* is clean (*svaccha*), is easily accessible (*sulabha):* dissipates doubt and delusion (*bhrama-samsayanasak*); looks upon the world with an inner vision (*antarlaksya bahirdsti*); is all knowing (sarvajna); knows the mysteries of time and place (*desakalavid*) knows the meaning of gestures (*ingitakaravid*); knows past, present, and future (*trikalajna*): is capable of penetrating to the inner depths of the devotee's being (*vedhaka*); is the illuminator (*bodhaka*); is peaceful (*santa*): is compassionate to all creatures (*sarvajivadayapara*); can control the movement of the organs (*svadhinendriya sancara*); has conquered the six enemies—desire, anger, greed, delusion, jealousy, and pride (*sadvargavidjayaksama*); can distinguish between the fit and unfit disciple (*patrapatravisesavid*); is stainless (*nirmala*); is ever content (*nityasantusta*); is independent (*svatantra*); is endowed with the power of mantra (*mantrasaktimana)*; is a lover of genuine devotees (*sadbhakta-vatsala*); is steadfast (*dhira*); is merciful (*krpalu*); speaks with a smile (*smitapurnavak*); is dear to devotees (*bhaktapriya*): is ever generous (*sadodara*); is profound (*gambhira)*; is an excellent practicant of the spiritual sciences (*sistasadhaka*); is free from attachment, hate, fear, pain and ostentation (*dambha*); can distinguish between what is good and what is bad (*gunadosavibhedaka*); is unattached to the opposite sex and wealth, and dislikes bad company or other vices (*anasakta*); has a feeling of Oneness with all (*sarvahambhavasanyukta*); has the power to be silent (*mauni*); is free of preferences (*nirapeksa*): is unaffected by praise or criticism (*tulyuaninidatuti*).[47]

Meaning of *Guru*: The *Kularnava Tantra* following the list of the *Guru's* qualities of (which the above is a selection from a greater list), the *Kularnava Tantra* suggests methods for assessing the aptness of the *Guru*. It first proposes that the disciple examine the competence of the *Guru* by analysing his "capacity for the transmission of knowledge, perfection in the science of mantra, and the ability to make a subtle impact.[48] If the *Guru* possesses these abilities, only then should one consider discipleship. If in studying with a *Guru*, one does not experience a subtle transformation of consciousness, then such a teacher should not be considered a *Guru*. According to the above quotation, a *Guru* is endowed with the power to assist the student to transform slowly or quickly (depending upon the capacity of the student) from a dualistic vision to the vision of the Self. Secondly, the *Kularnava Tantra*, in describing the consciousness of the *Guru*, states that it is infused with bliss, or *Ananda*. The scripture explains that upon contact with a *Guru*, bliss, happiness, joy, or the student or person present automatically experiences peace.[49] If irritation or agitation ensues, then one should not choose tutelage under that particular teacher. Thirdly, and of particular importance, the *Kularnava Tantra* warns that if a *Guru* imparts teachings contrary to the essence of those enunciated in the Vedas, particularly the Upanishads, then both teacher and student are doomed to great suffering.[50] "He who imparts an instruction that is not sanctified is a sinner; his mantra is lost like paddy-seed in the sands".[51]

This injunction presents an interesting question regarding the relationship of the enlightened consciousness to scripture. Does the enlightened consciousness live and reflect the accepted scriptural teachings? Or, does the possibility exist of the enlightened consciousness authoring a scripture whose knowledge differs from the Upanishads? It also inspires an inquiry as to whether the enlightened consciousness would teach a dogma, philosophy, or practices not advocated in the Upanishads? The above injunction explicitly denounces those teachers profess to be *Guru* who propagate spiritual teachings contrary to the accepted and honoured Vedic scriptures namely *brahma-vidya*, and emphasizes that a new message or philosophy could only be rooted in a dualistic intellect not entirely absorbed in the absolute reality. *Brahman*, as has been quoted from the Upanishads, it is only the purified intellect, transformed into Self-Consciousness, which perceives the *Suddha-cetana*, the basis of enlightened consciousness, the *Guru*. Only a person transformed into the state of unconditional realization is entitled to interpret and transmit the ancient teachings, because he has become the living Upanishad. In the same stance, the *Kularnava Tantra* warns that the spiritual knowledge of *mantra* cannot take root in a student who is devoid of potential; therefore, the *Guru* must test the applicant. If a *Guru* imparts knowledge without testing the capacity of the student then both teacher and student will suffer if the student proves to be an unfit vehicle.[52]

Guru Gita and Other Texts

The *Guru Gita*, a significant section of the *Skanda Purana* and an authoritative scripture about the *Guru*, states that unless one has understood the *guru-tattva*, or the *Guru* principle, the Vedas, Sastras, Puranas, Smrti, *mantras*, yantras, vows, penances, and pilgrimages will not be comprehensible or beneficial. Those who attempt the study of the sacred texts without comprehending the *guru-tattva* will not be able to penetrate the essential meaning of its teachings, and licence will be prone to misinterpret them. Those who practice vows, penances and charity will do so as fools, unless they know the *Guru*.[53] These verses isolate the *Guru* as the foundation of scripture and contact with the *Guru* as fundamental to scriptural interpretation. Self-proclaimed teachers who have not trained under a *Guru* and who attempt to discern the more esoteric scriptures, such as the Saiva treatises can be led into great errors and meet with their downfall, because, according to the *Guru Gita*, their intellects are fundamentally deluded.[54] Misconceptions can lead to the founding of sects, who do not uphold the intended precepts of the text and to forging ideologies equipped with religious observances and ordinances based on the misconceptions of an unrealised intellect, all in the name of truth and realized perception. Such teachers can malign the purity of the knowledge tradition conveyed in the texts, and cause severe damage in the lives of innocent seekers. Thus the *Guru Gita* cautions that only the initiates of an authentic *Guru* should represent the *Guru* Tradition and lends *bhashya*, or commentary, to the revered scriptures.

The *Guru Gita* identifies the *Guru* as the bearer of light, and states: "He by whose light (true knowledge) arises is known by the word *Guru*".[55] The enlightened intellect is the instrument by which an *avidya*-ridden intellect can be illumined; much like a lit candle can be used to light an unlit one. This process of enlightenment cannot take place without the flame contacting the wick. In this respect, the *Guru*'s very presence is potent with knowledge and contact with it transforms the disciple into *Guru*. The *Guru Gita* claims that even by remembering the *Guru*, knowledge will spontaneously arise in the devotee.[56] The power of the *Guru* to illumine the devotee is so heightened that even through the subtlety of thought, illumination can be attained.

Tapas and Nyasa

In the development of the Indian cultural tradition during the time of Upanishads and even afterwards in various *Bhakti* movements, the model that came into prominence is centred on *Gurus*. What is strikingly explicit is that the general orientations of this culture were predominantly rooted in two important Upanishadic concepts—*tapas* and *nyasa*. The reason why this culture pays great respect to *sannyasins* is that the Indian tradition holds in high esteem the life of *tapas* (austerity, penance, asceticism) and *nyasa* (renunciation).[57] In fact, *tapas* and *nyasa* are the two leading doctrines of the Upanishads. *Tapas* or ascetic life is raised to a special vocation (*dharma-skandha*) in the *Chandogya Upanishad*.[58] In the *Brihadaranyaka Upanishad*, we find men like Yajnavalkya departing to the solitude of wilderness for doing *tapas* and contemplation of the *Atman*.[59] The *Chandogya* describes the *tapas* of Upakosala, the *Brahmacharin*.[60] The same Upanishad, again, speaks of *tapas* as the most important (*Prathamas tapa eva*).[61] Yajnavalkya instructs Gargi that one wins Svarga (a temporary heaven) if one performs *tapas*, sacrifice and worship even though one has not known the *Atman*.[62] The *Brihadaranyaka* imparts the noble idea that the patient bearing with sickness (*vyadhi*), taking part in a funeral procession and cremation ceremony etc. are the best sort of *tapas* (*Paraman tapas*).[63] The *Mahanarayanopanishad* regards renunciation (*sannyasa*) as superior to all forms of *tapas*.[64] The *Kathopanishad* speaks of *tapas* as the *pratistha* (foundation, basis or prerequisite) of *Brahma-vidya*. The *Svetasvatara* declares that *Paramatman* is intuited through *tapas*[65]; *Atmavidya* is rooted in *tapas*[66]; *Brahman* is known through *tapas*; and the grace of God.[67] According to *Mundakopanishad*, the performers of *tapas* and Knowers of *Brahman* attain the "imperishable person".[68] The Prasna exhorts us that "those who practise *tapas* along with virtues of chastity, faith and knowledge will win the eternal goal.[69] Deussen maintains that it is *tapas* that later assumed the form of the V*anaprastha-ashrama* and *nyasa* became later the *Sannyasa Ashrama*.[70]

By Way of a Conclusion

These observations obviate the necessity to realize that the Hindu tradition must be considered as a tradition based on *Guru Cetana* whose foundations were built on *tapas* and *nyasa*. Accordingly, I may argue that this tradition rejected all absolute distinctions as it was rooted in the idea of an underlying unity that sustains all differences. Hence, this tradition was able to postulate and maintain that all realms of existence are continuous—the physical, the vital, the mental and the spiritual—and it is perfectly possible for one order of being to be transformed into another. In such a tradition and world-view where the pattern of life events is interdependent, *Guru* is seen as unitary consciousness—variously called *Brahma-Jnani, Brahma-saksatkari*, and *Brahma-anubhavi* etc. What this tradition undergirds, therefore, is the experiential realization where the *guru cetana* is the *Brahma cetana*. *Guru*, therefore, in this tradition is not merely a person from the Western perspective, but a unitary consciousness whose identities have achieved self-expression.

This positive notion of the *Guru* has always had an identical or unchanging meaning in both the Indian Philosophical tradition as well as culture. More than by mere accretion, the notion has managed to incorporate the great achievements of human self-discovery for which, in turn, it has been both the stimulus and the goal. Having looked into this cultural tradition as based on the *Guru* Consciousness vis-à-vis *Brahma cetana*, we have examined the nature of the *Guru* through reflection on a series of paired and progressively deeper dimensions: first, as a role, and as the one who lives out this role; second, as free self-consciousness that realizes itself as the IDENTITY and as the subject of that freedom; and third, as moral agent who fulfils that plenitude of consciousness. Accordingly, a philosophical and cultural tradition, which is rooted in *Guru* Consciousness as an image of the transcendent principle transforms and sensitises its culture. *Guru* remains part of nature but rather than being subject thereto as a mere producer or consumer, is a creative and transforming centre. This is an affirmation of existence as sharing in *Sat*, *Cit* and *Ananda* and reflects the meaning of the transcendent for man and of man in the Transcendent.

It would seem, therefore, that the *Guru* power or *Guru* consciousness is a creative stance reflecting the content, not only of the past, but of the time in which one stands and of the life project in which, one is engaged. It is a creative unveiling of the content of the tradition as this comes progressively and historically into the present and through the present, passes into the future. Conversely, it is this sense of the good or of value, which emerges through the concrete, lived experience of a *Guru* throughout his history and constitutes his cultural heritage as the rich cumulative expression of meaning evolved through the times to the point of normative and classical perfection. It is embodied personally in a Ramakrishna or a Vivekananda; Aurobindo or a Gandhi, a Sankara, a Ramanuja or a Karunakara *Guru*. Variously termed charismatic personalities, paradigmatic individuals or characters that mould role and personality in providing a cultural, epistemic, political or moral ideal, they supersede mere historical facts. As concrete universals, they express the harmony and fullness of perfection, which is at once classical and historical, ideal and personal, uplifting and dynamizing; in a word, liberating.

Notes

1. The word "psyche" is used as the word which in English comes closest to capturing the meaning of the Sanskrit word *Antahkarana*, the mental mechanism comprising the ego, intellect, mind and emotions.
2. Miller, David (1977). "The *Guru* as the Centre of Sacredness", *Studies in Religion*, pp. 517-523. Also Williams, Monier Sir; (1899), *A Sanskrit-English Dictionary*, reprint, Delhi: Motilal Banarsidass 1990, p. 359.
3. Subramanian, N.S. (1985). Trans, *Encyclopaedia of the Upanishad* (Delhi), Sterling Publications, p. 385.
4. Weber, Max (1958). *The Religion of India*, Trans. By Hans Gerth and Don Martindale Glencoe: The Free Press, p. 58.
5. Deshmukh, P.S. (1933). *Religion in the Vedic Literature*, London: Oxford University Press, p. 156.
6. Keith, A.B. *The Age of the Rig Veda, Oxford History of India*, Vol. 1, p. 95.
7. *Ibid.*, p. 95.
8. Venkateshwara, S.V. (1928). *Indian Culture Through the Ages*, London: Longmans Green, Vol. 1, p. 81.
9. *Ibid.*, p. 82.
10. Venkateshwara, S.V., *Indian Culture through the Ages*, *op. cit.*
11. Weber, *op. cit.*, p. 57.
12. Miller, David (1977). "The *Guru* as the Centre of Sacredness", *Studies in Religion*, pp. 517-523.
13. *Chand*, VI, 2, 1.
14. *Yoga-Tattva*, 15; Deussen, 2: 716.
15. Here it may be noted that while the Upanishads have several orthodox (*astika*) acceptable to the wide array of Indian Philosophical traditions, this chapter is founded primarily on *Advaita Vedanta*.

16. The person of the *Guru* is referred to throughout this chapter with the male pronoun only as the *Gurus* discussed were or are male and not because women *gurus* did not or do not exist in contrast, the aspirant, disciple, or *Sisya*, is referred to with both male and female pronouns as traditionally both have been admitted into the *Gurukulas*, and thus are part of the *Guru* Tradition.
17. *Brih.* IV, 4, 17; Radhakrishnan, 277.
18. *Kath*, I, 2, 18; Radhakrishnan, 616.
19. *Brh.* IV, 4, 7; Radhakrishnan, 273.
20. *Katha,* I, 3, 15; Deussen, 1: 289.
    44 *Yoga-Tattva*, 15; Deussen, 2: 716.
21. The Upanishads are a body of scriptures which contain the esoteric knowledge of the Vedas; traditionally, they are explained to be the Vedanta, literally the end of the Vedas, or the final compendium of the Vedas, in which the essential knowledge of the Self, *Brahman*, as revealed by the Vedic *Guru* has been recorded. The word 'Upanishad" literally translates into "sitting down near" the *Guru* to receive the esoteric teachings sit (verbal root *sat*), down (prefix *ni*), near (prefix *upa*). More specifically, and esoterically, in the Upanishads the word "Upanishads" is defined as *rahasya* "secret" to indicate that these mystical teachings should be secret because their content is too elevated for the one who is not trained to receive them. In total there are proximately 108 Upanishads, with the oldest, the *Brihadaranyaka Upanishad*, dating as far back as the ninth century B.C.E., and newer Upanishads, dating as the late fifteenth century C.E. The common ground of all the Upanishads is their exposition of *Brahman*, the self, and of *Brahma-Vidya* or self-knowledge.
22. For example, in the *Brihadaranyaka Upanishad*, *Guru* Yajnavalkya engages in teaching the disciple king Janaka; in the *Chandogya Upanishad*, *Guru* Uddalaka Aruni enlightens his disciple, Svetaketu: in the *Katha Upanishad*, Yama instructs Nachiketa; in the *Maitri Upanishad Guru* Sakayanaya appears to king Brhadratha after his thousand days of austerities, performed with the wish to receive self-knowledge from a *Guru*.
23. *Maitri*, VII, 7: Radhakrishnan, 854.
24. *Katha*, 1, 2, 21-22: Radhakrishnan, 618.
25. *Ibid*., II, 2, 14-15: Radhakrishnan, 641.
26. *Taitt*., II, 1, 1; Radhakrishnan, 542.
27. The concept of "Sheaths", or Mayas, is first introduced in *Brihadaranyaka* IV: 4; 5, and then in the *Chandogya* III, 14, 2. It is most fully elaborated in the *Taittiriya*, in the form that Sankaracharya latter incorporated into his *Viveka-Cudamani,* where he defines them as *Kosas*, or sheaths. The *Sarvasar Upanishads* of the Krishna Yajurveda speaks clearly of the five *Kosas* and their mechanisms.
28. *Taittiriya*, 1, 1.

29. *Ibid.*, II, 2, 1.
30. *Ibid.*, II, 3, 1.
31. *Ibid.*, II, 4, 1.
32. *Ibid.*, II, 5, 1.
33. *Ibid.*, 6, 2; Radhakrishnan, 534.
34. *Svet.*II, 12; Radhakrishnan, 722.
35. *Hamsa*, 11; Deussen, 2:721.
36. The *Patanjali Yoga Sutras* dedicates a whole chapter to the discussion of the *Siddhis*, or powers, attained by the practicant and the realized one. It is even entitled *Vibhuti Pada*, or the chapter denoting the powers attained through the practice of *yoga*.
37. *Chand*, 16; Deussen, 2:681.
38. *Katha*, I, 3, 12; Deussen, 1:288.
39. *Tejobindu*, 12-14; Deussen, 2:707.
40. *Svet.* II, 13; Radhakrishnan, 723.
41. *Chand. Up*, 13, 8; Radhakrishnan, 390.
42. Weber, *op. cit.*, pp. 380-428.
43. *Ibid.*, p. 319.
44. *Ibid.*
45. The charismatic presence of the *Guru* is central to the pure tradition of *tantra*; a rigorous set of Hinduism which, contrary to modern Western portrayal, aims at attaining *moksha* through complete mastery of the senses. Inauthentic teachers, posing as *Gurus*, advocated indulging the senses.
46. Roy, Ram Kumar (1983). trans., *Kularnava Tantra*, Varanasi: Prachya Prakashan, p. 257.
47. *Ibid.*, 36, XIII, 38-50: 247-248.
48. *Ibid.*, XIV, 25-26; 266.
49. *Ibid.*, XIII, 110.
50. *Ibid.*, XIV, 12.
51. *Kularnava Tantra*, XIV, 13; *op. cit.*; 264.
52. *Ibid.*; XIV, 11.
53. *Guru Gita*, 6-8; Swami Muktananda, 9.
54. *Ibid.*, 7; 9.
55. *Ibid.*, 10; 10.
56. *Ibid.*, 69, 26.
57. It is observed that probably *Tapas* in the forest were the forerunner of *Vanaprastha* and renunciation was the forerunner of *Sannyasa-Asrama*.
58. *Chand.up*; 2.2.3.
59. *Brh.* IV; 2.4.
60. *Chand. Up.*, 4.10.
61. *Ibid.*, 2.2.3.

62. *Brh.* IV. 3.8.10.
63. *Ibid.*, 5.11.1.
64. *Mahanarayanopanishad* 62.1.
65. *Enam tapasa anupasyati ... Svet.*II; 1.15.
66. *Atma-vidya tapo-mulam...Svet.Up*; 1.16.
67. *Ibid.*, 117.
68. *Mund. Up.*; 1.2.11.
69. *Prasna Up.*; 1.10.
70. P. Deussen. *Philosophy of the Upanishads*, p. 367.

4

Buddhist Preceptor Tradition and Social Transformation

The Hermeneutics of a Historical Legacy

C.D. Sebastian

The Buddhist preceptor tradition is one of the most significant among all other traditions in India that gave a considerable impetus to social transformation. The Buddha had exhorted his disciples to go forth for the welfare and well-bẹing of all: *Carata bhikkhave cārikam bahu-jana-hitāya bahu-jana-sukhāya lokānukampāya atthāya hitāya sukhāya deva-manussānam.*[1] The Buddhist tradition believed in 'virtue ethics'[2], and not so much on deontology and consequentialism.[3] This chapter is an attempt to bring out the hermeneutics of the Buddhist preceptor legacy in relation to social change and cultural creativity. In this chapter I firstly delineate what is meant by *the hermeneutics of a historical legacy*, as it has been mentioned in the title of the chapter. Subsequently, I take up two most important facets of Buddhist preceptor tradition for social transformation, namely, the *Bodhisattva ideal* and the *egalitarian principle*. They are seen in Buddhism as catalysts for social transformation and repudiation of caste-hegemony and subjugation. For this purpose I make use of the some of the Buddha's discourses, later texts and treatises to hypothesise, speculate, and then deduce conclusions from the analysis of such texts.

Towards Defining the Hermeneutics of a Historical Legacy

As the present chapter has been titled as 'Buddhist Preceptor Tradition and Social Transformation: The Hermeneutics of a Historical Legacy', it is an imperative to spell out what I mean by *the hermeneutics of a historical legacy*. The transition of Siddhartha Gautama to Gautama

Buddha is a historical event; likewise the inception of Buddhism is a historical event, and the successive contributions (moments) by the Buddhist *Acharya*s are also historical events. In order to look at and into these historical events in the Buddhist preceptor tradition and interpret it, we take recourse to the theories of 'historicism' and 'hermeneutics', which are interrelated in its approach and goal. Historicism or *historism* emphasises the importance of historical context to the interpretation of texts of all kinds. The first focus of historicism is hermeneutical. It signifies that any past legacy "is to be understood on the model of interpreting a text; and texts, literary or otherwise, only have meaning within an economy of other texts, which both limits their possibilities and facilitates the distinctiveness of their utterances."[4] In this connection, hermeneutics is the art and device of interpretation, and it offered a methodological alternative to empirical sciences by analysing and understanding historical events in interpretation. Hermeneutics "stresses the individuality of each human expression, and against scientific generalisations, claims that we choose between several meanings any utterance might have in the light of the special circumstances under which it is made."[5] Furthermore, the *social world* in which utterances are made gives meanings to such utterances as Bakhtin had stated and that communication happens only in specific "social situation."[6] Hence, in our present study we take a careful notice of the social situation and cultural milieu to fathom the richness of Buddhist preceptor legacy.

Historical explanation or the hermeneutics of a legacy is concerned with events and individuals that are particular, rather than instances of the application of a scientific law (where generalization plays a vital role). In it what is significant is not the empirical record of historical facts alone, but as Immanuel Kant had proposed in his "Idea for a Universal History with a Cosmopolitan Purpose" that interpretation of events of history is "to conform to certain rational ends."[7] Philosophically understood, such hermeneutics of historical legacy has a purpose "of attaining a civil society which can administer justice universally."[8] Similarly, when we look at the Buddhist preceptor tradition, we can see that it had *certain rational ends* and *purpose* for social transformation. Hence, the Buddha had exhorted his disciples to go forth for the welfare and well-being of all: *bahu-jana-hitāya bahu-jana-sukhāya lokānukampāya atthāya hitāya sukhāya deva-manussānam.*[9] He himself lived and worked for the social change and transformation from the ills of the society, and his disciples down through the last twenty-six centuries have been doing the same. He was a detractor of social ills and evils, caste hegemony, subjugation, exploitation, war and violence. The Buddha was not an essentialist in the strictest sense of the term as existential predicaments mattered to him, and he advocated a philosophy of *becoming*, where change and transformation are inevitable and they are at the core of the things. In this sense, there is "no 'essence' behind or beyond the interrelatedness of practices that might determine the choice of possibilities."[10] This interrelatedness (*pratityasamutpāda*) as the mark of reality calls for an abnegation of essence and all that related to it, whether it is the social stratification in terms of birth (*jāti*) and the like.

The Ideal of *Bodhisattva* and Social Transformation

The Buddhist ideal of *Bodhisattva*[11], which is the prime ideal in the Mahayana Buddhist preceptor tradition, if hermeneutically analysed, could be seen as a catalyst for social transformation. Individual transformation should lead to a social transformation, or in other words, individual transformation was a prerequisite for social transformation. If we search for the background as to why there was a need for the development of *Bodhisattva* Ideal, the answer becomes clear for the probing minds. Early Buddhism imparted the double ideal of *Arhatva* (in Pāli: *arahatta*) and *Nirvāna* (in Pāli: *nibbāna*). An *Arhat* was a liberated being, and s/he would not be re-born. S/he had accomplished what was to be done; s/he had lived the holy life; s/he attained final emancipation of mind and heart. S/he was alone, secluded, zealous, earnest and master of her/himself.[12] Such an *Arhat* went forth as a preacher and taught the doctrine of Buddha to the people. Buddha had exhorted his disciples to wander and preach the truth for the welfare and liberation of the people, as he loved his fellow creatures and had compassion for them.[13] Such was the great ideal of the *Arhat*, as it was understood during the three centuries after the death of Gautama Buddha. But the Buddhist monks, it seems, began to neglect certain important aspects of it in due course, and they became too self-centred and contemplative. They confined themselves to the four walls of the monasteries and sought for their personal liberation. They began to overlook the zeal for selfless activity among the people. They seemed to have cared only for their own liberation from sin and sorrow. They became indifferent to the great command of Buddha in fulfilling the obligation of teaching and helping all human beings. In this context, may sometime around second century BC, the *Bodhisattva* doctrine was promulgated by some earnest and diligent Buddhist leaders as a protest against this lack of true fervour and altruism among the monks of that historical moment. "The coldness and aloofness of the *arhats* led to the movement in favour of the old gospel of 'saving all creatures'. "The *bodhisattva* ideal can be understood only against this background of a saintly and serene, but inactive and indolent monastic Order."[14] In this sense, the social concern and transformation was the primary motif for the development of the *Bodhisattva* ideal.

There was a tendency towards spiritual selfishness among the monks. Besides the ideal of *Arhat*, the singular ideal of a *pratyeka-buddha*[15] also evolved during the early centuries. The *Bodhisattva* ideal was taught in order to counteract this tendency to a cloistered, quiet, inert and inactive monastic life.[16] A *Bodhisattva* is the one who condemns the spiritual egoism of *Arhats* and *Pratyeka-buddhas* and is always active and even gives his life for the well-being of all the sentient beings. The *Bodhisattva* doctrine was modified in its essential features in the course of several centuries. This course of time is from second century BC to seventh century AD. It should be noted that in the early Mahāyāna[17] Buddhism, the *Bodhisattvas* are inferior and subordinate to the Buddhas; but they acquire greater importance in the course of time, and they are at last regarded as equal to the Buddhas in many respects. They are also worshipped like Buddhas.

Let us also analyze the altruism of the Bodhisattva: which could be taken as a philosophy of life. In contrast to the ideal of *Arhat* in Theravāda Buddhism who rests satisfied with achieving her/his own personal liberation, and not necessarily and actively interested in the welfare of others, the *Bodhisattva* is actuated by the motiveless altruism. A *Bodhisattva* helps all beings not only to attain spiritual goal of *Nirvāna*, but also to obtain the more material advantages of happiness and welfare in the world (*sukha*). The austere and negative attitude to the world is abandoned in favour of a more humane aim. The most significant element in the altruistic character of a *Bodhisattva* is that s/he refuse to enter *Nirvāna* her/himself, as s/he cannot apparently render any service to the living beings of the world after her/his own *Nirvāna*. S/he wishes to help all beings to attain *Nirvana*. S/he thus finds herself/himself in the rather illogical position of pointing, revealing and elucidating the way to *Nirvāna* to other beings, while s/he herself/himself stays in this world of suffering in order to do good to all creatures. This is her/his great sacrifice for others. S/he takes the great Vow: "I shall not enter into final *Nirvāna* before all beings have been liberated."[18] Further s/he says to herself/ himself, "I must lead all beings to Liberation. I will stay here till the end, even for the sake of one living being."[19] The *Bodhisattva* aims at the *highest good* for herself/himself and also for others. Thus, we find the ideal of *Bodhisattva* in Mahāyāna Buddhism as a very charitable being who gives his life for others. There is no trace of selfishness in her/him. S/he shuns retiring into the final state of *Nirvāna*, though fully entitled to it, preferring by her/his own free choice, to toil for even the lowest of beings for ages.[20]

The *Bodhisattva* is unwilling to be satisfied by securing her/his own liberation, as s/he is deeply moved by the sight of the sufferings of other sentient beings. S/he feels compassion for the living beings, and determines to remain in the world so as to be able to provide the maximum benefit to others. S/he makes the great Vow to be in the world in order to free all beings in the universe from suffering regardless of how many beings there are, or how many aeons this might require.[21] Her/his goal is the welfare of all sentient beings, their liberation from suffering. S/he wishes and strives for the attainment of Buddha-hood together with all sentient beings. S/he does not look for her/his personal liberation alone, but s/he strives to make everyone attain the final release of *Nirvāna*. Thus, there is *the communitarian or universal outlook in all what s/he does*. The altruism of the *Bodhisattva* is so sublime and noble that s/he even forgets about her/himself. This is a great ideal for the world order. The following passage from the *Bodhi-caryāvatāra* highlights the altruistic attitude of the *Bodhisattva*: May I be the protector of the helpless! May I be the guide of wayfarers! May I be like a boat, a bridge, a causeway for all who wish to cross a stream! May I be a lamp for all who need a lamp! May I be a slave for all who want a slave! May I be a *cintā-mani* (wish fulfilling gem) for all creatures, a *bhadra-ghata* (pot of fortune) and a potent medicinal herb! May I be for them a *kalpa-vrksha* (wish fulfilling tree) and a *kāma-dhenu* (cow that yields all that one desires).[22]

There are three important metaphors popularly illustrated in Buddhist literature about the *Bodhisattva*'s altruistic activity. It is said that some *Bodhisattvas* become Buddhas in manner of a king, who first ascends to the throne and then provides for the welfare of his subjects. In the same way, the *Bodhisattvas* first become Buddhas and then lead all beings to *samyak sam-bodhi*[23] or perfect Enlightenment. Other *Bodhisattvas* are like a boatman, who arrives at the far shore at the same time as his passengers. These *Bodhisattvas* are said to achieve *samyak sam-bodhi* along with all other beings. Thirdly, the *Bodhisattvas* are said to be like a shepherd, who makes the sheep enter the sheep-shed safely at night and then enters himself. Such *Bodhisattvas* become Buddhas after all other sentient beings attain *samyak sam-bodhi.*

The philosophical bedrock of the *Bodhisattva* ideal is the theory of *Tathagata-garbha*[24], that means all beings possess the essence of Buddhahood, in other words, all are potential Buddhas. Logically speaking if all the sentient beings do not possess the *Tathagata-garbha,* then the path of the *Bodhisattva* who tries to help all beings reach *Bodhi* would be useless and her/his work would be a futile attempt. It is owing to the presence of *Tathagata-garbha* that s/he perceives the unity of all beings. Her/his expression of *maha-karuna* is due to her/his realization of *Tathagata-garbha.* S/he realizes the *advaya(ta)* (non-duality) between her/him and other living beings. The essence of this consists in the inner realization of unity of all beings and the utter negation of egoism. The realization of *Tathagata-garbha* in every sentient being will enable us to think in terms of equality, fraternity and unity. Only this realization can bring forth a fundamental unity of existence and at the same time make room for differences. This realization will enable us to have the genuine feeling for our fellow humans, and genuinely aspire for universal brotherhood. Furthermore, it will lead us to live and work for the happiness of others. All beings are part of us, for we all share in the common heritage of living beings.

The Egalitarian Principle and Social Transformation

The Buddhist preceptor tradition was not an essentialist philosophy. There is no hard essence of things. By birth (*jāti*) one does not get one's *being* in an essentialist sense, but one becomes what one is in the constant process of *becoming.* There is no caste in which one is born; and there is no divine origin of caste at all. Buddhism advocated egalitarianism in all respects: equality of human beings and equality of sexes. However, it is fact that when it came to the entry of women in the Buddhist Sangha, the Buddha denied their entry. But the good sense and insistence of Ānanda, the most important preceptor after Buddha, prevailed and Buddha gave his consent.[25] Ānanda asked the Buddha: "O Lord, is woman not capable of leading houseless state or realising the fruit of conversion?" and to him the Buddha replied: "No Ānanda, they are capable."[26] Let us leave aside the equality sexes here as it was upheld in Buddhist tradition, and consider the vital catalyst for social transformation in Buddhist preceptor tradition, namely, the equality of human beings in birth (*jāti*).

In the large canvas of classical India, one could trace out two clear-cut identity narratives, namely, the *varna vyavastha* narrative of Vedic tradition and the counter narrative of *varna* in the Buddhist tradition. These two identity narratives can be deduced from a number of texts and documents most of which were composed or compiled in the period between 500 BC and 500 AD. In the identity narrative of the Hindu tradition, a *metaphysical* framework was provided by the *Law Books*[27], which ascribed an identity on the basis of birth (*jāti*). *Varna* and *Āśrama* divisions were schemed to maintain the orthodoxy and orthopraxy of Vedic tradition. "It is not, therefore, surprising that both Buddhism and Jainism challenged the orthodoxy and orthopraxis of this period."[28] According to *Varna Vyavastha*, society is organized into "a fourfold (but originally threefold) functional division or 'class', called *varna* (literarily 'colour' or 'category')."[29] But in due course there was an emergence of a system of sub-divisions in the form of castes[30] (*jāti*) which "further proliferates the class function, gradually turning *varna* into discriminatory hereditary-based institution."[31] At practical level there was a separation of ritual-purity status of *varna* from the actual status of *jati*.[32] There were four major ones, *brahmana* (priest), *ksatriya* (warrior), *vaiśya* (trader) and *śudra* (the agriculturist or any low profession). Later on to these four, another was added, the untouchable, who were in fact outside the *varna* framework.[33] The theory of *varna* is about the social and professional (occupational) division in the society where the duties of the four *varnas* (classes, castes) get enunciated. "According to the theory, a set of duties, or *dharma*, called *varnadharma*, are prescribed for everyone as a member of the *varna* he belongs to, i.e., as a *Brahmana*, a *kṣatriya*, a *vaiśya*, or a *Śudra*."[34] *Varna* has the benefit of providing a model which is applicable all over India, and 'castes' are divided into castes and numerous sub-castes.[35] The economy of *varna* system espouses a hierarchical structure of the society. "Each person is born into a caste and is thereby either superior or inferior to someone else."[36] In theory, *Varna Vyavastha* is eternal and inviolable. There is an essence to it, as it is a social ordering institution, and casteism is an essentialist position which is abnegated in Buddhist preceptor tradition.

In the Buddha's discourse there is no *absolute and no difference between varnas*. According to the Vedic narratives (or Brāhminical theory), *varna-vyavastha*, with its social gradation therein, is an absolute one, and one has to abide by the duties of the *varna*. The Buddhist narratives considered it nothing but a relative division. We read the narrative in *Kannakatthala-sutta* (*Majjhima Nikaya*: 90), where King Pasenadi of Kosala asking the Buddha whether there is any distinction among the four *varaas*, and the Buddha telling King Pasenadi that there is no distinction among the four *varnas,* their activities, and the effect to the society. The narrative goes like this:[37] "Now, revered sir, could there be any distinction, any difference between these four castes (*varnas*)?" The Buddha said: "I, sire, here speak of no difference that is to say in freedom as against freedom. It is as though a man, sire, bringing dry sticks from a teak tree were to produce a fire and heat were to result. Then another man, bringing dry sticks from a sal tree... another man bringing dry sticks from a mango tree... another man, dry sticks from a fig tree were to produce a fire and heat were to result. What do you think about this, sire? Because of the different woods used for the fires, would there be any difference in what is produced, in flame as against flame, in hue as against hue, in brilliance as against brilliance?" Then the king said: "No, revered sir." The Buddha said again: "Even so it is, sire, with heat created by energy, produced by striving. I do not speak of any difference there, that in freedom against freedom."

Further, the Buddha had an *emergent view on the four professional stratification of the society*. The Vedic narrative presents a static conception of society based on the *varna-vyavastha*. In the Buddhist narrative, on the other hand, we find in the *Agga—a Sutta* of *Digha Nikaya*[38], the Buddha presenting an emergent view. Vasettha and Bhardvaja, two Brahmin youths, after receiving instruction from the Buddha, become his disciples. But they get the disparagement from their former upper castes in this manner: "you have given up the best *varna* (rank and social grade), and have gone over to the low class, to shaven (heads), to the vulgar, dark complexioned fellows, to those born of Brahma's foot. We are the pure breed, the sons of Brahma, born of his mouth.'[39] However, when Vasettha and Bhardvaja tell the Buddha about the vilification they face from their erstwhile fellow *Brahmins*, he does not engage a theoretical debate about divine origin of *varnas*, but rebuts the Brahmanical claim of *varna* system. It goes like this: There was an emergence of agricultural life, and on the basis of which human families formed into households. Subsequently there was a rise of rights on private property (land) and creation of boundaries, disputes, and settlements. As situation worsened, people together selected a ruler from among themselves who was an agreeable person to all, and was called "Mahasammata" or "the person agreeable to all" or "the Great Elected One." He was also called Kshatriya, and also Raja. They are the people of fields (*kshetra*, *khettiya*), and they are the Kshatriyas. Then the people who went into forest, mediated, and spend time on study began to be called *Brahmana*. Those who took up trade and business were called the Vaiśya (Vessa). Some of the people went for hunting, and such occupations, were called sudra (Sudda). All these four came from the same beings. All the four classes were from the people of the field (Khettiya, Kshatriyas or the farmers and field owners). This *sutta* clearly gives the Buddha's account of "how various social identities developed in the course of historical development"[40] and it sounds to be a verity.

In the Buddha's discourse again, *one from any family whatsoever can hear, take recourse and follow* the Buddhist way and become part of the Sangha. We read this in the *Majjhima Nikaya*: A Tathagata appears in the world, accomplished, fully enlightened, perfect in wisdom and conduct, sublime, knower of worlds, incomparable leader of men to be tamed, teacher of gods and humans, enlightened, blessed. ... He teaches the *Dhamma* good in the beginning, good in the middle, good in the end, with the right meaning and phrasing, and he reveals a holy life that is utterly perfect and pure. A householder or householder's son or *one born in any family whatsoever* hears that *Dhamma*. On hearing the *Dhamma* he acquires faith in the Tathagata. Possessing that faith, he considers thus: "Household life is crowded and dusty; the homeless life is wide open. It is not easy while living in a home, to lead the holy life utterly perfect and pure as a polished shell. Suppose I shave off my hair and beard, put on the yellow robe, and go forth from the home life into homelessness." On a later occasion, abandoning his affairs, whether large or small, abandoning his circle of friends and relatives, whether many or few, he shaves off his hair and beard, puts on the yellow robe, and goes forth from the home life into homelessness.[41] "One born in any family whatsoever" is mentioned in the above passage and it would imply that the Buddha's teaching is open to all, not *varna*-based. Anyone can follow the Buddha's teaching, and the hierarchical distinctions implied in *varna*-system shall not be there in Buddha's *Dharma* and the society built on that *Dharma*.

When it comes to the Buddhist narrative the purity-pollution discourse gets a different turn. Untouchability in any form is denied in Buddhism. The Buddha says in the 'Vasalasutta' of the *Sutta Nipata* that by birth no one is an outcast, but one is an outcast only because of her/his actions.[42] Buddhist narratives do not approve of the notions of purity and impurity when it comes to human beings and their inter-relatedness. In the Buddhist perspective it is one's own body that is the locus of impurity and purity. And "it is impossible to place the burden of impurity on another human body while appropriating a discourse of purity for one's own body. ... In this sense, the metaphysics of Buddhism is indeed one that negates the metaphysics of untouchables."[43] Buddhist narrative gives ontological equality to human beings irrespective of their birth and status. As Gopal *Guru* says "every body is worthy of respect simply because it is constitutive of five principles—air, fire, earth, water and orbit—that are present in every organic body in equal quantity. These are earth, water, fire, air and *akaśa* (space)."[44] Thus, there is "an ontological unity among bodies across time and space."[45] And human beings' existence demands this ontological equality. "Ontological equality as an underlying principle, there should make all organic bodies worthy of respect without discrimination. Thus, any cultural construction dividing egalitarian bodies into pernicious gradations could be decisively refuted by invoking the metaphysics of body."[46] Thus, all human beings are equal and this egalitarian principle of the Buddhist preceptor tradition paved way for social transformation in Indian society.

Conclusion

The *Bodhisattva ideal* and the *egalitarian principle* enshrined in the Buddhist preceptor tradition which paved way for social transformation glow elegantly if we look at the hermeneutics of this historical legacy. These two catalysts in the Buddhist preceptor tradition has much to do with the contemporary discourse on 'engaged

Buddhism.' The term 'engaged Buddhism' is in vogue today which stands for the social, political and environmental application of the Buddhist principles in order that they bring one to a responsible and resilient relationship to all beings around us. It must be said that, though it came into light with Vietnamese Buddhist teacher Thich Nhat Hanh, as far as I am concerned, the foremost figure of engaged Buddhism in the world in our times was B.R. Ambedkar.[47] Today both women and men are involved in engaged Buddhism, and the spirit of it could be seen in the recent book *Buddhist Women and Social Justice: Ideals, Challenges and Achievements* by *Karma* Lekshe Tsomo[48], and it focuses on women working for social justice in a wide range of Buddhist traditions and societies. In order to conclude let me quote the first line of the *Dhammapada:* "All that we are is the result of what we have thought."[49] It implies that the transformation of sociological and psychological structures must take place initially in our own minds, and those of others, if we truly hope to address the root cause of social maladies in order to usher in a social transformation. For this social transformation and cultural ingenuity, the Buddhist preceptor legacy stands out among all other traditions.

Notes

1. The *Vinaya* 1, 21.
2. Virtue ethics has a long history and heritage. In the Greek thought, it goes back to the classical times. It had a specific place in the discussions of the "classical writers like Plato and especially Aristotle" [Christopher Bennett, *What is this thing called Ethics?* (London and New York: Routledge, 2010), 91]. Aristotle's *Nichomachean Ethics* was written sometime in c. 350 BC. "Aristotle in his *Nichomachean Ethics* argued that the best life for a human being—eudemonia—consists in the existence of the virtues (or the 'excellences'). Indeed his is perhaps one of the most radical virtue ethics ever, since he can be understood to be saying that there is nothing worth having in life except the exercise of virtues"[Roger Crisp and Michael Slote, "Introduction" in their *Virtue Ethics* (Oxford: Oxford University Press, 1997), 2].
3. Utilitarians are consequentialists with welfares' theory of value, where welfare is taken as the relevant consequence.
4. Hamilton, Paul (2007). *Historicism*, 2nd Edition, London and New York: Routledge, 3.

5. Hamilton, Paul *Historicism*, 44.
6. Bakktin writes: "Not only the meaning of utterance but also the very fact of its performance is of historical and social significance, as, in general, is the fact of its realization in the here and now, in given circumstances, at a certain historical moment, under the conditions of the given social situation. The very presence of the utterance is historically and socially significant" [M.M. Bakhtin/P.N. Medvedev, *The Formal Method in Literary Scholarship: A Critical Introduction to Sociological Poetics*, Albert J. Wehrie (ed.) (Baltimore, MD, and London: The John Hopkins University Press, 1978), 120].
7. Kant, Immanuel (2003). "Idea for a Universal History with a Cosmopolitan Purpose", In: Kant *Political Writings*, Hans Reiss (ed.), Cambridge: Cambridge University Press, 51 (full essay in pp. 41-53).
8. Kant, Immanuel, *Idea for a Universal History with a Cosmopolitan Purpose*, 45.
9. As stated above in note 1: The *Vinaya* 1, 21.
10. Ginev, Dimitri (2009). "From existential conception of science to hermeneutic phenomenology of scientific research", *Journal of Philosophical Research*, 34, 366 (full chapter 365-389).
11. The Ideal of the *Bodhisattva* has to do with the finest title and noblest role to which any Buddhist, for that matter any human being, can aspire. A *Bodhisattva* is the one who will certainly become a Buddha (literally means "An Enlightened One"), as the state of being enlightened is essential to the concept. A *Bodhisattva* is the one who is constantly active in the service of all beings. Out of great love and compassion for the sentient beings, a *Bodhisattva* makes the vow to work to liberate all sentient beings. With the noble ideal of *Bodhisattva*, a deeply religious element, and at the same time a sound philosophy of life, got introduced into Buddhism. The *Bodhisattva*—doctrine brings us to the topic of Buddha's universal compassion, the *leitmotiv* that runs through all the schools of Buddhism, Mahāyāna in particular. In this concept of *Bodhisattva,* we have the ideal person without any trace of ego. For a detailed study see: C.D. Sebastian, "The Bodhisattva Ideal as Philosophy of Life", in *Indian International Journal of Buddhist Studies*, 9 (2008), ISSN 0972-4893, pp. 185-198.
12. The *Dîgha-nikāya* 1, 1-46.
13. "*Caratha bhikkhave cārikam bahu-jana-hitāya bahu-jana-sukhāya lokānukampāya atthāya hitāya sukhāya deva-manussānam*" (The *Vinaya* 1, 21).
14. Har Dayal (1978). *The Bodhisattva Doctrine in Buddhist Sanskrit Literature,* Delhi: Motilal Banarsidass Publishers, p. 3.
15. In Pāli it is called *Pacceka-buddha*. Such a Buddha is "one enlightened by himself". He is the one who has attained the supreme and perfect insight, but dies without proclaiming the truth to the world.
16. One can find a similar strand of thought in Rabindranath Tagore, the mystic

poet of modern India and Noble Laureate for Literature 1913, as it goes in the eleventh song of the celebrated *Gitanjali*:

"Leave this chanting and singing and telling of beads;
Whom doest thou worship in this lonely dark corner of a temple with doors all shut?
Open thine eyes and see thy God is not before thee!
He is where the tiller tilling the hard ground and where the path maker is breaking the stones;
He is with them in sun and shower, and His garment is covered with dust!
Put off thy holy mantle and even like Him come down to the dusty soil!
Deliverance! Where is this deliverance to be found?
Our Master Himself has joyfully taken upon Him the bonds of creation; He is bound with us all for ever.
Come out of thy mediations and leave aside thy flowers and incense! What harm is there, if thy clothes become tattered and stained?
Meet Him and stand by Him in toil and sweat of thy brow."

17. The origin of the term Mahāyāna may be traceable to an earlier school known as *Mahasanghikas*. In the Council of Vaishali, a hundred years after the *mahaparinirvana* of Buddha, the *Sangha* was divided into two opposing camps, the *sthaviras* (Pali—*Thera*) or the order of elders and the *Mahasanghika*s or the order of the majority. The elders (*sthavira*s) denounced the *Mahasanghika*s as *papabhikkus* (sinful monks) and *adharmavadins* (propagators of untruth). In turn, the *Mahasanghikas* called themselves as Mahāyāna (the Greater Vehicle) and others as Hinayana (the Lesser vehicle). The word Mahāyāna is to be found in the *Mahayano±raddhotpada±astra* (Awakening of faith) of Aṣvaghoṣa. Aṣvaghoãa calls himself as a Mahayanist and he is known as the systematic expounder of the Mahāyāna School.
18. *The Lankāvatāra-sutra* 66, 6.
19. *The Öikãa-samuccaya* 14, 8.
20. "*Nāham tvaritarûpena bodhim prāptum ihotsahe, Parānta-koæim sthāsyāmi sattvasyaikasya kāraṇāt.*"—*The Öikãa-samuccaya* of Śāntideva 14, 19.
21. For a detailed account of the Bodhisattva vow see: Vasubandhu, *Vasubandhu's Treatise on Bodhisattva Vow: A Discourse on Bodhisattva Vow and Practices Leading to Buddhahood,* Bhikshu Dharmamitra (tr), (Seattle, WA: Kalavinka Press, 2009). In this text, Vasubandhu discourses on the causality behind the origination of the Bodhisattva vow (*bodhicitta*) and on each of the six perfections through which that vow reaches its fruition in Bbuddhahood.
22. *The Bodhi-caryāvatāra* of Śāntideva III, 6-19. One could see a different translation in *The Bodhi-caryāvatāra of Śāntideva: Entering Path of Enlightenment*, Marion L. Matics (tr), (Delhi; Motilal Banarsidass Publishers, 2007), pp. 153-155.

23. In Buddhist philosophy, "the term *bodhi* appears to indicate the predominantly static wisdom, the predominantly kinetic aspect of the spiritually positive content of *Nirvana*. *Bodhi* is the insight into the true nature of things. More abstractly, *Bodhi* is the state of Supreme Knowledge, imperturbable and absolute, which arises, in the concentrated mind as a consequence of *samadhi*. In this sense *Bodhi* is the antithesis of *avidya*. There are two qualifying adjectives commonly associated with the term *Bodhi*: *samyak* and *anuttara*. *Samyak* means right or perfect, whereas *anuttara* means 'nothing higher, or without a superior, incomparable, unsurpassed, pre-eminent, and supreme.' The usual appellation is *anuttara-samyak-sambodhi*. The prefix *sam* is also placed before the word *bodhi* in order to emphasize its excellence and fullness. Thus, *Bodhi* or *Sambodhi* is the *summum bonum* of a *Bodhisattva* and it is essentially and primarily equivalent to Omniscience, though it has been analysed into its constituent elements and its various aspects have been elucidated by Buddhist philosophers.
24. For an exposition on the theory of Tathagatagarbha see C.D. Sebastian, *Metaphysics and Mysticism in Mahayana Buddhism: An Analytical Study of the Ratnagotravibhago Mahayanottaratantra±astram* (Delhi: Sri Satguru Publications, 2005), pp. 99-162
25. Mahaprajapati Gotami (Siddhartha Gautama's maternal aunt, who had nursed him after his mother's death) requested the Buddha to admit women in his Sangha, but he denied admission. She did not give up, even after she was refused thrice. Together with five ladies, she cut-off the hair, wore yellow garments, and travelled from Kapilavastu to Vaisali to meet the Buddha. Ānanda convinced the Buddha and Ānanda and Mahaprajapti became the founders of Bhikkhuni Sangha (H. Oldenberg, Vinaya Pitakam, Vol. II, p. 253).
26. H. Oldenberg, *Vinaya Pitakam*, Vol. II, p. 254.
27. The *Dharmaśastra* literature is the codification of Hindu laws; they mainly include the *Dharmaśastras* of *Manu*, Yajnavalkya, and Narada.
28. Balasubramanian, R. (2005). *Primal Spirituality of the Vedas: Its Renewal and Renaissance*, New Delhi: PHISPC, Centre for Studies in Civilizations, p. 20.
29. Bilimoria, Purushottama (2008). "Early Indian Ethics—Vedas to the Gita, rites to 'Right' ", In: Purushottama Bilimoria, Joseph Prabhu and Renuka Sharma (ed.), *Indian Ethics: Classical Traditions and Contemporary Challenges*, New Delhi: Oxford University Press, p. 35.
30. The term *Caste* was used by the foreigners for *varna* system of India. L. Dumont writes: "...caste is of Portuguese and Spanish origin: '*casta*, properly something not mixed, from Latin *castus*, chaste'... The word seems to have been used in the sense of race by the Spaniards, and to have been applied to India by the Portuguese in the middle of the fifteenth century. In English, there is a use (*cast*) in the sense of race in 1555, and the Indian sense is encountered as the beginning of the seventeenth century; the French

spelling, *caste*, is scarcely found before 1800... There are four castes... The derived sense of 'exclusive group', as in the expression 'caste spirit', is found ... 'Its distinctive mark is birth', as opposed to 'aristocracy' which designates 'the chief men' "[Louis Dumont, *Homo Hierarchicus: An Essay on the Caste System* (Chicago: The University of Chicago Press, 1970) pp. 21-22].

31. Bilimoria, Purushottama, *Early Indian Ethics—Vedas to the Gita, rites to 'Right'*, p. 35.
32. Thapar, Romila (2010). *Ancient Indian Social History: Some Interpretations*, 2nd edition, New Delhi: Orient Blackswan, pp. 38-43.
33. See note 7 in Romila Thapar, *Ancient Indian Social History: Some Interpretations*, p. 34.
34. Prasad, Rajendra (1999). Varnadharma, *Niskama Karma and Practical Morality: A Critical Essay on Applied Ethics*, Utkal Studies in Philosophy-VII, New Delhi: D.K. Printworld, p. 7.
35. Louis Dumont (1970). *Homo Hierarchicus: An Essay on the Caste System*, Chicago: The University of Chicago Press, pp. 72-75.
36. Mani, Braj Ranjan (2008). *Debrahmanising History*, Delhi: Monohar Publishers, p. 52.
37. *Majjhima Nikaya* 2004. II: 128-130 (*The Collection of the Middle Length Sayings* (*Majjhima-Nikaya*), Vol. II, I. B. Horner (tr), Delhi: Motilal Banarsidass Publishers, pp. 310-311.
38. *Digha Nikaya* 3: pp. 84-96.
39. *Agga—a Sutta*, verse 3.
40. Swaris, Nalin (2011). *The Buddha's Way to Human Liberation: A Socio-Historical Approach*, New Delhi: Narayana Publishing, pp. 285.
41. The *Majjhima Nikaya* 51: pp. 12-13.
42. '*Na jacca vasalo hotti na jacca hoti brahmano; kammuna vasalo hoti kammuna hoti brahmanoti.*' ("Not by birth is one an outcast; not by birth is one a *brahmana*. By deed one becomes an outcast, by deed one becomes a *brahmana*"). (*Sutta Nipata* I, 7, 21 and 27 or in Pali Text Society Version I, 7, 142). See *Sutta-Nipata*, P.V. Bapat (ed.) (Delhi: Sri Satguru Publications, 1990), 20.
43. Sarukkai, Sundar (2012). "Phenomenology of Untouchability", In: Gopal Guru and Sundar Sarukkai, *The Cracked Mirror: An Indian Debate on Experience and Theory*, New Delhi: Oxford University Press, 157-199, 172.
44. Guru, Gopal (2012). "Archaeology of Untouchability", In: Gopal Guru and Sundar Sarukkai, *The Cracked Mirror: An Indian Debate on Experience and Theory*, New Delhi: Oxford University Press, 200-222, p. 205.
45. Guru, Gopal, *Archeology of Untouchability*, p. 205.
46. *Ibid.*
47. See Christopher Queen and Sallie B. King (1996). *Engaged Buddhism: Buddhist Liberation Movements in Asia*, Albany, NY: SUNY Press, pp. 45-120.

48. *Karma* Lekshe Tsomo (2004). *Buddhist Women and Social Justice: Ideals, Challenges and Achievements*, Albany, New York: SUNY Press. In this book one could see the attempts made by people to actualize Buddhism's liberating ideals of personal growth and social transformation. Dealing with issues such as human rights, gender-based violence, prostitution, and the role of Buddhist nuns, the work illuminates the possibilities for positive change that are available to those with limited power and resources. Integrating social realities and theoretical perspectives, the work utilizes feminist interpretations of Buddhist values and looks at culturally appropriate means of instigating change.
49. The *Dhammapada* (2004). 1: 1 (The *Dhammapada, The Sacred Texts of the East*, Vol. 10, Max Mueller (tr), Delhi: Motilal Banarsidass Publishers, p. 3.

5

Spiritual Evolution of Life with Reference to Sri Aurobindo

Panneer Selvam

The gnostic individual would be the consummation of the spiritual man; his hole of being, thinking, living, and acting would be governed by the power of a vast universal spirituality. All the trinities of the spirit would be real to his self-awareness and realized in his inner life.

—Sri Aurobindo in *The Life Divine*

I

The Life Divine, the work of Sri Aurobindo represents the spiritual evolution of the universe. The spiritual evolution which has to proceed from matter to life and from life to mind and from mind to supermind shows that divine life is possible in this life itself. It is a kingdom of God on earth. The uniqueness of Sri Aurobindo is that he is concerned about the aspiration of the individual. He has examined the spiritual beings in one's own self and help others in similar evolutionary ascent which is considered as real service to the mankind. His integral philosophy takes into account the problems of man. He considers man as the part of the cosmic evolutionary process. Man is an ideal combination of matter, life and mind. As because mind is finite, he is bestowed with limited powers of consciousness. The nature of evolution indicates that mind is followed up with a higher integral consciousness or the supramental consciousness. Man, according to him is a transitional being. By this, he means that man is not a final. Man is mind-imprisoned in a living body. Mind is not a highest power of consciousness. This means that mind is not in possession of truth. It is only an ignorant seeker. Thus Sri Aurobindo presupposes that beyond mind, there is Supermind, the gnostic power of consciousness, which is in eternal possession of truth. This Supermind is the Superman. The Supermind is in the eternal possession of Truth. Aurobindo says that it is the Gnostic growth. This conception gives a new hope and a new prospect of life for the future of mankind. Man must awake himself to the divine person to overthrow the desire-soul or the little ego. The desire-soul is the egoistic existence. It is shut off by the egoistic walls. In the surface-soul or the desire-soul there is no real soul-life. How to proceed from desire soul to Divine soul? This is a basic issue in Sri Aurobindo. He says that it is possible by a psychic man. He says that mental man has evolved but a spiritual man is yet to evolve. In this context, Sri Aurobindo talks about three levels of existence. They are: (1) the level of the being, (2) the level of the being and non-being, and (3) the level of the non-being. Man is born into the world at the level of being and non-being. This non-being is a process of becoming. This implies a new departure for both man and the world. Thus man's progress consists in his ceaseless aspiration to transcend himself. According to Sri Aurobindo, it is always the future of man, which is more important and significant than his present and the past. Thus in Sri Aurobindo, the concept of man is the genetic evolutionary one. Man is not only engaged in his own greater perfection and happiness but also in the general liberation and higher evolution of his fellow creatures. The lower life of plants and animals are conditioned by nature, the material life of man and his species tend to harness the forces of nature to make the human life both happier and nobler. Man has to evolve his capacities of knowledge with greater mastery over them. This is the extension of consciousness.

Consciousness is the expression and the manifestation of the Spirit-in-Man. It is the medium of the Divine in Man. So it is the absolute and the fundamental determinate of the Divine Satchidananda. Man is bound to undergo the extension of consciousness. The extension of consciousness demands openness on the part of the individual. Consciousness is absolute and fundamental. It is the creator of the whole world. It is Satchidananda. It is also evolving Supermenal Process. For Sri Aurobindo, man is a spirit using the mind, life and body for an individual and a collective experience and self-manifestation in the universe. The Satchidananda itself descends in the finite for the delight of self-manifestation. Self is as real as the Absolute. This means that in the integral philosophy of Sri Aurobindo, the individual is as much real as the Universal. The ultimate reality is a unity manifesting in triunity—of essentiality, commonality and individuality. The unity is an inseparable one. Here the individual is related to the Universal and cannot exist without. The Universal is closely related with the Transcendent, which expresses Himself through individual, and Universal. Sri Aurobindo in *Ideal and Progress* says as follows: "For the particular, the individual can have no self-existence, no truth, no valid force except in so far as it reflects rightly and relates and confirms itself justly to the universal, to the all-being, the all-knowledge, the all-will and follows its true drift towards self-realization and vast delight in itself."[1] Further he says that the universal also has no self-existence, truth or validity except as it expresses the Divine Being, Knowledge, Will, Power, Delight of Him who surpasses all universe.

Sri Aurobindo's concept of the future of mankind depends on his concept of evolution. The future of mankind actually depends on the success of *yoga* as a method of social development. The gnostic consciousness, like the mental consciousness, will create a race of gnostic spiritual beings. Let us see the nature of the future transformation of man otherwise, known as gnostic being. Sri Aurobindo, in search of a divine being who is governed by universal spirit. He feels divine everywhere and also in part of his own being. He would be universal but free in the universe, individual but not limited by a separate individuality. He would be a perfect individual fulfilling individuality, commonality and complete self-mastery. The supramental being would act as a cosmic individual. His awareness, will and action would be in union with the Absolute. The gnostic being will have a complete knowledge of all existence. How to achieve this is a fundamental question for Sri Aurobindo.

The ascent of the mind into the Supermind, through the descent of Supermind into mind is possible by removing the veil, which separates them, yet veil can be removed by our intense aspiration for the light and through *yoga* with the help of the divine *sakti*. The process of evolution continues from mind to Supermind through the intermediate strategies of higher mind, illumined mind, and intuition and overmind. With the descent of the Supermind, nature becomes transformed into Supernature and human beings into gnostic beings. It is not sufficient for individuals to achieve their own divinization. It is necessary that larger and larger groups of people can be divinized. Does this mean that the whole human race is raised to the higher level? The answer is in the negative. Sri Aurobindo remarks: "There is not the least probability or possibility of the whole race rising in a block to the supramental level—but only in the capacity in the human mentality when it reaches a certain level or a certain posit of stress of the evolutionary impetus, to press towards a higher place of consciousness and its embodiment in the being".[2]

The uniqueness of Sri Aurobindo is that his notion of the Superman is something original in the Indian philosophical tradition. Sometimes, it is argued that it is similar to that of *jivanmukta*. But the concept of Superman has a wider scope than that of the *jivanmukta*. Very correctly, Haridas Chauduri says in his book, *Sri Aurobindo: The Prophet of Life Divine*, that there have been numerous instances of *jivanmukti* in the past, but the Supermanhood is yet to blossom forth in the course of further evolution.[3] A *jivanmukta* attains the supreme spiritual excellence and makes no further attempt to bring down the higher light and power into the flux of evolution. He fails to see the descending movement of God towards self-objectification, and as a result, misses the significance of the cosmic process. The Superman on the other hand has grasped the reality in its fullness. He has perceived the spirit in its splendour and in matter. He feels himself one with the creative impetus. He sees the true meaning of evolution in the involvement of spirit in matter. The Superman of Sri Aurobindo is that it is the synthesis of different aspects, human and divine. Superman presents certain divine and harmonious Absolute, of all that is essential in man. To take all that is essential in human beings and to lift him higher to light and joy is the essential function of divinity.

The central concept in Sri Aurobindo's philosophy is evolution. It is a basic concept and all other doctrines centre round it. No doubt, the concept of evolution has the following important questions: Is evolution an automatic drive of material forces to known or unknown or knowable ends? Does it involve a rigorous mechanical necessity? Is there any teleology underlining the evolutionary process? Is man the final product of evolution? What is the aim and end in view of evolution? Sri Aurobindo posits on the authority of his spiritual experience the fundamental presence of Divine consciousness in all things. This Divine consciousness has a static poise and a dynamic poise. It has seeped into all the different strata of the evolutionary process. This is the involution of the Divine in all. It is because of this involution, inert matter is able to break its life and that in turn is succeeded by the formation of mind. Evolution does not stop with the emergence of mind. It is not the highest product. Man is not the final product of evolution. It is not an aimless inconsequential process. It is a purposeful unfolding of the spirit.

The unification of mankind is inevitable for human evolution, according to Sri Aurobindo. He says: "If a spiritual unfolding on earth is the hidden truth of our birth into matter, if it is fundamentally an evolution of consciousness that has been taking place in nature, then man, as he is, cannot be the last term of that evolution".[4] What is interesting is that his concept of evolution is significantly concerned not only with the physical or cosmic evolution from matter to life and mind but also with the parallel evolution of consciousness. If evolution of consciousness is only a kind of an uncoiling process of what is coiled in involution, humanity, he says, is but a penultimate stage in terrestrial evolution. The involution of the spirit into matter, marking the beginning of terrestrial evolution must inevitably culminate in the ultimate evolution or the emergence of the spirit out of the mental man in the form of a spiritualized Superman or Supramental being, otherwise, known as the "gnostic being".

According to Aurobindo, man cannot transcend his *svabhava* beyond certain limitations. Man according to Sri Aurobindo, is the most complex that has been created, the riches in content of consciousness and the curious ingeniousness of his building. He is the head of the earthly creation, but he does not exceed it. If a Suprememtal being is to appear, says Sri Aurobindo, in the terrestrial creation, it must be a new and independent manifestation, just as life and mind have manifested in matter, so Supermind must manifest there. Such a divine manifestation in man, according to Sri Aurobindo, did really occur once already in a body and mind adequately evolved or prepared for the reception of the divine spirit of the highest order, when man first appeared on this planet earth. For Sri Aurobindo, man is essentially a spiritual being with spiritual aspirations to exceed his mental status and therefore his mental evolution is only an additional aid for his spiritualization. This spiritual man is the sign of the new evolution.

Man's urge towards spirituality is to reach the final manifestation of the spirit on earth and the goal of humanity is a spiritual religion. The goal of spirituality is the flowering of the Divine in collective humanity. In *The Ideal of Human Unity*, this has been emphasized by Sri Aurobindo as follows: "A religion of humanity means the growing realization that there is a secret spirit, a divine Reality, in which we are all alone."[5] Sri Aurobindo argues that that only can evolve which was involved. Something cannot emerge of nothing. There is involution of consciousness in matter and there is a gradual unfoldment of that consciousness into varied forms of matter and also into life in matter and into mind in life. It is this consciousness in different grades and at different levels, which evolved, and as a complementary part of process the forms which are essential for its operation take shape. Thus, life evolved out of matter, mind out of life, because they are already involved there; matter is a form of veiled life, life a form of veiled mind. Sri Aurobindo supports the view that present man is the summit of evolution. He is a transitional being and is bound to grow further and consciously transcend himself and so to rise to a higher level of consciousness and to become higher being than what he is today. Till now, evolution was a spontaneous and apparently unconscious process determined by the working of nature; it was moving slowly and inadvertently as things in nature normally move. But man has now reached a stage when he can consciously evolve and so compress centuries into years. But the change depends on an awakening within man by conscious effort of his latent or unborn higher powers and by bringing his psychic being into active participation. Sri Aurobindo's contribution here is that he foresees that the ideal of human unity would be no longer an unfulfilled ideal but an accomplished fact, whatever may be the uncertainties and dangers which face the world today. There is Divinity waiting to be manifested. There is essential unity in the apparent diversity and the many are now moving towards the realization of the Oneness.

For Sri Aurobindo, the past evolution indicated that nature and its processes have created larger and more complex human aggregates from family to clan or tribe, to city, and other larger groups of varied kinds and finally to national units. He claims that the nation, the largest natural unit which humanity has been able to create and maintain for its collective living, is not its last and ultimate unit but that greater and ever greater aggregates will be formed until all nations will be ungloved in the united totality. He says that the world government is inevitable and that may take the form of a world union of free and independent nations, with unity in diversity as the major principle of life and freedom as its basic principle. He traces in *The Human Cycle,* the social and cultural development of the human race and envisaged the advent of a spiritual age evolving out of the present rational age. His argument is interesting. "If the spiritual change of which we have been speaking is to be effected, it must unit be two conditions which have to simultaneously satisfied but are most difficult to bring together". He says that there must be the individual, and, the individuals who are able to see, to develop and, to recreate themselves in the image of the Spirit, and to communicate both their idea and its power to the mass.

The main message of Sri Aurobindo is about the evolutionary process on the earth, and the growth of consciousness, which both process and growth, man is not in a position to accelerate. His greatest life work, which is supremely unique collaboration with the Mother, was the descent of the Supramental consciousness. The supramentalism of consciousness, is the goal towards which, nature is aiming at, and for which man is striving. It is the next step the earth and man are destined to take in their evolutionary ascent. The important step in his evolution is that, which raises man to a higher and larger consciousness. His dream about the next step in evolution, has been fulfilled by the descent of Supramental consciousness on the 29th February, 1956 as has been declared by the Mother of the Sri Aurobindo Ashram. She gave a message on the 24th April 1956, which goes as follows: "The manifestation of supramental upon earth is no more a promise, but a living fact, a reality. It is at work here and a day will come when the most blind, the most unconscious, even the most unwilling shall be able to recognize it." As the Supramental consciousness has contacted the earth's atmosphere and has begun its realizing power, the evolution of a spiritual society becomes easier than ever before. It will mean in due course, the emergence of Spirit in Mind, even as mind emerged in life and life emerged in matter. It prepares the ground for the evolution of a spiritual man and ultimately of Supramental being which will resent to the world a major transformation. This Supermind is something beyond mental man and his limits. On the 29th February, 1956, the foundations were laid for an evolution of a supramental race, which will be as much higher than the present humanity, as the present humanity is higher than the animal world. This means that the world will move towards the manifestation of Spirit in matter, the establishment of divine life on earth and the evolution of a new race, though in terms of earth time it may take several centuries of its full manifestation.

Sri Aurobindo's understanding of evolution of consciousness is something novel and ideal. It is self-aware force of existence. It is neither a mere mechanical nor unintelligent force as the scientists and the Sankhyas think, not a mere vital force or the *elan vital* of which Bergson speaks, which cannot be aware of itself, but a conscious self-aware force. In *The Life Divine* it is said: "A conscious-Force, everywhere inherent in Existence, acting even when concealed, is a creator of the worlds, the occult secret of Nature".[6] This conscious-Force is present everywhere. Consciousness is not restricted to the higher forms of life only. It is present, below the mental level, in the vital and material existence as a sub-conscious energy and above the mental level as Super-conscious energy. Consciousness is invisible in the material sphere, appears at the vegetable level and dominates at the human level. This energy, Sri Aurobindo calls it the Mother or the Divine sakti. Sri Aurobindo says: "Consciousness is a Force, inversely force is consciousness and all the forces are conscious. Consciousness is a Force; it is inseparable and convertible. Force is inherent in Existence. Therefore it is *Cit*. *Cit* is the essence of Existence. Therefore all is *Sat* here. Consciousness is both *Sat* and *Cit*, it is also Blisss or *Ananda*, for to be conscious means joy. Hence Consciousness is *Sacccidananda*—Existence, Consciousness-Force and Bliss. In Sri Aurobindo's understanding, to understand the reality of the universe we must also know the process by which the Reality manifests itself in the universe. The process of manifestation of the Absolute, otherwise known as "involution", wherein the consciousness aspect of *Brahman* conceals itself in the universe and slowly evolves out of it. In the words of Sri Aurobindo, it is "a self-involution of *Brahman* from its involved conditions, "a self-involution of consciousness in form and a self-evolution out of form".[7] It is because of this involution, evolution has not become a transformation. it is because of this matter is not unconscious but inconscient or consciousness veiled itself in it. "The Inconscient is the Superconscient's sleep", says Sri Aurobindo.[8] As a result of this, evolution becomes meaningful and possible. Ascent without descent, evolution without involution is unthinkable. Evolution means making more and more manifest, the unmanifest consciousness that dwells in every being. Thus for Sri Aurobindo, it is a progressive self-manifestation of the Spirit or Consciousness in material conditions. It is a creation, a self-creation and a bringing out of what is implicit in Being. Spirit or Consciousness is the source from which everything emerges and into which everything disappears. Sri Aurobindo makes evolution both continuous and emergent. A continuous evolution without emergence is a contradiction in terms. There is continuity in evolution, for it is the same Consciousness that evolves throughout the process. This means the different stages of evolution between

Matter and Spirit are not entirely different from one another. They are related by one Conscious-Force, which is present everywhere in different organizations. If they are different from each other, we cannot talk of the evolution of the one from the other. But at the same time, there is the emergence of the new capacities, which were once in unmanifest condition. Here the word emergence means the arrival of higher, spiritual and supramental grades of beings, consciousness and powers in successive order. In the process of evolution, their emergence is unpredictable and miraculous. Thus, evolution is emergence in this sense. It does not conform to the fixed path determined by our mental logic. One principle is different from the other, not in its potentiality, but in the manifestation of this potentiality. It is by rising to a new higher state of consciousness a real unification of the world is possible. This new consciousness will not be an elevated ordinary human mentality but a new higher spiritual consciousness. This new spiritual consciousness can be reached only by a spiritual endeavour or spirituality. If this is accomplished, then humanity will not be an ordinary one but a spiritual one with an entirely new mode of thought and knowledge. By this stage, man becomes a Superman. Unity, mutuality and harmony will be the new basis of this new Supramental consciousness.

Sri Aurobindo develops an ideal of social development, which requires a clear conception of the nature of subjectivity, both at the individual and collective level. He sees certain parallelism between the individual and the group. He is of the view that the self is neither a body or the vital ego, nor the rational mind. Similarly, the self cannot be identified with any one-sided expression of our mind, ethical or aesthetic. The true self, according to him, is the spiritual individual. The individual self as well as the group, he claims has also a body, a living organism, has a mind has ethical ideals. But he is more than this. His inner being is exhibited in three levels: the infra-rational, the rational and the supra-rational. The infra-rational is exhibited in the bodily sensations and vital instincts. The rational is exhibited in the intellectual, ethical and the emotional. The supra-rational also is a complex structure having its own inner stratification. The infra-rational requires to be sublimated, which is possible only through the supra-rational. No doubt, reason is useful here; but it cannot be the role master. Further Sri Aurobindo says that the individual is not only himself but is in solidarity with all of his kind.[9] An ideal order of social development must recognize the mutual interdependence—an interdependence that does not annul the autonomy of each—of three terms: the individual, the community and humanity. "The individual has to live in humanity as well as humanity in the individual: but mankind is or has been too large an aggregate to make this mutuality a thing intimate and powerfully felt in the ordinary mind of the race, and even if humanity becomes a manageable unit of life, intermediate groups and aggregates must still exist for the purpose of mass-differentiation and the concentration and combination of varying tendencies in the total human aggregate."[10] These are the foundations on which the future order of social development depend.

II

Sri Aurobindo exhibits the ideal social order in his *The Human Cycle.* This takes into account the three poles of human existence: the individual, the community and mankind in general. Each has its own destiny, its own needs, its own law of growth. According to Sri Aurobindo, mankind is marching towards a far-off ideal of perfection. But within the fold of this common destiny of mankind, each individual and each community has to follow its own unique line of development. The law of social development requires a harmony between the needs and the interests of these three terms of existence. The ideal relationship between the individual, the community and humanity provides the perspective from which Sri Aurobindo offers valuable comments upon the various social and political theories. He says: The perfect social state must be one in which governmental compulsion is abolished and man is able to live with his fellow man by free agreement and co-operation."[11] But how to bring about this ideal state of affairs? He talks about two methods: (1) intellectual anarchism by which he means the method of enlightening man's reason of appealing to 'natural human sympathy to the love of comrades or the principle of fraternity with a view to bring about a free equality founded upon spontaneous cooperation. His criticism of this method gives expression to one of the toughest problems with which he was concerned. Unless a solution to this problem was found out, all methods would be useless. He feels that the intellectual anarchism does not realize the pull, which the infra-rational in man's exercise, the way in which it disturbs all the intentions of the higher reason. Therefore, there should be some means of dealing with this aspect of human affairs, and for this purpose, Sri Aurobindo suggests a method, which he calls "spiritual anarchism". This method should concentrate upon a growing number of spirituality evolved individuals who would channelize their spiritual energy in the direction of uplifting both the community and mankind at large. In such spirituality-developed, individuals should recognize a spiritual evolution as the destiny and therefore it is the great need of the human being.

III

No doubt, Sri Aurobindo's concept of the future of mankind is based on the concept of evolution. But the theory of evolution can be challenged on the basis of insufficient foundations. Can we say that man has the capacity to develop into a higher evolutionary being? Seeing the earthly nature, it is difficult to believe in the evolution of the Supramental consciousness. Moreover, why evolution should stop at man? This is the view of the many Positivists, Pragmatists, Instrumentalists etc. Not only in the present, in past also this type of philosophical thinking is uncommon. It is argued by many critics that man has to attain his manhood and not the Supermanhood. Even if the superman is born, he shall be a different species, not an evolution out of man.

Another criticism is that even granting that Sri Aurobindo's metaphysical contentions about the nature of creation, there is no guarantee about the spiritual evolution of man. The principle of evolution has not been sufficiently and finally established in science and hence cannot be accepted in metaphysics. Moreover, it is argued that evolution is not proved by observation. The principles of creation appear to be permanent and unchanging. The evolution of life and mind does not prove the evolution of Supermind, since mind and Supermind belong to quite different levels. There is succession but not evolution in species. No human race exhibits signs of Supramental nature. Psychoanalysts like Freud argue that man hardly advanced from the animal in his motives and impulses. Man's progress is only in degree and width.

IV

The above criticisms cannot be valid. First of all, it should be understood that theory of evolution is based on Sri Aurobindo's deep, personal, *yogic* experience. The personal experiences differ. Since the validity of the experience can be established by sufficient training and sincere self-analysis. His theory of evolution is based on his *yogic* experience. He shows the limitations of science. The integral theory affirms other theories and improves upon them. The evolution of the unevolved principles on earth, as well as the descent of the higher powers from their own bases, is quite compatible with the perfection of the whole.

Moreover, the theory of evolution is proved by observation and by reason and intuition. The scientific theory of evolution is itself an argument in favour of the spiritual evolution. Man's future evolution has its roots in his own type, since the impulse towards self-exceeding is also his fundamental principle. To be a man fully, he should be a gnostic being, a Superman. The spiritual human society will realize the three essential truths of existence—God, Freedom and Unity, which are the three aspects of one and same truth. None of the three can be realized without the realization of the other two. Sri Aurobindo says: "When man is able to see God and to possess him, then he will know real freedom and arrive at real unity, never otherwise."[12] The spiritual society will live as collective soul and not as a collective ego. It will be the outcome of the realization of God within and on this earth. To find the Divine self in the individual and collectivity and to realize spiritually, mentally, vitally, materially its greatest, largest and deepest possibilities in the inner life of all and their outer action and nature.[13] Since the inner divine compulsion grows in the individuals, society will lift the outer compulsions. In a perfect spiritual society, all will be perfectly free.

Notes

1. *Ideal and Progress*, p. 16.
2. *The Life Divine*, Vol. II, Part II.
3. Chaudhuri Haridas (1951). *The Prophet of Life Divine*, Calcutta, p. 169.
4. *The Life Divine*, p. 1009.
5. *The Ideal of Human Unity*, 1962, p. 775.
6. *Life Divine*, 1960, p. 352.
7. *Ibid*., p. 18.
8. *Savitri*, X.I.
9. *The Human Cycle*, p. 54.
10. *Ibid*., p. 82.
11. *Ibid*., p. 110.
12. *Ibid*., pp. 283-84.
13. *Ibid*., p. 286.

6

Discourse on Religion and Secularism

Approached through Guru Tradition

P.I. Devarajan

Religions have played a very important role in the evolution of human civilization and culture. They evolved a set of beliefs concerning the cause, nature, and purpose of the universe and grew as an organized system of beliefs that bound people to become a close knit society. It can become an enormous unifying force in a world torn by suspicion and hatred. As stated by Swami Vivekananda, "Religion, to help mankind, must be ready and able to help him in whatever condition he is, in servitude or in freedom, in the depths of degradation or on the heights of purity; everywhere, equally, it should be able to come to his aid."[1] It may be described as the quality of life which is characterized by a fearless, single-minded and vigorous pursuit of truth that transcends phenomenal human existence. Religion, in its real sense, is self-discovery. Again, according to Swami Vivekananda, "Religion is the manifestation of the divinity already in man." Elsewhere he says, "Religion is realization; not talk, nor doctrine, nor theories, however beautiful they may be. It is being and becoming, not hearing or acknowledging; it is the whole soul becoming changed into what it believes."[2] We have to realize the immense value of the inner meaning and significance of religion. The essence of religion is truthfulness, love and not hatred towards others. In the words of Swamiji, "...if one religion is true, all others must be true. There are differences in non-essentials, but in essentials they are all one."[3] Therefore, religion becomes an effective medium for human brotherhood and not social alienation. Religion has thus supplied some deeply felt inner need of human nature, and the vast majority of people all over the world cannot do without some form of religious belief. It was made clear by Pundit Jawaharlal Nehru when he stated that "the religions have helped greatly in the development of humanity. They have laid down values and standards and have pointed out principles for the guidance of human life."[4] Thus we find that religion serves a great deal in achieving self-security, change of heart and renunciation in its unceasing attempt to create a new social order through love.

When we go into detail, we find that organized religion has more harm than good to offer and it even hinders the moral and spiritual progress of man. Religion, as practiced, deals with matters unrelated to our normal lives and thus adopts an ivory-tower attitude, or is allied to certain social usages, which do not fit in with the present age. It often seems to stand for blind belief and reaction, dogma, bigotry, superstition and exploitation, and the preservation of vested interests. We find in religion pre-conceived notions because of which it deliberately shuts its eyes to reality might not tally with its notions. It seems very often to be the enemy of clear thought, for it is based not only on the acceptance without objection of certain fixed and unalterable theories and dogmas, but also sentiments, emotion and passion. So people's involvement with organized religion has brought comfort to innumerable human beings and stabilized society by values, it has checked the tendency to change and progress inherent in human society.

One of the greatest threats that the world faces today is that of international terrorism, which to a great extent, is fomented by this type of organized religion. Terrorists are a group of people sharing common goals and objectives determined by certain requirements towards the achievement of which each and every member puts in his or her competent skill. Religion, which is actually a great refuge of man in distress, has thus become a source of torture and wickedness and has created religious fanatics throughout the world. They consider their religion as the only true religion and their activities are guided by an urge to punish those who do not believe in it. In this way religion has led to terrorism. Violence in the name of religion, caste, and language has caused untold harm whenever it has occurred. So these fanatics are the greatest enemies of humanity as they do not tolerate the views of others.

Religion is the expression of the permanent nature of man—the aspect of divinity, the element of essential goodness present in every man. When we go through the teachings of various religions we find that none of them neglect this innate goodness in man. This belief in the essential spirituality and goodness of every man led Gandhi to believe in the essential unity of mankind. So he says, "I believe in absolute oneness of God and therefore also of humanity though we have many bodies, we have but one soul. The rays of sun are many through refraction, but they have the same sources."[5] All religions have their basis on the same principles of truth and non-violence and they propounded the law of love or *ahimsa*. Hence all religions are to be considered as different paths leading towards the same goal. A study of different religions shows that they have philosophical depths, spiritual intensity, holiness, purity chastity, charity and above all, the idea of universal brotherhood. All of them try to build up a fellowship of believers and are bound together in a holy partnership to advance the cause of peace, justice and freedom. As Dr. S Radhakrishnan said about the goal of religion, "Universality, social service, practice of religion and transformation of the human individual are the goals of religion. These are the lessons which Vivekananda taught us in is great life. These lessons have a purpose, a validity and relevance even today."[6] These are the basic ideas upheld by humanism also. Such a way of thinking undergirds the idea that one can as well postulate humanism as a new religion which mankind can rely upon. When the human element in man is highlighted, we firmly believe that most of the problems we are facing today can be solved.

Secularism in India was woven into the fabric of her ancient society. From the dawn of her history, India has given to the world the message of brotherly love and universal compassion. It is because of this ethos of tolerance and culture of secularism that century ago, Christians, Jews and Parsis found no difficulty in finding a home in India, the tradition of tolerance was thus found existing in India since time immemorial. Secularism has been the most effective cementing force in the context of meeting the demands of multi-religious, multicultural, and a multi-lingual society like India. The concept of secularism is also relevant in the process of nation building. Without secularism as a binding force, uniting the citizens of India, we cannot imagine to construct the polity in the right perspective. Secularism besides being a prerequisite to the presentation of the new nation's integrity is also a necessary aspect of modernization. As far as modern India was concerned, it was impossible to go back to that conception which the world had outlined and that which was completely out of tune with modern outlook. The necessity of the secular state arouse also from certain practical considerations. The government of a country like India with its plurality of religions can function satisfactorily in the modern age only on a secular basis. The progress of a state depends on national unity and solidarity. If special status was given to one particular religion, it would create a feeling of suspicion among the adherents of other faiths and it will inevitably lead to friction and conflict. Thus, secularism in India was the need of the society and country as a whole. It was essential for peace, unity integrity and progress. This form of secularism which respected the religion of all individuals was designed to ensure the emergence of a strong and cohesive polity in India. In simple words, Indian secularism means a protection and equal treatment of all religions and absence of state religion. "It (secularism) does not obviously mean a state where religion is discouraged. It means freedom of religions and conscience, including freedom of those who have no religion, subject only to their not interfering with each other or with the basic conception of our state."[7]

Hence we can say that it does not stand for the abolition of religion, but only for the separation of state and religion. Secularism is a philosophy of life and its ideal is progress in human life in the present world irrespective of man's religion, sect, caste, colour and creed. It does not accept anything which makes difference between man and man. Humanism based on reason and not on religious dogmas is the silent feature of secularism. The ideal of secular state implies a social structure in which the individual is not subject to the social inequalities imposed by religious sanctions. Religious attitudes may hamper the growth of a free atmosphere, necessary for the building up of a democratic and secular state. Religions were not debarred from public life but it was dissociated from the state. The spirit of religious tolerance was thus combined with strict neutrality of state to all religions and a clear demarcation of religious and secular spheres with autonomy of the latter. Thus, Indian secularism does not exclude religion, but promotes peaceful co-existence of all religions.

Social Philosophy: Reformative Thinkers of Kerala

All great thinkers come forward with some relevant answer to any major challenges that face the nation. This happens because such challenges facing the nation cannot be faced with the help of prescribed formulae. In India, a supreme challenge of this kind existed in the form of foreign domination, economic exploitation and social evils like caste, untouchability, *sati*, child marriage etc. The last decade of the 19th century saw the rise of powerful social and religious reform movements among the people in Kerala. This movement has their aim of the eradication of untouchability, the break-down of inter-sub caste barriers and the abolition of many costly and wasteful social practices and customs. These social reform movements were led by outstanding leaders like Sri Chattambi Swamikal and Sree Narayana Guru in Travancore and Brahmanada Sivayogi, Vagbhatanada and *Ananda* Thirtha in Malabar and recently the awakening task is taken by Navajyothi Sri Karunakara Guru. They revolted against the existing social evils in which *Brahmins* enjoyed a monopolistic position and eventually helped in ushering a new social order in which the non-Brahmin communities came to have their legitimate place. In these social reformers Sri Karunakara Guru played a unique and innovative role. Unlike the other philosophers, his activities were not radical or academic but it is purely mystical and elevates his followers to a higher plane of consciousness. Without an organized community based association, *Guru* empowered his followers to a world of experiential transcendental heights by simplicity and purity of heart. It is really a reformation which is beyond petty emotions of caste, religion or any sects. A serious and thorough study is required to unfold the transcendental philosophy of Sree Karunakara Guru. A mystic-philosopher who is not interested in constructing a system of philosophy or any abstract metaphysical or epistemological or any logical arguments *Guru* is a visionary, and therefore, communicate the truths that are revealed to him directly through his 'Guruvani'. "A seeker or a follower of *Guru* goes beyond the explanations in the Guruvani at a realm of experiential plane for apprehending the absolute truth, i.e. 'World is *Guru*, *Guru* is Truth, Truth is God." But it is really unfortunate to see that no serious attempts have been made to expose the philosophy of *Guru* in the Indian academic scenario. I hope a seminar like this will help us to fulfil this mission. Here in this chapter, I would like expose some ideas of *Guru* along with the thinkers like Chattambi Swamikal, Sree Narayana Guru, Brahmanada Sivayogi, Vagbhatanada and Swami *Ananda* Thirtha.

Chattambi Swamikal

Of the spiritual masters and reformers that Kerala has given birth after Sankara, Chattambi Swamikal is the most important figure. The religious and social reform movements in Kerala initiated by him have opened the doors of temples and spiritual knowledge as well as social and political power to all castes and creeds and all classes of people. He and his disciples have captured the cream of content of the basic religious and philosophical texts and translated it into the language of the common man and provided correct interpretations.

At a period when the elite claimed that the study of Vedas was the monopoly of the *Brahmins*, Swami boldly argued that all such barriers in the realm of knowledge and thought were baseless and illogical. He effectively established this through his speeches and writings. Swami by correctly interpreting the concerned Vedic texts established the eligibility of all, irrespective of caste or sex, for the study and teachings of Vedas. His vision of unity (*Samadarsana*) was the outcome of his belief in and adherence to the *Advaita* principle that '*Atman is Brahman',* each man is potentially divine, that all existence is one. So Swami argued that Vedic knowledge and temples should be open to all.

Chattambi Swamikal boldly fought against caste system. His influence on Kerala society on this account was unique. His first attention was in removing unjust customs and practices of Hindu society. His religious views gave an equal position to women also in the society and religion. He believed that religion should contain everything one might expect for a good life. He believed that the task of religion is to guide man in his spiritual and moral development. Swami initiated a new era of religious reformation through his symbol of love. He considered that for material as well as spiritual upliftment, love towards all living beings is essential and so he upheld *ahimsa* as the ultimate *dharma*. He defined the highest state of *ahimsa* as *Moksa.*

Thus we see that the message of Chattambi Swamikal; endeavoured all through his life to spread and inculcate was the self-realization of godliness is the modest of material pursuits. Swami has taught that *Advaita* has solutions for sustainable material progress as well as for attaining spiritual goals. The first person to revolt the inequalities and suppression of human rights in Kerala was Chattambi Swamikal. The fire lit by him in that repressive society has given to the people of Kerala the strength to clear new paths to freedom and equality.

Sree Narayana Guru

Like Chattambi Swamikal, Sree Narayana Guru also revolted against the existing social order in which the *Brahmins* enjoyed a position of primacy. He tried to uplift the social, economic position of the lower caste people and struggled against the upper caste domination in the society. His philosophy is basically a revaluation and restatement of *Advaita Vedanta*. Reintroducing the same wisdom in the modern age of science giving full recognition to the scientific midst of the days in which he lived, was what Narayana *Guru* did.

The caste system prevalent in India brought untold miseries to the *avarnas* or lower castes in Kerala. The writing in his works '*Jati Lakshanam*' and '*Jathinirnayam* advocated the messages of 'One caste, One religion, One God for man.' He called on the people to strengthen them through organization and to free them through education. According to *Guru*, the basic objective of every religion was to elevate the moral character of the individual and hence no religion or caste was inferior to another. He also advocates intermarriages between different castes as a means of evolving a classless and casteless society.

Sree Narayana *Guru* initiated a series of measures to mitigate the rigorous of the caste system and also to bring about a social and moral advancement in the society. For making an ideal society he advocated an eight-fold path which consisted of education, cleanliness, piety or *swarabhakti*, organization or Sanghatana, agriculture, trade, handicrafts and scientific and technological training. Thus, we see that Narayana Guru's message was full of love for humanity and it was not restricted to one community alone. Within a short span of time, the works and message of Guru touched all the castes of Hindu religion and paved for a greater social reform movements in Kerala.

Brahmananda Sivayogi

Like Chattambi Swamikal and Sree Narayana *Guru* in Travancore, in Malabar Brahmanada Sivayogi and Vagbhatanada started spirituality and ended in reform movements that became a stream joining the modern national movement. It is this reform movement having an external form of spirituality, but internally a movement of democracy, that became the forerunner of the political movements in Malabar.

Swami Brahmanada Sivayogi was one of the greatest social reformers who dedicated his life to the upliftment of the downtrodden people. He was one of the first persons to put an end to the Brahmin dominance in Malabar. He was of opinion that all faiths in the world should preach love and goodness. Religion, according to him, was not to be made an instrument of hate or hostility that build barriers between the people and divide them into separate narrow groups. He wanted people to practice a universal religion, a religion of Bliss that would bring into its fold the flowers of several religions and also the atheist. He hopes that it will help us to live amicably a life of harmony and peace. Sivayogi's entire life was spent in a fervent and untiring effort to place before the common man the glorious and scientific path of *Raja yoga* in an easily and intelligible manner.

We see that Brahmananda Sivayogi was the first spiritual leader of Kerala who emphasized the need of morality and ethics in every aspect of life. His beliefs and concepts of man and mind were very much different from his contemporary thinkers. We, the people of Kerala, owe much to him as he was an inspiring force to the socio-religious movements in Kerala society.

Vagbhatanada

Vagbhatanada was a disciple of Sivayogi. He stood apart as a glorious personality for his noble thinking and for practicing what he preached. He accepted *Advaita* philosophy but it was not a negation of material life for him. He said that the primary duty of an *Advaita* follower is to fight against the caste system and its bye-products such as evil customs, rituals and superstitions. He raised his voice against the inequalities existing in the society. He argued that women are inevitable part of society and so they must be respected and granted equal rights like men. Hence he founded the 'Atmavidya Sangha' women's organization. The sharpest weapon of Vagbhatanada was poems and articles, which aimed at the ignorance and conservation of the society. He aimed not only to refine the socio-religious fields but also tried to introduce humanism in the society which was deeply rooted in feudalism and social evils. He exhorted the people to follow a life based on righteousness and morality, thereby leading men to cleanse their minds. The cleansed minds pave the way to social welfare and upliftment. The contribution of Vagbhatanada through his Atmavidya Sangha is noteworthy as he had taken pains for renaissance and fought for maintaining justice. Even today his ideologies are propagated by the followers of the Atmavidya Sangha.

Swami Ananda Thirtha

Swami Ananda Thirtha, the disciple of Sree Narayana Guru, fought against untouchability in temple, schools and other public places. His works extended beyond the borders of Kerala to the parts of Tamil Nadu and Karnataka. To build a democratic community out of a caste ridden society is an historic task. It requires a full-scale religious-cultural revolution in the consciousness of Indian people. This was really a huge task for a single man to achieve. But Swami aimed at this as his desire was to build a democratic culture against the prevailing values of the caste ridden society.

Swami wanted the caste Hindus to get rid of their attitude of superiority while the economically poor and ignorant *Harijans* had to be enabled to overcome their feelings of inferiority. Payyanur was chosen by Swami Ananda Thirtha to start his work of *Harijan* education not because people there were sympathetic to the cause but because it was one of the most conservative centres of orthodox Hinduism in Kerala. *Jati Nasini Sabha*, an association for the abolition of caste was started under the leadership of Sri Kelappan and Swami Ananda Thirtha. The movement argued that the age-old religious beliefs should be modified according to the demands of the modern times and that a social revolution was imperative to build a modern India, and to liberate people from their caste mentality.

Swami held that caste had destroyed the rationality and humanity of the 'Caste Hindus' as it dehumanizes people and makes them worse than animals. As long as caste consciousness and caste discrimination remains, the nation will never attain freedom and progress. Only if the caste structure is destroyed Hindus will become one community. He took practical steps for this. But he was well aware of the limited values of legal solutions to problems of religious and social nature like untouchability. What he wanted to achieve through these legal battle was to pose a public challenge to the age-old myth in the popular mind that *Brahmins* were people with special privileges and religious status. His religion was that of service and dedication to the down-trodden. It was this religion which made him to look at untouchability as intrinsically evil, contrary to goodness, religious truth and God. Hence he took upon himself to the removal of untouchabiltiy as his special religious vocation. He was equally concerned about the economic and educational development of *Harijans*. Hence we can say that Swami Ananda Thirtha brought about a significant socio-religious change which further strengthened the struggle of the Scheduled Caste in Kerala for social equality.

The socio-religious movements under the leadership of the above thinkers were revolutionary in their practical plane. The most important aspect of these reform movements was the awakening of lower caste people and their struggle against the evils of the contemporary society. The social reformers before the advent of these thinkers regarded the situation of lower caste with 'sympathy' but did not try to liberate them from the centuries old social tyranny. There was very little or no stress against economic inequality and exploitation. But the above said thinkers have all fundamentally subscribed to the humanist philosophy and they recognized the value or dignity of man. In order to get rid of the evils of caste system or emancipate the downtrodden masses they brought about certain social reforms and the basis of this was the humanism in them. It was again this humanism which caused them to undertake a secularist attitude so as to save the downtrodden masses from the grip of religious fundamentalism. They thought that the spread of secularism was necessary to bring about a unity in a multi-religious country like India. These were the basic tenets of the *Guru* tradition in Kerala and Karunakara *Guru* was no exception. But he was not a social reformer like the leaders which we have mentioned earlier and his philosophy is not much familiar as the above thinkers. And many of the books of all these thinkers are written in regional languages and hence not familiar in the academic circle. Since we are living in a period in which humanism is least regarded, and religious rivalries are becoming a daily routine of our life, it is highly important that we must do all our best to revive the secular and humanistic tradition of these great thinkers and bring them to light. This will help a lot in solving many of the religious problems faced by our country and bring about equality leading to progress and development.

Notes

1. Vivekananda, Swami (1989). *The Complete Works of Swami Vivekananda.*, Vol. II. Calcutta: Advaita Ashrama, pp. 300-301.
2. *Ibid.*, p. 396.
3. *Ibid.*, p. 318.

4. Nehru, Jawaharlal (1980). *Discovery of India.* Bombay: Asia Publishing, p. 622.
5. Gandhi, M.K., *Young India,* 25.9.1924.
6. Dr. S. Radhakrishanan, (1988). *Our Heritage,* Delhi: Orient Paperbacks. p. 90.
7. Gopal, S. (1983) (ed.). *Jawaharlal Nehru*, Delhi: Oxford University Press, p. 327.
8. Nair, Raman, R. and Devi, Sulochana (2010). *Chattambi Swami: An Intellectual Biography*, Trivandrum: Centre for South Indian Studies.

7

The Religious Thoughts of Narayana *Guru*

Tradition Modernity Dualism

P. Chandramohan

The present chapter is purported to discuss in detail the religious ideas of Narayana Guru in the context of modernity and tradition. It may be stated at the outset that I am not alluding to tradition and modernity as either binary opposites or do I seek to counterpose them as referents with watertight boundaries. However, these concepts have been conceived as binary opposites in all contemporary societies. Given such an understanding, it has become customary to classify any practice in terms of the made-up opposition between tradition and modernity. As for example, traditional knowledge and modern knowledge; traditional dress and modern dress; traditional education and modern education; traditional customs and modern practices; traditional culinary practices and modern food habits; the static tradition and dynamics in modernity; this is certainly a list that would seem endless. But it may be possible to bypass this opposition between modernity and tradition. For instance, one could portray Narayana Guru as traditional in the sense that he followed *Advaita Vedanta* but, on the other hand, it is also possible to say that he was modern for he believed in equality and negated all caste distinctions. Therefore, what is important is to examine the intertwined strands of his thoughts and ideals. In this context, it is necessary to visualize the Guru as a synthesizer of the desirable aspects of modernity and tradition.

Most of the academic writings on the socio-religious history of Kerala have generally viewed the emergence of modern ideas and the development of a critical attitude towards religious superstition and social obscurantism as a consequence of the introduction of English education[1] and institutions[2] and the activities of Christian missionaries.[3] While emphasizing the role of missionaries and Western knowledge and ideas, the writers, have however, overlooked the potentialities of socio-religious ideas that were rooted in what is called as 'the Indian intellectual tradition'. Had these changes been due to the impact of Western thought and ideas, instead of modernization, our society would have undergone a process of Westernization.[4] The intellectual's quest to re-shape or reformulate the society and community did not fructify mainly because of their ambivalent, often contradictory, attitude towards tradition and modernity. If tradition served as a powerful weapon in the efforts to realize modernity, modernity did not involve a complete rejection of the past. There is a belief that the Western influence automatically leads to 'progressive' social and political consciousness and the traditional influence invariably develops 'conservative' attitudes. One of the arguments that gained predominance has been that Narayana *Guru* was the product of Indian intellectual tradition mainly based on the *Advaita* philosophy of Sankara[5], and that the sources of the evolution of his intellectual thought were derived from traditional knowledge. Nevertheless, rationalism and religious universalism, the two important intellectual and ideological strands of the nineteenth century, were the binding principles of Narayana *Guru*'s socio-religious reform activities. This may perhaps help us to question the general belief that the Western influence automatically leads to 'progressive' social and political consciousness and that the traditional influence invariably promotes 'conservative' attitudes. Here the attempt is to place as well as portray *Guru*'s ideas as a combined outcome of both tradition and modernity as Western education had already been mediated through the former.

A lot has been written on Narayana *Guru*[6], not strictly with the aid of an academic approach, but mainly journalistic, and often devoid of a critical historical perspective. Some of these writings have been undertaken with the aim of appropriating the legacy of Narayana Guru for legitimizing one or other sectarian interests.[7] To some extent, the fairly extensive literature on Narayana Guru owes its existence to the efforts of Malayalees to orient themselves towards their contemporary social, cultural and religious needs in order to legitimize themselves with the help of the 'past', that is, what happened in the late nineteenth and early twentieth centuries of their society.

Narayana Guru belonged to a family of cultural and intellectual tradition and a community of some standing, notwithstanding his low position in the caste hierarchy. He inherited considerable cultural and social capital which made him an 'exception' within the general social hierarchy. Perhaps, this could have qualified him to transcend the binary mentioned above. As a result of this intellectual inheritance and cultural background Narayana Guru possessed a mind which combined brilliance and incisiveness in a finely balanced proportion. Almost all the biographers of the *Guru* have narrated in detail that Nanu as a boy used to reveal his innate nature very often by reacting to affairs related to religious rituals and caste sensibilities in his own naughty way.[8] Evidently, even at that young age, when education and conscious thinking had little influence on his actions, the two significant aspects of the future *Guru*'s mental makeup which could be discerned even in his childhood were *rationalism* and humanism[9] or humor and skepticism about the present.

There are no sources to enlighten us on whether he was associated with any teacher other than Raman Pillai or educational institutions and their curricula that may have shaped his education. The paucity of information about the formative influences on Nanu makes it difficult for us to understand his evolution as a spiritual-intellectual with a vision for the future socio-religious transformation of society.

In 1884, after the death of his father, he left home in search of Truth.[10] During 1884-1888, he travelled extensively in South India[11] when he came in contact with Chattambi Swamikal and Taikkattu Aiyyavu, who influenced his intellectual contours.[12] It was possibly from Chattambi Swamikal that he acquired a critical attitude towards the scriptures; he understands the painful truth that the Vedas were the sole preserve of the *Brahmins*. It was possibly also from him that he learned that non-*Brahmins* too had the right to consecrate idols in temples.[13] From Taikkattu Aiyyavu[14], he practiced *yoga* which helped him to 'open the inner eye[15].' It is strongly believed that the *Guru*'s famous dictum "*Oru Jati, Oru Matham, Oru Daivam Manushyanu*" (one caste, one religion and one God for mankind) was borrowed from Taikkattu Aiyyavu who had propagated, much earlier, in Tamil, *Oru Jati than Manushyanu, Oru Matham than Manushyanu, Oru Daivam than Manushyanu*[16]." During this period he had developed deep knowledge in Sanskrit and Tamil lore and had acquired himself with various provincial cultures and also familiarized with Buddhism and Jainism.[17] It is still an enigma as to from where or from whom he acquired his vast knowledge in Sanskrit and Vedas. One can only say that the long existing historical knowledge considerably influenced the intellectual make up of Narayana Guru.[18]

Narayana Guru's socio-religious experiences during this journey also contributed, to some extent to his intellectual transformation. It was during this period that he became especially sensitive to the social problems, particularly to those of the low castes. Unique both in appearance and demeanor when compared to conventional *Sannyasi* or a *Sadhu*, he mixed with people of all veins without being touchy about whether one belonged to this or that caste or social status.[19] He lived in the midst of the poor and saw for himself their grinding poverty and superstition which added to their misery and brought about their ruin.[20] He witnessed the oppression and injustice to which they were subjected to. This close contact with the weaker sections of the society provided him with a clear understanding of their socio-religious and economic conditions and a conception of the remedial measures. By his sheer character, personal magnetism and homely wisdom he stormed the hearts of thousands and earned the respect of even those who could not agree with his ideas and activities.

The widespread missionary activities in Travancore at a time he was socially active[21] and his tour to Malabar, a predominantly Muslim area[22] might have familiarized him with the dieta of Christianity and Islam. His ideas for the social and economic uplift of the lower castes might or might not have been derived from Christianity; nevertheless he was inspired by the activities of Christian missionaries.[23] It is possible that missionary activities and the subsequent changes in society helped Narayana Guru to introspect about the strengths and weaknesses of traditional culture and its institutions, but it would be far-fetched to assume that the missionaries were mainly responsible for his socio-cultural ideas. It would be more appropriate to propose that the socio-cultural ideas of Narayana Guru were occasioned by the missionary presence but not created by missionaries. There seems to be no casual link between the two; in other words. It is worthless to casually connect them because they had their own independent existence and functions in Travancore irrespective of their coexistence during the same historical time.

The social practices and religious beliefs prevalent in the late nineteenth century Kerala society were perceived as 'religious superstition' and 'social obscurantism'.[24] The popular notion was that Hindu religion was a compound of magic, animism and superstition.[25] Polytheism and idolatry made religion into ceremonious rituals. The commonsensical view was that the *Brahmins* established their monopoly of scriptural knowledge and interpretation of rituals. As the backward communities were not generally allowed to participate in the institutionalized pattern of worship followed by the *Savarnas*, the religious beliefs and practices of *Avarnas* followed the so-called 'abominable' practices: the worship of totems, guardian deities and demons of destruction replete with detestable rites and abhorrent practices.[26] The worship of the snake, very popular among the Malayalees, was such an instance and skin diseases, leprosy and sterility, for example, were believed to be caused by the wrath of serpents.[27] The practice of *Mantravada* or spells, offerings of fermented drinks and the sacrifice of cocks and goats, singing obscene songs about female genitals, copulation and masturbation and devil dancing were part of the rituals for the worship of spirits.[28] The religious beliefs and practices were thus a mixture of magic, sorcery, witchcraft, divination and several other forms of popular religion; the forms differed slightly between the *avarnas* and *savarnas*. But then, the content remained the same; they being common to both of the groupings. The rites and practices observed at the time of birth, death, puberty and pregnancy began to be treated as absolutely absurd and irrational.[29] It is often said that such practices had led to the 'decadence' of the society; it is at such sites that we find tradition becoming antithetical to modernity.

The most distressing factor, however, was caste. The practice of untouchability, inapproachability and unseeability affronted human dignity. Government offices, schools and courts were not open to low castes. They were prohibited from entering public roads, temples, palaces, etc.[30] Thus the rules and regulations relating to caste hampered social mobility, fostered social division and sapped individual initiative.

The Guru understood the interdependences and interconnections between religious and social life and also between religious beliefs and social stigmas—the implications of the prevalent form of worship on social institutions. Thus, Narayana Guru was quite aware of the material, psychological and spiritual problems that affected the deprived sections of Kerala society. The influence of this social experience in the transformation of Nanu from a school teacher to Narayana Guru, the reformer is entrenched in the non-duality between tradition and modernity.

Religious Reforms and Narayana Guru

The reformers of Kerala can be distinguished into two broad

categories; the first group believed that social behaviour can be affected through rearticulating the existent religious idioms. The second group of reformers organized themselves under non-religious leadership and gained their ends through constitutional means and secular organizations.[31] However, as elsewhere in India, the reformers who belonged to the first category were more successful in Kerala, than the second. This perhaps may be owing to the fact that religion was the dominant ideology of the time and it was not possible to undertake any social action without a referential relation with.[32] Though the English-educated people were respected by the masses, they were not accepted as their cultural ideal. This was mainly because of their alienation both from the existent culture and their partial affinity with the emergent cultures.[33]

Having realized the interconnection between religious beliefs and social practices, Narayana Guru started his activities by making reform resonant with religious idioms in order to legitimize the need to reform oneself and others. The Keralites met their religion at every turn—at birth, puberty, marriage, death, etc. As social life was strongly influenced by religious tenets, Narayana Guru realized that religious idioms were a necessary prerequisite for social reform. This is exemplified in the famous consecration of Shiva and the proclamation that he had consecrated “Ezhava Shiva”. In such instances, along with several others, we discern that Narayana Guru sought to replace the existing abominable religious beliefs and practices with a different form of worship. The establishment of temples and consecration of idols by the *Guru* was an expression of this alternative path. In contradiction to the attitude of the nineteenth century Indian intellectuals[34], except Sree Rama Krishna Paramahamsa, Narayana Guru conceded that idolatry and rituals and the practices of traditional religion[35] was necessary for people in the earlier stages of their religious understanding, before they could grasp the abstract truth embodied in spiritual philosophy. That is why, although he himself did not believe in idolatry[36], he sanctioned it as the nucleus around which an alternative form of worship could evolve.[37] The first step was the consecration of an idol of Shiva at Aruvippuram in 1888.

The words he inscribed on the temple wall eloquently declare his vision of universal brotherhood and oneness of man: ‘In this model place all inhabitants irrespective of caste and religion can dwell freely as brothers’.[38] Narayana Guru wished for this temple to symbolize the brotherhood of man and equality of all before God. One of the most striking features of the religious thoughts of his reformation was a universal outlook based on the unity of Godhead. By this consecration Narayana Guru unleashed an attack on the sacred order of *Varna dharma*. The consecration of Shiva thus symbolized a struggle between the *status quo* and change. It was on the basis of religious universalism that the *Guru* formulated in his 1914 doctrine, "One caste one religion and one God for mankind".[39] This underlines the fact that he was moving towards a universal religion based on the best tradition of Hindu theism. He indirectly declared that all believers in one God were his brethren and also advocated wide toleration in the tract on different modes of worship. To him the claim of superiority of one religion over the other stemmed from ignorance. He drew parallel with the story of the seven blind men who felt the parts of an elephant and each gave his own version as he distinguished.[40] The *Guru* advised his followers, "Whatever is one's religion it is enough that man become good... Whatever a man does for his own pleasure shall be for the benefit of others."[41] The *Guru*'s general interest in comparative religion led to the holding of a *Sarva Mata Sammelanam* (All Religions Conference) on 3-4 May 1924. He declared his objective in organizing the conference saying: "To know and to make known, not to argue and win".[42] When the principles of different religions were discussed on a common platform, the underlying unity was easier to grasp. The principal motives of this conference were: to search for universal truth in religion, to create interest in comparative religion, to bring home to people the essential unity of all religions, and finally to create an atmosphere for developing the idea of religious universalism. Soon after the conference, he decided to start a "School of all Religions" which he called "Mata Mahapathashala" at Sivagiri in order to teach the essentials of all religions.[43] In this sense, he was not against religiosity, but against differential treatment (often hierarchical) of people in terms of religion/caste one adhered to.

After the Aruvippuram consecration, Narayana Guru installed images in sixty-four temples in different parts of Kerala. Three distinct phases can be discerned in the establishment of these new places of worship. During the first phase gods of the Brahminical pantheon were consecrated in place of "lower satanic gods of primitive religion". He forbade the worship of evil spirits and keeping of images representing such beliefs in temples and houses of well-to-do

Ezhavas.[44] Their place was taken by the newly consecrated temples. He also brought about changes in the method of worship; animal sacrifices and offerings of fermented drinks were replaced by flowers and fruits.[45]

The second phase was marked by the establishment of simple and inexpensive temples. Though these temples had idols, *pujas* and celebrations were dispensed with. They were, in fact, conceived more as community places with gardens and libraries which provided a serene and educative atmosphere.[46]

The third category of temples had no idols or images, like the temples at Karamukku in which he had, in 1920, installed a lamp in place of an idol and pronounced the benediction, "Let there be light".[47] At Murukkupuzha, in 1921, he placed a granite slab with the inscription "Truth, Duty, Kindness and Peace[48]", and at Kalavancode in 1927 he installed a mirror which symbolically represented the fact that god is present in the self[49] or rather "know yourselves". According to Nataraja Guru, "A plain mirror and lamp was installed by him at one place, so that idolatry might come into line with Self knowledge, for at least one's own image in a mirror told no distorted lie in any hysterical terms".[50]

These innovations in his consecration not only differentiate his concept of temples from that of the Brahminical ones but also illustrate his precept that ideals are more important than idols. Narayana Guru was quite different in inspiration, character, and message to the traditional saints of pre-modern and also westernized reform movements. That was his uniqueness. But his active participation in the socio-religious movement in Kerala, during the late nineteenth and early twentieth centuries, endowed him with the halo combining a modern Indian reformer with that of a traditional Hindu Sannyasi.[51]

Our understanding of Narayana Guru will depend on our perception of the character of the socio-religious movements in the nineteenth century Travancore. A significant aspect of his religious reform was the freedom it afforded to an individual to be critical about one's own tradition and one's position within the unfolding of modern ideas and practices, without renouncing totally the former and selectively accepting the latter.

Irrespective of whether the consecrations were looked upon as sanskritization or protest, the fact that they sought to change the popular form and attitude of worship among the lower castes is undeniable. At the same time the system he created was not a replica of what the upper castes followed. It was an intervention intended to create a new mode, distinct from both the popular and the elitist. Unlike his successors in socio-religious reform, he was not demanding homogenization of identity among the lower and the upper castes through temple entry but was striving for the creation of a new religious ethos.

The objective of Narayana Guru's religious reform efforts does not seem to be to enable the low castes to have access to the Brahminical gods, as has been argued by Genevieve Lemercinier[52], but to create a system of worship of their own. That Narayana Guru initially consecrated the idol of Shiva, despite his disapproval of idolatry, was an indication of the influences of both the elite and the popular culture. At the same time, he was eager to create a system distinct from both which explains the changes he made in consecration during the later stages as he was himself transforming or reformulating his own selfhood.

The consecration of temples by Narayana Guru cannot be viewed either as an attempt to revive the past or as a rebuttal of it. His consecration of temples not only signified a rational approach to customary practices but also represented an effort to embellish faith with rationality. If religion did not keep pace with the demands of the times, it would get fossilized and justifiably relegated. While consecrating idols in the temples, Narayana Guru was least concerned about religious sanctions or bothered his head over whether such practices existed in the past. When the upper castes questioned his possession of scriptural authority to make him suitable to undertake consecration, the *Guru* replied "My consecration is of an Ezhava Shiva and not of a Brahmin Shiva".[53] Hearing this, the people, *Savarnas* and *Avarnas* alike, were torn between their retained sentiments and emerging commitment.[54] The important intellectual criterion which marked the consecrations was persuasive reason and convincing rhetoric. Not very many were able to match the uncompromising reasoning of Narayana Guru. On another occasion when the *Guru* was installing an idol in a temple in Trivandrum, a scholar very sarcastically expressed his doubt whether the time was auspicious for such sacred function. The *Guru* calmly replied, "A horoscope is cast after the birth of the child. The birth does not take place according to a pre-determined auspicious time. The consecration is over. Now you can do your calculation".[55] His only concern at that time was the effect the consecration has on society. He was concerned about creating social mobility and promoting individual initiative rather than toeing the scriptures. Thus his consecrations broke the rules of customary practices which resulted in emotional and sentimental ruptures in society; but then, the times was such that reason prevailed over both of them.

To Narayana Guru it was immaterial whether his consecrations had the sanction of religious institutions, as his reform activities were a struggle against cultures that ought to be relegated.[56] They posed a challenge not only to the Brahmin hegemony, but also to the senseless customs that had survived through ages as though by divine ordinance. A sense of freshness was generated through the *Guru*'s efforts, casting a seminal ray of light on the life of the untouchables and those unapproachable of Kerala who were, for centuries, wallowing in darkness and slavery. Temples were, to Narayana Guru, a means to an end. Once the end was achieved he did not bother about the proliferation of temples. In 1917, the *Guru* advised his followers, "Do not encourage construction of temples any longer; if at all any temple is to be constructed it should be a small one. The educational institutions should be the chief temples."[57] In the religious sphere his reforms sought to remove priestly monopoly of religious knowledge and also to simplify religious rituals on the basis of ideals of humanism, economic rationalism and perhaps nationalism as well. The social implication of his consecrations was to liberate individuals from conformity borne out of fear and from an uncritical submission to the exploitation by the priests. The religious activities of Narayana Guru were an explicit expression of his opposition to all distinctions based on caste and *Varna*. According to him there was no fundamental difference between a Brahmin and a Pariah; both belonged to a single human caste.[58] In "Jati-Mimamsa" he emphasized this oneness: terms like Brahmin and Pariah are churned out ideas and superimposed on the reality of the humans which is essentially and fundamentally the same.[59]

The greatness of Narayana Guru was that he practiced what he preached. In other words, he lived the life he wanted others to live. He started his crusade against *Varna dharma* by liberating himself from its bondage, not by demanding rights of others but by freeing himself of all dependence on caste practices and stipulations.[60] He was the practicing model of "how to take care of oneself" in the changing times. The uplift of the communities, who were lower in social status to the Ezhavas, was considered by the *Guru* as a part of his life's mission. He admitted people from all castes to temples consecrated by him. He maintained personal relations with those who belonged to the castes lower than his in the hierarchy. In order to uplift the conditions of the Cherumas and the Pulayas, he not only admitted them as students but also employed them as cooks, ignoring all caste taboos.[61] The *Guru* felt that it was paradoxical that while the Ezhavas were fighting against pollution practiced by the upper castes, they were themselves treating the Pulayas and Parayas as untouchables.[62] Narayana Guru reminded the Ezhavas that unless they changed their attitude towards the communities considered as inferior to them in caste hierarchy, they have no right to clamor for justice.[63] With this reform in view he encouraged intercaste marriages and interdining.[64] This goes on to show that 'going beyond' was an integral part of his reform lexicon. Narayana Guru's outlook on India was quite different from the upper caste elite thinkers of the Indian renaissance. As Hindu culture and the caste system rested upon Brahmanism, Narayana Guru geared his moves in opposition to cultural and ideological hegemony of *Savarnas*.

Consecrations of idols in temples by Narayana Guru were a move against the cultural hegemony of *Brahmins* and represented the first expression of social reform. To Gail Omvedt, "'caste struggle' like 'class struggle' could become revolutionary only when it poses as an alternative, a more advanced social system rather than being simply a negative protest or a competitive struggle for more economic or social-cultural rights within the framework of exploitation".[65] Narayana Guru's reform activities represented the fulfillment of the renaissance's desire for social transformation along revolutionary lines. In other words, Narayana Guru formulated a theo-ideology of reason in order to tilt social relations in such a way so that there are no 'up' and 'down' within the texture of sociality. His consecrations of idols, inscriptions and mirrors were re-formulating practices that have no precedents but gained prevalence as far as future freedom and self-fulfillment are concerned. Perhaps, that is why he was unique and has become an icon in all imaginable fields of social actions; as someone who could live a life without referential relations to both tradition and modernity. And live a life of his own as an exemplar being in this world for the future to come.

Notes

1. *Kerala Mitram* wrote, "....the study of English language has conferred great many benefits upon the natives of Malabar, who, having read various English books, have now begun to discover defects and flaws in their own habits and proceedings and evince an inclination to improve and reform...." (30, April, 1881, in *Madras Native News Paper Report*, for May 1881. See the speech of N. Kumaran in Travancore Legislative Council, *Proceedings of Travancore Legislative Council* Vol. VI, No. 2, October 1925, p. 310 and *Report of the Malabar Tenancy Committee* Vol. II Madras Govt. Press 1940, p. 316.
2. *Manorama, Malayala* (1898). 19 February.
3. Mateer, Samuel (1883). *The Land of Charity: A Descriptive Account of Travancore and Its People*, London 1871, pp. 141-157; *Idem, Native Life in Travancore*, London, pp. 396-413; Robin Jeffrey (1976), *Decline of Nayar Dominance*, New Delhi: Vikas Publishing House, p. 265; R.N. Yesudas (1977), *British Policy in Travancore*, 1805-1859, Trivandrum, p. 5; B.N. Nair (1977), "The Problematic of Kerala Society", In: *Journal of Kerala Studies*, Vol. IV, Part II, p. 213; P.G. Edwin, "British Impact in Kerala" in *Journal of Kerala Studies*, Vol. 5, June 1978, Part II pp. 271-286; Lawrence Lopez (1988). *A Social History of Modern Kerala*, Trivandrum, pp. 40-104; Dick Kooiman (1989), *Conversion and Social Equality in India: The London Missionary Society in South Travancore in the 19th Century*, Manohar, Delhi, p. 200.
4. Panikkar, K.N. (1985). "Breaking with the Past, Yet Looking Back to it", In: *The Telegraph* 7th June, p. 7. See also, Idem "Socio-Religious Reforms and the National awakening", In: Bipan Chandra etc. *India's Struggle for Independence 1857-1947*, Viking, Penguin Books, 1988, pp. 82-90.
5. Guru, Nataraja (1968). *The Word of the Guru: An Outline of the Life and Teachings of the Guru Narayana*, PAICO Publishing House, Ernakulum, Cochin, especially Chapter XX "More Intimate Jotting", pp. 241-266; M.K. Sanoo writes, "Advaita was Swami's declared character of faith. The influence of Raman Pillai should have been a deciding factor in Swami's progress to Advaita Philosophy" *Narayana Guru Swami*, Vivekodayam, Printing and Publishing Company, Irinjalakuda, 1976, p. 53. P. Chandramohan, "Popular Culture and Socio-Religious Reform: Narayana Guru and the Ezhavas of Travancore" in *Studies in History*, 3, 1, ns (1987), Sage Publications, New Delhi, pp. 57-74.
6. Sree Narayana literature can be divided into two broad categories as the works of and on Narayana Guru. The second one can again be divided into various categories such as Biographies, Memoirs and Reminiscences, Studies, Essays, Exposition/Commentary, Poetry/Songs, Anthology and Souvenirs. All these parts together there are about 250 Works on Narayana of which are 54 biographies, 45 exposition and Interpretations, 40 poetries/

songs, 80 essays/studies, 15 Collected Works and more than 20 souvenirs. Besides hundreds of articles published in Newspapers, Weeklies and Magazines. For a detailed accounts of Sree Narayana Literature See Champadan Vijayan "Sree Narayana Sahithyam Malayalathil in *Mathrubhumi Varanthappathippu,* 16 September, 1990, p. III.

7. There are some attempts by certain sections to appropriate for themselves his legacy—to paint him as a champion of revived Hinduism (P. Parameswaran, *Sree Narayana Guruswamikal Navothanathinte Pravachakan,* Jayabharath Publications, Calicut, 1971, Second edition 1979), to describe him as a crusader of the *Dalit* for their movement for "social justice, P.K. Gopalakrishnan, "Sree Narayana Guru—Torch Bearer of Enlightenment for Revolutionary Changes" in a Seminar on *History of Political Development in Kerala,* 11 and 12 December 1985, Sponsored by Indian Council of Historical Research and University of Kerala), M.S.A Rao, *Social Movements and Social Transformations*, Macmillan, Delhi, pp. 37-38) to another he was a messiah of Ezhava liberation in Kerala (see the First Annual Report of the Secretary of the SNDP Yogam in *Vivekodayam* 13 May 1904, pp. 15-19, see also the letter of P. Parameswaran to the Dewan of Travancore on the 18th January 1903, Travancore Government *English Records*, Cover No. 8338, Kerala Secretariat Cellar, now it is in Kerala State Archives, Thiruvananthapuram See also Stephen Fuchs, *Rebellious Prophets: A Study of Messianic Movements* in *Indian Religion,* Asia Publishing House, Bombay 1965, pp. 270-271 and according to Swami Dharma Threertha, Narayana Guru was the representative of "Hindu Nationalism" (Swami Dharma Theertha, *The Menace of Hindu Imperialism*, Har Bhagwan, Lahore, 1946, pp. 264-276.
8. N. Kumaran Asan's *Brahmasri Sri Narayana Guruvinte Jeevacharithra Samgraham,* the first biography of Narayana Guru serialized in *Vivekodayam* in 1915. The first chapter published in *Vivekodayam*, April-May 1915, Vol. XII No. I, pp. 416-18. In 1979, these *Vivekodayam* articles were compiled, edited and published in a booklet form by Kumaran Asan Memorial Committee, Thonakkal and its second edition came out in 1984. See 1984 edition, p. 88; see also M.K. Sanoo, *op. cit.*, P. Parameswaran, *op. cit.*, K. Damodaran, *Shri Narayana Guru Swami Tripadangalude Jeevacharitram,* Quilon, 1929, Kotookoikal Velayudhan, *op. cit.*, Vijayalayam Jayakumar, *Sree Narayana Guru: A Critical Study*, New Delhi, 1999, p. 44.
9. Sanoo, M.K. *op. cit.*, p. 37.
10. Sanoo, M.K. *op. cit.*, 179, P. Parameswaran *op. cit.*, pp. 36-37.
11. Guru, Nataraja *op. cit.*, 256-261, M.K. Sanoo, *op. cit.*, pp. 77-94. Kotookoikal Velayudhan, *op. cit.*, pp. 49-67, Parameswarn *op. cit.*, pp. 30-52.
12. Balakrishnan, P.K. Narayana Guru (An Anthology) Kottayam, 1969, p. 204; See also Nataraja Guru *Op. cit.*, pp. 258-60, M.K. Sanoo *op. cit.*, 89-90.
13. *Shri Chattambi Swami Shatabda Smaraka Grantham*, Quilon, 1953, pp. 14, 98-99 and 206-211.

14. Taikkattu Aiyyavu was a devotee of Lord Subramanian and well known for his knowledge of *Vedanta*, Tamil spiritual tradition and mysteries of *yoga*. See M.K. Sanoo, *op. cit.*, p. 90; see also V.T. Samuel (1977), *One Caste, One Religion* and *One God: A Study of Sree Narayana Guru*. New Delhi, p. 46.
15. Parameswaran, P. *op. cit.*, pp. 41-42; see also M.K. Sanoo, *op. cit.*, p. 90.
16. A.C. Raja, Sivarajayogi Thycaud Ayyaswami Thuruvadikal (1960); See also Wikipedia.
17. Samuel, V.T. *op. cit.*, pp. 110-15.
18. Nataraja Guru, *op. cit.*, pp. 254-61.
19. Nataraja Guru Writes, "Clean shaven, with no ornamental things about him, the Guru Narayana avoided even any stripes or colours in his clothing. He dressed in two seamless pieces of white cloth (in later years tinged orange at the request of his ochre-robed disciples of the Sannyasin tradition). He would sip clean pure water as if drinking a rich beverage, and extol simple foods like fruits or roots. Often he preferred to sleep on a cloth spread on stone for a couch under the clear starlight, with his own arms alone for a pillow; and likewise he preferred bathing in rivers and walking on foot; and he would eat any kind of food from the devoted hands that offered it in village homes as he moved among the people," in *op. cit.*, p. 248.
20. *Ibid.*, p. 258.
21. When Colonel Macaulay was the President of Travancore, Christian missionaries received considerable help from colonial government. As a result the London Missionary Society, The Church Missionary Society and Danish Mission started their evangelical activities in Travancore in the beginning of the 19th Century. By the last quarter of the 19th Century Salvation Army also started working in Travancore. T.K. Velu Pillai, *Travancore State Manual*, Vol. II, Trivandrum, 1938, p. 727.
22. For Muslim contact see Murkoth Kumaran, *op. cit.*, pp. 410-12.
23. Stephen Fuchi, *Rebellious Prophets*, p. 271. See also Swami Dharma Theerthan, *The Prophet of Peace*, Chempazhanthi, 1931, p. 91. After organizing inter caste dining with the Pulayas on 27 May 1917, when Sahodharan Ayyappan sought the blessing of the *Guru* for his endeavour for intercaste marriages and interdining for which he faced strong criticism and opposition, the advice of the *Guru* was, "Don't feel dejected by opposition. This would grow into a great movement. Just bear in mind to be as forgiving as Christ", Quoted in M. Prabhu "Sahodharan Ayyappan" in M. Govindan (Ed) "Poetry and Renaissance: Kumar Asan Birth Centenary Volume", *Sameeksha* Madras, 1974, p. 230 and M.K. Sanoo *op. cit.*, p. 260.
24. Barbosa, Durate (1866). *A Description of the Coast of Africa and Malabar in the beginning of the 16th Century*, tr. and ed. Henry E.J. Stanley, London, p. 129; See also G.A. Ballard, Resident to the Chief Secretary to the Madras Government, 9 March 1870, "National Archives of India", *Madras Residency Records, Madras Political Proceedings*, 13 April 1870, G.O. No. 143.

25. Webber, Max (1971). *The Sociology of Religion*, London, p. 25.
26. For their socio-religious practices see L.K. Ananthakrishna Iyer (1909). *The Cochin Tribes and Caste*, Madras, Vol. I, p. 310, See also Samuel Mateer, *Land of Charity* 1871, p. 194, Francis Day (1863), *The Land of Perumals*, Madras, p. 320, Edgar Thurston (1909), *Caste and Tribes of South India*, Vol. II, Madras, pp. 406-409, Nagam Aiya, *Travancore State Manual*, Vol. II, p. 55, M.S.A Rao, "Supernatural Possession in Kerala" In: *Man*, Vol. 66, No. I, March 1986, p. 4, *Census of Travancore*, 1876, p. 162.
27. Sanoo, M.K. *op. cit.*, 228.
28. *Ibid.*, pp. 229-30; see also *Vivekodayam*, 15 July 1904, Vol. II, No. 2. P. Chandramohan, *Social and Political Protest in Travancore*, pp. 178-180.
29. *Vivekodayam*, 15 November 1905, Vol. II, No. 4, pp. 73-74, *Census of India*, 1901, Report. p. 280; C. Kesavan (1968), *Jeevithasamaram*, Kottayam, Vol. I, pp. 126-28; P.K. Gopala Krishnan (1979), "Ezhavas", In: "*Kerala Charitram*", Ernakulum, History Association Kerala, Vol. I, 1979, p. 985.
30. See *Vivekodayam*, 16 September, 1907; Proceedings of *Sree Mulam Popular Assembly*, 1913, p. 163, 1920, p. 108 and 1921, p. 11; *Mitavadi*, February 1917, Vol. 5, No. 2, p. 4 and *Mitavadi*, November, 1918, Vol. 6, No. 11, p. 26; *File No. 66/1911, Judicial Dept.*, Travancore.
31. Heimsath, Charles H. "The Function of Hindu Social Reformers—With Special Reference to Kerala", In: *The Indian Economic and Social History Review*, XV(I): 21-22.
32. According to Charles H. Heimsath, the reason for the failure of other reform movements in Kerala was due to lack of religious premises, See *Ibid.*, p. 27; See also P.K. Balakrishnan, *op. cit.*, p. 108 and M.K. Sanoo, *op. cit.*, p. 170 or 175 and K.N. Panikkar "Socio-Religions Reforms and the National Awakening", In: Bipan Chandra (etc.) edited *India's Struggle for Independence 1857-1947*, Viking, New Delhi 1988, pp. 82-83.
33. Chandramohan, P. (2010). "Education and Social Consciousness in the Making of Modern Kerala", In: Dr. Suresh Jnaneshwaran (ed.) *Historiography: Structure and Practice, A Festschrift in honour of Dr. T.K. Ravindran*, Trivandrum, pp. 176-187; See also *Idem, Social And Political Protest in Travancore*" *op. cit.*, pp. 90 and 112.
34. The 19th Century intellectuals like Ram Mohan Roy believed that polytheism and idolatry negated the development of individuality and supernaturalism and the authority of religious leaders imbibed the habit of conformity born out of fear (see Ram Mohan Roy. *Tuhfat-ul-Muhawaddin*, J.C. Ghose (Ed), *The English Works of Raja Ram Mohan Roy*, 1906, pp. 945-46.
35. For nineteenth century Indian attitude towards idolatry See K.N. Panikkar, *Presidential Address*, Section III, Indian History Congress, Thirty Sixth Session, Aligarh, 1975, p. 20.

36. One day a few people approached the *Guru* with a request that he may consecrate an idol in their newly built temple. Instead of installing an idol, the *Guru* proposed to hang a lamp at the Sanctum Sanctorum of the temple. They insisted the *Guru* for installing an idol and finally he accepted it, as he knew that the people would not be satisfied with less than an "Aradhana Moorthy". For this conversation between the *Guru* and the devotee see P.K. Balakrishnan, *Narayana Guru*, p. 154.
37. Chandramohan, P. "Popular Culture and Socio-Religious Reform." in *op. cit.*, p. 62.
38. The actual translation of the words which Narayana Guru inscribed in Malayalam on the temple wall was:
    i. "Without differences of caste;
    ii. Nor enmities of creed,
    iii. All live like brothers at heart
    iv. Here is this ideal place"
39. Dharmatheerthan, Swami. "The Prophet of Peace", *Chempazhanthi*, p. 33. See also Nataraja Guru, *op. cit.*, p. 24.
40. Narayana Guru, "Jathinirnayam" stanza No. 2 in *Sree Narayana Gurudeva Krithikal, op. cit.*, p. 154, M.K. Sanoo, *op. cit.*, pp. 332-335.
41. See his poem "Athmopadesha Shathakam", stanza no. 44 in T. Bhaskaran (Ed), *Sree Narayana Guruvinte Sampoorna Krithikal,* Mathrubhumi Press, Calicut, 1985, p. 366.
42. *Idem* "Athmopadesha Shathakam" in *Ibid.*, p. 115. See also Pazhambally Achyuthan, *Sree Narayana Guru (Smaranakal)*, Sarada Book Depot, Thonakkal, 1960, p. 123.
43. Sanoo, M.K. *op. cit.*, pp. 385-386.
44. Prasad, Muni Narayana (2006). "*Narayana Guru's Complete Works*", "Introduction" NBT, New Delhi, p. xviii.
45. In 1915 the *Guru* removed twenty-one deities from Kottattu Arumukam Pillayar Koil and the temples in nearby streets; See *Vivekodayam*, January 1915, Vol. II, No. 10, p. 354. See Pazhampally Achuthan, 'Guruvinte Karmapadharthy' *SNDP Yogam Platinum Jubilee Souvenir*, Quilon, 1978, p. 57. See also P.K. Gopalakrishnan, 'Samudhaya Pariskarna Prasthanangal' in *Kerala Charitram*, Vol. I, p. 1208. Apart from removing the evil spirits, Narayana Guru also took initiative to clear the 'Sarpakavu' or snake park with the intention of removing the superstition in connection with snakes and also to avoid the expenses for Sarpathullal, which was a special ceremony for the propitiation of snakes. Generally this *thullal* lasted one week. See M.K. Sanoo, *op. cit.*, p. 228 and P.K. Balakrishnan, *op. cit.*, p. 155.
46. Chandramohan, P. *Social and Political Protest in Travancore*, *op. cit.*, pp. 178-181.
47. The Sarada Temple at Varkala is the best example of this; see M.K. Sanoo *op. cit.*, p. 121.
48. Parameswaran, P. *op. cit.*, p. 122; Kotookoikal Velayudhan, *op. cit.*, p. 319; M.K. Sanoo *op. cit.*, p. 550.

49. *Ibid.,* p. 550. Kotookoikal Velayudhan, *op. cit.,* pp. 96 and 319.
50. *Ibid.,* p. 97, P. Parameswaran, *op. cit.,* p. 149 and M.K. Sanoo *op. cit.,* p. 550.
51. Guru, Nataraja *op. cit.,* p. 258.
52. Chandramohan, P. *Social and Political Protest in Travancore*, p. 172.
53. Lemercinier, Genevieve (1984). *Religion and Ideology in Kerala*, New Delhi, pp. 248-52.
54. *Vivekodayam* April-May 1917, Vol. XIV Numbers 1-2 (medam Edavam 1092 ME) pp. 57-5. See also Murkoth Kumaran, *op. cit.*, 2nd ed, Calicut 1971, p. 131, P.Parameswaran, *op. cit.*, 2nd ed, Calicut, 1979, p. 50; M.K. Sanoo, *op. cit.*, p. 123. Even the Ezhava leaders like Cherunelli Krishnan Vaidyar and many others seriously doubted whether the *Guru* had the authority of scriptural sanction for consecrating an idol in a temple, see P. Parameswaran, *op. cit.,* pp. 57-58.
55. Balakrishnan, P.K. "Religion, Temple and God", In: *Narayana Guru* (*An Anthological Compilation*) *op. cit.*, p. 154; see also M.K. Sanoo, *op. cit.*, pp. 532-33.
56. K.N. Panikkar has explained in detail the two dimensions of cultural-ideological struggle in colonial India in his first Damodaran Memorial Lecture delivered at Trivandrum on "Rationalism, Humanism and Secularization". This was reproduced in *Social Scientist* under the title "Culture and Consciousness in Modern India: A Historical Perspective" Vol. 18, No. 4, April 1990. See also *idem* "Culture and Ideology: Contradictions in Intellectual Transformation of Colonial Society in India", *Economic and Political Weekly*, Vol. XXII, No. 49 December 5, 1987.
57. For this message of 1917 see P.K. Balakrishnan, *Narayana Guru, op. cit.*, p. 76; see also P.K. Gopalakrishnan, *Keralathinte Samskarika Charitram,* Trivandrum 1974, pp. 529-30.
58. The *Guru* writes, "Of the human species even a Brahmin born, as is the Pariah too. Where is difference there in caste as between man and man?" in "Jati Mimamsa" in *op. cit.*, see also Nataraja Guru, *op. cit.*, p. 283 and 287.
59. See "Jati Mimamsa" in *op. cit.*
60. Swami Dharma Theerthan *op. cit.*, p. 99.
61. Achuthan, Pazhampally *op. cit.*, p. 11; P. Parameswaran, *op. cit.*, pp. 107-108.
62. *Vivekodayam*, June-August 1906, p. 5 and December-January, 1908-1909, Vol. 5, No. 9, p. 5 *Kerala Kaumudi,* 14 June, 1923, p. 4. See also P.K. Balakrishnan "Kerala Navothanathinu Charithraparamaya Oru Mukavura" in *Yoganadham*, October 1977, Vol. 3, No. 7, p. 32; See also *Idem* "Oru Madhyasthan" in *Narayana Guru op. cit.*, pp. 150-51.
63. He told them, "You must look upon the Pulayas and the like with love. The Ezhavas should behave towards their inferior in such a way that those who deem themselves superior to the Ezhavas should see and learn from it. This is a matter you should pay special attention to", Quoted in P. Parameswaran, *op. cit.*, p. 108.

64. Ayappan, A. (1945). *Iravas and Cultural Change, Bulletin Madras Government Museum*, 1945, p. 156; *Kerala Kaumudi*, 2nd June 1921, p. 2. See also M.K. Sanoo, *Narayana Guru Swami*, p. 261.
65. Omvedt, Gail (1971). "Jotirao Phule and the Ideology of Social Revolution in India", *Economic and Political Weekly*, Vol. VI, No. 37, September 11, pp. 1969-1979.

8

Navajyothisree Karunakara *Guru*

Continuity and Change in the Wisdom Tradition of India

K. Gopinathan Pillai

Context

I

In Indian spiritual tradition *Guru* is the epitome of the Supreme Light. *Guru* is perfection and cosmic consciousness. The dictum '*Guru sarva dharmatma*" denotes this truth. A *parama Guru* is concerned only with the material well-being and spiritual attainment of disciple. India had a tradition of such *Guruparamparas*. It was this *Guru*-disciple tradition that provided the foundation of *Sanatana dharma*.

Guru Tradition represented by *atmajnana Guru paramparas* has historically played supreme role in the evolution and development of the core spiritual wisdom and philosophy of *Sanatana dharma* which gifted to humanity whole embracing life vision and path towards perfection.

Wisdom accumulated over the past several centuries of progress and evolution of human societies reveals the fact that the life and teachings of great spiritual visionaries had been instrumental in the social awakening, spiritual upliftment and civilizational growth of humanity. The influence of these great *Gurus*, Prophets and preceptors in the cultural milieu of the land is visible in almost all civilizations, be it that of India or other civilizations of the world. As far as India is concerned, it is evident that the comprehensive life vision and philosophical insights of these masters have contributed to the cultural creativity and unity of the country, and in fact it is this *Guru* tradition and its legacy transmitted down the tradition that was instrumental in preserving and sustaining values and ethos at both the individual and community levels. While Veda Vyasa, Sree Buddha, Mahavira the Jina, Acharya Sankara, all have laid the foundations of this great tradition, their modern counterparts like Swami Vivekananda, Sree Narayana Guru, Chattambi Swami and Navajyothisree Karunakara Guru have sought to regenerate and rejuvenate this cultural legacy and integrate virtues of modernity with that of our ancient culture. Thus, the cultural creativity consequent upon the life and mission of great spiritual visionaries during the intervals in history has been instrumental in preserving and transmitting values from generations to generations, which preserved the continuity and change of culture and social order.

Though the onslaught of modernity has visibly challenged this cultural legacy and spiritual unity of India, she could withstand and preserve her identity only due to the dedication and sacrifice of *Guruparamparas*. Our inattentiveness to this cultural continuity has caused great mishaps in our country, like communalism, class and religious conflicts. Hence, it is necessary that the consciousness of India's own distinctive life-force of spirituality is awakened, which has the potency to bind the people of the land with the single string of spiritual oneness beyond castes and religious sectarianism.

The *Guru* tradition or wisdom tradition that was handed down from generations to generations by *Guru Paramparas* of India was thus instrumental to the continuity and change of Indian culture, society and polity. This tradition periodically ignited social awakening and contributed to cultural creativity which rejuvenated and sustained tradition not being fossilized. This is validated by the living instances of several *Gurus* and ascetics across India even during this modern scientific age. The ascetics continue to bloom in the spiritual garden of India even today and have been instrumental in preserving her traditions and practices alive.

II

All beings in this cosmos, according to the spiritualistic worldview are moving towards perfection. This voyage towards perfection is governed by specific laws of Nature or principles which are engrained in the evolutionary process of nature. Wisdom tradition otherwise called *Sanatana Dharma* refers to the knowledge tradition of fully realized *Gurus* and Atmajnanies who revealed to humanity the cosmic will and design and guided humans in their spiritual and material life. However the materialistic worldview and the emergence of modern Western civilization marked a major shift in the thinking, perception and value systems of humanity. The past more than three hundred years of human activity on earth guided by modern science and technology for achieving economic progress, material prosperity, peace and happiness, despite its remarkable contributions, is a narrative of irreparable damage done to Nature and human culture.

But this materialistic civilization was a necessity for human progress towards perfection as Aurobindo notes: "this materialist phase was not without its significance. Perhaps it is a necessity for the emergence of the Spirit and fulfillment of the secret divine purpose guiding the evolutionary development. By materializing everything up to the intellect itself it (Modern civilization) has given the life in Matter an importance which the spirituality of the past was inclined to deny to it."[1] An observation of Navajyothisree Karunakara Guru is pertinent in this context. *Guru* Notes, "In due course there will be a stage, when anyone can pursue any type of learning. When man acquires learning and affluence and a certain control over his circumstances he will think about peace. In fact his further striving will be for peace once he has achieved wealth and power in equal measure."[2]

Human effort to unravel truth through intelligence and reason bespeak the spectacular advances of modern science in quantum physics, biology, neuro science, experimental psychology etc. Declaring that there is only light and light of consciousness, Hans Peter Dhurr notes that matter is not made out of matter. Matter is made of energy, light. Thus, an analysis of the relentless efforts of past spiritual visionaries and materialist civilization to raise humanity to a righteous life and higher planes of consciousness brings out two things:

(i) Human life is not an accident but it is guided by a cosmic design and its perfection depends on the way of life and thinking one chooses.

(ii) Past spirituality and modern materialistic civilization are unable to resolve human problems and save humanity from the present predicament. The most fascinating irony of our times is that we are seeking solutions to the multitude of problems in which we are enmeshed, within the framework of the self same thought patterns, value systems and lifestyle which have created them.

We are living at a time in which the irrelevance of past spirituality and modern technological civilization in providing us the basic needs of life, a decent standard of living for all instead of an increasing standard of life for few, and real peace, love, happiness and secure future for our children has been more or less crystallized. Aurobindo notes that "when all is said, Love and Force together can save the world eventually, but not Love only or Force only. Therefore, Christ had to look forward to a second advent and Mohamed's religion, where it is not stagnant, looks forward through the Imams to a Mehdi."[3]

It is in this context, the significance of the life and teaching of Navajyothisree Karunakara Guru assumes planetary importance.

Navajyothisree Karunakara Guru

Several *Gurus* and *Acharyas* took birth in India to restore *dharma* by eliminating the superstitious beliefs and practices based on religion and the resultant social segregation which is otherwise not the culture of this tradition exalted by Vedas and Upanishads. However, it has been a tragedy to find that these seers could not fulfil their mission and restore equilibrium by eliminating the basic deviations and distortions that ever caused social disintegration and made human life vitiated. Moreover, many of them confused the real meaning of *dharma* as constituting the distinctive duties of the four *Varnas* and the four *Ashramas* so that the term *Varnashrama dharma* has been misconstrued and looked upon as the *Sanatana dharma*. What they have lost sight was *dharma* as reflective morality.

Many of the world's great seers have prophesied the advent of a great spiritual master by the end of 20th century to save the world from the possible holocaust of wars, ecological tragedies and wild epidemic diseases.

Buddha told his disciples that the next great world teacher who would be known in the name 'Medheya'(*Karuna*) would appear around the year A.D. 2000 and will restore momentum and power to all those seeking after spiritual truth. Nostrodomus predicted the flowering of a new religion which would denounce all the familiar established faiths. Nostradamus says that an Eastern teacher who strikes out at the world would be called 'temple breaker' and therefore, be unpopular. He might be unusual and unorthodox devices would be employed to stir people up, disturbing the status 'codes' of social and religious behaviour of our times.

Shri Aurobindo was frequently awakening and cautioning his disciples and others of the imminent descent of the Supramental Light on earth and how it would mercilessly destroy the dark powers and its evil design and pervasive influence on human consciousness. A few observations of Aurobindo will help us in understanding the relevance and importance of *Guru's* advent and scheme of things. Aurobindo notes, "Something more drastic, more radical than moral and religious change is imminently needed if the tide of darkness and falsehood which is now threatening to engulf the world and plunge it into catastrophic disasters is to be turned back. The need of the hour is for a power which will work out a change in the inner consciousness of man more drastic and decisive that cannot be achieved through moral and religious reform[4]."

Revelatory Spirituality of Navajyothisree Karunakara Guru

Navajyothisree Karunakara Guru started his spiritual pursuit in the line of Hindu worship order. *Guru* passed through inexplicable vicissitudes of spiritual experiences which the mendics whomever he met could not explain and guide. In 1973 at a particular point of his spiritual pursuit, *Guru* realized the contradiction and inadequacy in the prevailing faith and worship system of God. *Guru* entered into a deep *tapas* without heeding to the appearance and words of divine powers whom we believe as God. Spiritual developments leading to the spiritual fulfillment of *Guru* and the revelatory words and vision received thereupon marked a turning point in human understanding of spirituality and religion. **On the occasion of the spiritual fulfillment of Navajyothisree Karunakara *Guru* in 1973 it was revealed from *Brahma Prakasham* that "what I wished for ages has been fulfilled" which makes out the historical relevance and importance of *Guru's* birth and mission.**[5] Disciples got revealed on the occasion on the vision and mission of the *Guru*. They also got revealed the hitherto untold truths on many of the vexed riddles in spirituality, the reasons of unabated miseries and peace lessness despite the sacrificial life of Great Preceptors, the future of humanity etc. It was revealed that the *Jeeva* or soul of *Guru* was the one preserved by *Brahman* and it was sent for accomplishing the unfulfilled Will of *Brahman*, i.e., the restoration of Yugadharmam by rectifying an initial error occurred in *Manudharma*.[6]

Guru's long drawn search and *Tapas* for unraveling the basic causations of lingering human miseries, India's spiritual decay, social degeneration and disintegration as well as material poverty thus found fruition. *Guru* proclaimed to the world that *Manudharma*, otherwise called *Sanatana Dharma*, was the Fountain of Spiritual Knowledge of humanity. It was Due to an **Error occurred in Spiritual vision** to a Great *Rishi* in the *Manu* lineage, *Manudharma* was eclipsed and *Manu's* memory was vanished. The revelation that human miseries and peacelessness lingers despite the advent and sacrifice of innumerable great spiritual visionaries in different parts of the world due to an error in spiritual vision to a *Kalanthara Guru* in the 3rd *Chaturyuga* of 7th *Manwanthara* is a new knowledge to the world.

When we examine the teachings of Navajyothisree Karunakara Guru, it is found that most of the concepts found in *Guru*'s teachings had already been there in existence. *Manu dharma*, concepts such as *Yugadharma*, *Jnana marga*, spiritual stages, Astral powers, Demonic worship, *Pitru Suddhi* or *Gurupooja* etc. are all part of Indian spirituality and religion.

One may naturally ask what the original contribution of *Guru*'s teaching is. *Guru*'s revelation that non-observation of *Yugadharma* for the last 25 *Chaturyugas* due to an error occurred in Spiritual vision to a Great *Rishi* in the *Manu* lineage and its non-rectification was the singular reason for the unabated miseries and peacelessness of humanity is a new knowledge to the World.

Basic Philosophy of *Guru*

***Guru's* teaching is premised on the revelatory words and visions that were received on the occasion of *Guru's* spiritual fulfillment in 1973.** *Guru* did not subscribe to any existing spiritual streams or religious teachings and traditions. *Guru* said, "Whatever I pass on to you have been received from that Supreme Light or *Brahma Prakasham* by way of revelatory words and vision". His teaching marked a shift in the existing notions on God, faith, worship and religious practices and demystified the organized religions.

The basic premises of *Guru*'s teaching originate from the revelatory knowledge that:

1. The inability of humanity to progress towards a righteous life and bring about a humane social order and to resolve the

human predicament are the inevitable consequence of the initial error occurred to a *Kalantara Guru* in *Manu* lineage which contributed to termination of *Yugadharma* and the resultant non-observance of *yugadharma*.

2. The spiritual and religious systems that exist today had evolved as part of the initial Error. Hence, the restoration of *yugadharma* and conduct of *dharma, karma* and a way of life accordingly alone is the solution for the liberation of man from his materially and spiritually fallen state.
3. Spiritual purification *karma* of *Gurupooja*, which means cleansing of soul of the inherited impurities, which got accumulated on account of humans' living deviated from *Yugadharma*, is the solution that the *Guru* received from the Suprme Light to wash away the impurity from human souls. This spiritual purification *karma* called *Gurupooja* in Santhigiri is the spiritual instrumentality to liberate humans from the inherited *vasanas* embedded in genetic order and soul. It is how *Guru* envisions the emergence of a new generation and ushering in of a new human civilization. Thus, the spiritual purification *karma* known as *Guru* pooja is the greatest gift that humanity received from *Guru* for achieving this new generation having no parallel in spirituality. Though there have been in all religions spiritual practices aimed at the cleansing of souls, a purification *karma* as done in Santhigiri is unknown.
4. A way of life as enunciated by the teaching of *Guru* and Family life in accordance with the words and guidance of *Guru* is the inalienable part of the order that *Guru* has initiated through Santhigiri *Guru parampara. Guru* has initiated almost all *karmic* realms in Santhigiri for initiating, nurturing and nourishing a new work culture, attitude and orientation in the people.[7]

First Error and Spiritual and Material Fall

Revelation on first error and the consequent deviation in *dharma* had its inconceivable impact on the subsequent spiritual and material life of humanity. Following the error a curse from *Brahman* ensued leading to the eclipse of *Jnana path.* It is revealed that three *chaturyugas* since the curse went on in spiritual darkness. From seventh *chaturyuga* onwards spiritual pursuit was initiated and on reaching *Trimurthy* stage it again was stuck. The time calculus and worship was placed under *Trimurthy* and the *karma* of creation was attributed to Brahmavo, one of the *Trimurthis*.[8] Thus a grave mistake was again committed in the pursuit of *dharma* and the only Transcendent *Brahman* was again distanced and made unapproachable. Human worship deviating from *yugadharma* gave birth to alarming multiplication of dark forces in the astral plane which contributed to astral pollution. Astral pollution and its impact on human life constitute a major area of research.

"Innumerable souls are there in the astral planes that after worshipping in wrong way without knowing god and devil, constitute astral pollution. It is equally true that the bad effect of this astral pollution affect us all, i.e. the whole humanity. I don't know how many of us have such knowledge? I am stating that this pollution can be eliminated while it remains just like that. This is a great subject."[9]

"Crores of souls who lived in the past hundreds of years on earth doing bad *karmas* remain as astral pollution in the *sookshmam*. It is not the pollution of thousand or ten thousand years. There is twenty five *chaturyugas* pollution. Even though we will have to undergo a lot of pain and face a lot of problems, this pollution could be eradicated."[10]

Guru proclaimed that restoration of *yugadharma* necessitates the purification of the astral plane and doing away with the influence of this *asuric* forces on human thoughts and deeds. Astral pollution consequent on the existence of these dark forces are instrumental in creating wars, violence and negative activities in human society, *Guru* noted. All spiritual visionaries have focused on this aspect of dark forces in astral plane. However it is the *Guru* who vividly has explained the unbelievable deeds and influence of astral *asuric* forces on the spiritual and material progression of humans. It has been an irony that the past messengers of God could not transcend the astral planes of mighty dark forces and restore the lost path towards Supreme light. The *Guru* noted that since they did not get reveal the first error, that they were unable to fulfil their mission. In 1973 on the occasion of *Guru*'s spiritual fulfilment, *Guru* received permission from *Brahman* to perform the purification *karma* of astral powers which is designated in Santhigiri as *Gurupooja*.[11]

This spiritual cleansing that *Guru* performs, for the creation of a new generation and evolution of a new human civilization is the methodology or path that translates *Guru's* teaching into practice making it, thus, the *dharma* of the time to come. *Guru* visualizes Cultural creativity and social change through the birth of children devoid of genetic impurities. *Guru* refers to his experience in the following words: "I have got this revealed from the Supreme Light. It is what I inform you. The bad effects of our ancestors' *karma* spread out as ignorance and arrogance all over the world. You can firmly believe that God has given me the knowledge capable to rectify and eradicate these bad effects. Do not feel that I am saying this to let you know that I possess this gift from the Supreme. I am stating this to caution you about the depth of responsibility rests with you."[12]

Gurupooja, Astral Purification and the Emergence of a New Human Civilization

"Those who speak of changing the modern man's consciousness by moral and religious means fail to understand that the powers that now rule that consciousness are too formidable and treacherous to be dislodged by any such means. Aurobindo believed that his mission was to facilitate the descend of the Supramental Light on earth which is imminent and which will raise humans to the highest stage of spiritual evolution[13]."

The principle, "Ulpathi karmagathipole varum jagathil" is subscribed by almost all Indian spiritual traditions. The *karmagathi* is the quintessence of the good and bad effect of one's *karmas* embedded in soul in the preceding lives which guides the vicissitudes in one's future life. Just as every object is accompanied by a shadow, even so every volitional activity is inevitably accompanied by its due effect. The Puranas state that even the trinity of gods, Brahma, Vishnu and Siva attained their current status by virtue of their deeds in the previous cycles of creation. The law of *karma* is inexorable, neutral and impartial. The wheel of *dharma* knows no discrimination. All beings, which manifest, irrespective of their cosmic status, are subject to the laws of *dharma* and being and becoming. Only the supreme *Brahman* in His formless state is eternal and changeless and beyond the state of beingness. In His formless and transcendental state He is immutable.

All religions exhort man to do right actions. The actions deviated from *dharma* contribute to *karmadosha* or sins in *jeeva* and to the resultant miseries and sufferings in life. The scriptures say that it is the accumulated vices and virtues in *jeeva* inherited over the past lives that determine the fortunes and misfortunes in the present life. This is *Karma* theory. Therefore all religions prescribe different means for the elimination or reduction of sins or *karmadosha* in *jeeva* and to achieve peace and happiness. But *Jnanis* say that the impurities in *jeeva* transmitted from past lives could not be wiped out by the means prescribed usually by religions. The bad effects resulted from wrong actions are to be removed by leading a righteous life and earning *punya*.

Awareness of the law of *karma* is an important step in the religious life of any individual. *Karma* is responsible for our becoming and being. Our problems of existence and the law of *karma* become active only when we enter into the state of beingness. Through *karma* we perpetuate this state of beingness and create our own future existence. *Karma* is supposed to be a corrective mechanism, meant to refine us gradually through our own actions. But if *karma* is not performed in accordance with *dharma* of the *Yuga*, it turns out to be the cause for our bondage and sufferings in life. The law of *karma* makes it abundantly clear that the solution to our liberation lies in our hands and how we go about it is left to ourselves.

The hereditary transmission of good and bad effects of actions accumulated in the course of the evolution of *jeeva* in previous births known as *karmadhosha* or sins is a truth which exercises considerable influence in the fortune and misfortune of human life. Heredity and its importance in human life have been testified by modern science of genetics. It seeks solutions by genetic interference. While the whole world clamors about wars, violence inequalities, vices and cruelties of individuals and nations, we are conveniently sidelining the basic causation.

The accumulated wisdom borne out of our past experiences inform us that either religious solutions such as prayer, rites, penances, *yoga*, and several other spiritual mechanics and spiritual discourses or modern ways of problem solving by socio-economic restructuring based on revolutionary doctrines and scientific analysis and solutions, will not eliminate the inherited impurities and genetically transmitted instincts and bad effects that are ingrained in *jeeva*. Various means have been prescribed by religions for the elimination of impurities in *jeeva*.[13] But they have been insufficient in promoting and leading man to a righteous life by eradicating his negative genetic imprints so as to purify his *jeeva*.

It is true that there are innumerable instances in Hindu scriptures that shed light into the impact of *karmadosha* in *jeeva* in determining the course of life in the subsequent births and how the influence of *karmadosha* of the ancestral manes in astral planes is a basic reason for human sufferings and tragedies in life. But it is found that the spiritual means prescribed for the eradication of these impurities in Hindu *sastras* are inadequate and permanent solution cannot be achieved by them. It is found that the solutions prescribed like performance of rituals, *homa* and *poojas* bring in only temporary relief and misfortunes do not end with such *karma*. No satisfactory explanation to this issue has yet been given by the divine spiritual masters who take birth periodically in Hinduism.

"In the past twenty five *chatur yugas* innumerable great men have incarnated. They themselves could either change themselves or others in accordance with the *dharma* of *Kali yuga*. Then what would be the situation of others? Innumerable souls are there in the astral planes that after worshipping in wrong way without knowing god and devil, constitute astral pollution. It is equally true that the bad effect of this astral pollution affect us all, i.e. the whole humanity. I don't know how many of us have such knowledge? I am stating that this pollution can be eliminated while it remains just like that. This is a great subject."[14]

The distinctiveness of *Guru*'s teaching is to be examined and understood in this context. He revealed the reasons that contributed to the inability of previous preceptors who came to guide humanity to virtues. "Let our ancient doctrines be right or wrong. We are not to correct it by discussing its rights and wrongs. We have born. What could we do for the redemption of these? You are not benefited, if some miracles or *siddhis* are performed. We must not put faith in any such things" (pp. 63-73 J). The disappearance of *Manu dharma* consequent upon a spiritual lapse occurred to a great *Rishi* in *Manu* lineage caused a curse from the Supreme Light which led to the deviation of *Yugadharma*. We and our ancestors have been striving and following the footsteps of a great mistake occurred 25 *chaturyuga* back. I reveal all these to you for the rectification of the same. It is not possible to do it today and tomorrow. This is something which could not be accomplished by thousands of past great souls.[15]

It is in this context, *Guru's* teachings assume global significance. The greatest gift that *Guru* has given to humanity is the gift of *Gurupooja*. *Gurupooja* is the spiritual purification *karma* by which the astral pollution is eliminated and a new progeny devoid of impurities in *jeeva* is born. Such a generation will be free from any genetic aberration. In all religions, some rites are performed for the tranquility and redemption of manes. But a spiritual means for the purification of manes as well as the powers they worshipped as god has never existed in any spiritual tradition or order. Thus the *gurupooja* performed at Santhigiri is basically different as far as it leads to the liberation of *pitrus* in every family lineage from the inherited impurities called *karmadosha* and influences of other astral powers. The children born after this purification *karma* are believed to be free from impurities in soul and thereby genetic disorders also. *Guru* notes, "The myriad of powers such as *devi* and *deva*, *rishi*, *sannyasi*, *Jnani*, devout that our ancestors have worshipped for long are purified and the most impure powers are eliminated by this spiritual performance. How will you know whether their impurity is vanished and have become pure? You can know it either through your faith and experience or by the divine means available in each religious order like astrology among the Hindus. Since this *karma* remains beyond the reach of other religious practices, it is difficult to verify. The truth and untruth alone can know by such means."[16] When the ancestral or genetic transmission of negative qualities is ceased and ancestral manes and other powers are purified, environment is created for the growth of a generation with noble qualities.

Regarding the eligibility of a Guru who can perform Gurupooja by which powers remaining at different astral planes are purified it is observed: "A *rishi* and his lineage destined for this mission by the supreme alone could be the authority for elevating through the stages of visions by seeing into, the evolutionary process of *jeeva* and the spiritual stages and the highest plane of salvation. By owing thus authority from the Supreme, *Gurupooja* in the Santhigiri, which is based on monotheism, is the corner stone of a spiritual *karma* that rectifies the knots of accumulated *karmas* transmitted from past births. The sacrificial *karma* that a *rishi* undergoes to rectify the accumulated *karmas* in the past births and correct the layers of *karmas* of previous births by spiritual radiance is inexplicable and inconceivable."[17]

This eventually leads to the emergence of a new civilization. It is for first time that spirituality has been democratized and made popular. All strata of population have been brought under an oneness. Every man according to his ability and living situation can participate on equal basis without religious, caste, racial, linguistic and regional distinction. *Guru* has explicitly made it clear that observation of *yugadharma* in spiritual and material life is the means for getting out of the impending calamity that may engulf the whole humanity at any time.

Notes

1. Sri Aurobindo, *The Human Cycle*, Aurobindo Society, Pondicherry, p. 138.
2. Navajyothisree, Karunakaraguru (1993). *The Path of Culture*, Thiruvananthapuram: Shantigiri Ashram, p. 35.
3. Aurobindo, Sri. *The Supramental Manifestation Upon Earth*, Pondicherry: Aurobibdho Society, p. 231, Vol. 16.
4. Aurobindo, Sri. *The Supramental Manifestation Upon Earth*, Pondicherry: Aurobibdho Society, p. 305, Vol. 16.
5. Karunakaraguru, Navajyothisree (1980). *Dialogue on Human Prospectus*, Thiruvananthapuram: Shantigiri Ashram, pp. 27-34. (Vijayan, O.V., *Introduction*, tr. Usha, O.V.).
6. Karunakaraguru, Navajyothisree (1992). *Gurupuja in Shanthigiri*, Thiruvananthapuram: Shanthigiri Ashram, p. 37.
7. Navajyothisree, Karunakaraguru (1980). *Dialogue on Human Prospectus*, Thiruvananthapuram: Shantigiri Ashram, pp. 27-34. (Vijayan, O.V., *Introduction*, tr. Usha, O.V.).
8. Navajyothisree, Karunakaraguru (1988). *Birthday Messages*, Thiruvananthapuram: Shantigiri Ashram, p. 75.
9. 73rd Janmajayanathi edition, p. 171.
10. 75th Janmajayanathi edition, p. 112.
11. Karunakaraguru, Navajyothisree (1980). *Dialogue on Human Prospectus*, Thiruvananthapuram: Shantigiri Ashram, pp. 27-34. (Vijayan, O.V., *Introduction*, tr. Usha, O.V.).
12. 75th Janmajayanathi edition, p. 137.
13. 73rd Janmajayanathi edition, *Ibid.*, p. 73.
14. *Ibid.*, p. 171.
15. Karunakaraguru, Navajyothisree (1980). *Dialogue on Human Prospectus*, Thiruvananthapuram: Shantigiri Ashram, pp. 27-34. (Vijayan, O.V., *Introduction*, tr. Usha, O.V.).
16. *Ibid.*, p. 198.
17. 73rd Janmajayanathi edition, p. 53.

9

Navajyothisree Karunakara Guru

The Source of Revelation to Social Evolution

C.V. Babu

Introduction

This chapter is an attempt to look into the First Error that happened in *Manu* tradition as revealed to Navajyothisree Karunakara Guru from *Brahman*, the Almighty, and to the Curse from *Brahman* as consequence of this error that lead to the downfall of *Manu* lineage. *Guru*'s entire teaching is anchored on this point of revelation identifying the two elements of Error and Curse as the two fundamental undercurrents of socio-cultural manifestation of Indian spirituality and philosophy. *Guru*'s teaching signifies the necessity of overcoming the overwhelming cultural undercurrents of the Error and the Curse for proper spiritual development and thereby an effective evolution of the society leading to the development of the country.

Indian scriptural writings are divided into two sections such as *Sruti,* what is heard, and *Smriti,* what is remembered. *Manusmriti* is the oldest and the most important one of all other *smriti*-s and sacred next to *Sruti.* It is considered as the oldest Indian law-book and the basic law-book of *Manu* lineage. Though both scriptural writings are revealed in nature *smriti* is regarded as secondary to *Sruti* since the former is recorded by mediation of men whereas the latter is preserved in its original form of revelation. *Manusmriti* is revealed by *Brahman* to *Manu*, the son of the Supreme, as shown in verse I.3 that the entire ordinance belonged to the supreme Self-existent: "for you alone, Master, know the true meaning of the duties contained in this entire ordinance of the Self-existent One, an ordinance beyond the powers of thought or cognition." It was the occasion of request of the Seers, the sons of *Manu*, to him to deliver the laws of the self-existent *Brahman*. This verse, indeed, shows the revelatory nature of Brahman. However, the word *smriti,* what is remembered, itself signifies that the revelation is not preserved in its original form but as remembered from generation to generation. This, to a large extent, justifies the charges levelled against *Manusmriti* that the text had undergone large scale interpolation especially to safeguard the self-privileged dominance of certain social groups for their clannish survival and egoistic satisfaction, though it unfortunately and inevitably led to social divisiveness and disintegration. This chapter is an attempt to look into the very cause of the social deterioration by means of this law-book from the point of view of revelation from *Brahman* to Navajyothisree Karunakara Guru. According to Navajyothisree Karunakara Guru, the word, *Vak,* revealed from *Brahman* signifies the will of *Brahman*, *Brahmanischayam*. This very concept as formulated out of his experience can be considered as a novel contribution to Indian philosophy.

Before beginning of the text, *Brahman* is paid homage in the additional verse before the verse 1.1: "To the Self-existent One, to *Brahman* of boundless energy, I pay homage, as I set out to promulgate the diverse and eternal Laws proclaimed by *Manu*." *Brahman* is characterized in this verse as *svayambhu,* self-existent, as well as of boundless energy. The concept "self-existent" is used to refer to *Brahman* throughout the text. Especially in the first chapter, various other characteristics of *Brahman* are also given such as super-sensuous, unthinkable, eternal, subtle, imperishable, unmanifest, etc. Though Brahman is unmanifested and consequently super-sensuous, ungraspable and unthinkable, verse 1.7 discloses that He is graspable by *yogic pratyaksa,* super-sensuous perception. The verses 1.6 and 1.7 reveal that it is the very Unmanifested who self-manifested manifesting the world. The entire first chapter shows the creative nature of *Brahman* such as self-manifestation, manifestation of the world, creation of other beings and entities as depicted from verse 6 onward. Though in *Manusmriti* the self-manifestation of *Brahman* is with reference to the manifestation of the world, it does not mean that *Brahman* self-manifests only at the time of creation. *Kena Upanishad* depicts another occasion of self-manifestation of *Brahman* in order to teach the deities, *devas,* that their egoistic attitude of considering themselves as supreme is an erroneous notion that can bring devastating effect.

The created world is temporal in the nature of its existence from an evolutionary perspective that it begins with creation and culminates into total dissolution constituting the cosmic cycle that recurs eternally. The aeon of one cosmic cycle is called as *Kalpa* and is divided into the epochs of 14 *Manus*. Epoch of one *Manu* contains 71 divine ages as disclosed in verse 1.79.: "The divine Age mentioned previously as lasting 12,000—that multiplied 71 times is here referred to as an "Epoch of a *Manu*". "One Age-quarters, *Chaturyuga*, contains 12,000 divine years as disclosed by Navajyothisree Karunakara Guru based on his vision, *yogic pratyaksa*": "A *Manu's* epoch is considered as over seventy-one *Chaturyugas* (*yuga*-quarters). One *Chaturyuga* consists of 12000 divine years. This is what the scriptures say and this is what we know. One divine year is equal to 365 human years."[14] One epoch of *Manu* is known as one *Manvantara.*

A *Chaturyuga* means a cluster of 4 Y*uga*-s, ages, such as *Satya* or *Krta*, *Treta*, *Dvapara* and *Kali*. *Satyayuga* is the first age of one *Chaturyuga*. According to Navajyothisree Karunakara Guru, it is the most perfect age of the *yuga*-quarters because the light of *Brahman*, *Brahma prakasam,* can be perceived by everybody in that era. The Light is manifested in the gross dimension of the universe. Since everybody receives word from the supreme Light there will not be error in human actions. The change in nature indicates the change of *Yuga*. When *Satyayuga* changes to next *Yuga*, the light of *Brahman* can no longer be perceived by everybody. It unmanifests into the subtle dimension.

In the following *yuga*-s only the seers who take birth according to the will of *Brahman*, can perceive the Light and receive Word from it. Hence, they become the masters leading humanity through the path of evolution to the Supreme. This process of evolution becomes more significant in *Kaliyuga* since it is the last age of that *Chaturyuga* and needs to be evolved up to the perfection of the following *Satyayuga* in which the divine Light is manifested. Whatever mistakes had occurred in the entire *Chaturyuga* is to be corrected and evolved up to the perfection of the light of *Brahman* by truthfulness. This mission is carried out through the masters born according to the will of *Brahman*.

Manu tradition included the order of such masters who takes birth from time to time maintaining the evolutionary order of *Chaturyugas* and *Manvantaras*. In every *Yuga* there will be five *Gurus*, masters.[15] The last one is known as *Kalantharaguru*[16], *Guru* in the times of transition, since he takes birth at the end of one *yuga* and the beginning of the next *yuga*. This particular period is known as twilight, *sandhikalam*[17], the joining period of two *yuga*-s. The mission of such a *Guru* is something special that he has to convert all the *karmic* streams that are carried over from the previous *yuga*-s into the next *Yuga* within the same *Chaturyuga*. The twilight in between a *Kaliyuga* and the following *Satyayuga* is still more special since the whole of the *karmic* streams of the entire *Chaturyuga* has to be carried over into the utmost perfection of the next *Satyayuga* of the following *Chaturyuga*.

The First Error in *Manu* Tradition

Manu is the first seer, *Adiguru*, of a *Manvantara*. *Manusmriti* speaks of such 7 *Manus* in verse 1. 61 and 62, indeed, belonging to 7 *Manvantaras*. At present is the 7th *Manvantara*. Vavasvata *Manu* is the first seer of this *Manvantara*. Now, it is the 29th *Chaturyuga* of this *Manvantara*. The current age is *Kaliyuga* of that *Chaturyuga*. In the past *Manvantaras* as well as up to the end of 3rd *Chaturyuga* of the present *Manvantara* everything went well according to the Will of *Brahman*.

The will of *Brahman* was erred in the last twilight of the third *Chaturyuga*. It was the transition period from the *Kaliyuga* to the *Satyayuga* of 4th *Chaturyuga*. In the order of that *Manu* lineage a *Kalantharaguru* called Satyatranan took birth in this age. Satyatranan was the 16th *Guru* of the *Manvantaram* of Vaivasvata *Manu*.[18] He was entitled to transform all the *karmic* streams of that *Chaturyuga* purifying them up to the perfection of the next *Satyayuga*.

A *Kalantharaguru*[17] who takes birth in the twilight of a *Kaliyuga* belongs to both the previous and the following *yuga*-s. He is the first *Guru* of the coming *Yuga* and the last *Guru* of the last *Yuga*. It is in accordance with his task of transforming the whole *karmic* streams of the previous four *yuga*-s into the next *Chaturyuga*. Such was the task of Satyatranan at the end of the *Kaliyuga* of the 3rd *Chaturyuga*. Rather he was entitled to perform that mission according to the order of the *Manu* tradition as per the will of Brahman.

A *Kalantharaguru* with that mission has to evaluate all the *karmic* streams of the previous *yuga*-s. In order to evaluate them he has to perceive them in his power of vision and analyze them. Then only he can purify and transform them into the perfection of the next

Satyayuga. Satyatranan was also supposed to look back into the history of *karmic* streams in order to evaluate them. He by the power of his vision looked back into the history of Vaivasvata *Manu* since he is the first seer of that *Manvantara*. That task was part of his performance of his duty up to the perfection.

He looked back up to 10 *Chaturyuga*-s in his vision. Out of these 10 *Chaturyuga*-s 3 belonged to the Vaivasvata *Manu* and the remaining 7 belonged to the 6th *Manvantara*.[19] He wanted to observe utmost perfection in his duty. He wanted to know what does it mean by *Manu* or *Manvantara*.[20] He was so enthusiastic to discover the fundamental truths and structure of *Manvantara* with which it function.

Satyatranan wanted to perceive the reality in its gross as well as subtle dimension so as to get the wholesome structure in which it functions. He wanted to evaluate different kinds of *karmic* streams that have been in the process. He also wanted to find out which is the order that those streams belong to. He looked at the traditions in which the different streams of activities are preformed. He also wanted to determine the ages in which they are carried out.

He perceived different *karmic* streams even from the spaces of *Saptarshis*, the seven seers of seven spaces beyond the gross dimension of the universe. According to the revelation to Navajyothisree Karunakara Guru, Satyatranan perceived from there up to the times of *Manu* and visualized the order of *Manvantara,* the way it functions.[21] The tradition of *Manu* includes the structure that keeps the order of *Chaturyuga*-s and *Manvantara*-s. The difference between the different ages is kept in well maintained order within the structure of *Manu* tradition. There was no error that ever prevailed in it.[22]

He could realize that the tradition of *Manu* is quite unique in the sense that it is all inclusive and all pervading.[23] He could not see any other stream of activities that is not included in the tradition of *Manu*. The *karmic* streams of both the planes of gross as well as subtle are conceived in *Manu* tradition.[24] Both the cause of subtle plane and the effect of gross plane are functioning within *Manu* tradition.

Satyatranan could realize that everything merges into the order of *Manvantara*. He could also realize the way that everything is merging into the order of *Manvantara*. The functioning of *Manvantara* is according to this structure of *Manvantara*. The structure has got a nucleus into which everything is centred in to. Satyatranan could realize that this nucleus is the *Manu*, the *Adiguru*.

It is the way everything got centred into the order of *Manvantara*. *Manu* is the centre of the functional structure of *Manvantara*. Hence, Satyatranan concentrated on the nucleus of *Manvantara*.[25]

Satyatranan could see that how does *Manu* function as the nucleus of the order of *Manvantara*. All *karmic* streams are merging into *Manu*. He is the authority of all activities that are carried out in that temporal dimension. The time scale of *Manvantara* is such that it is centred into its first seer. Everything in that temporality merges into the nucleus of *Manu*, the merging centre, the beginning of that time order.[26]

Manu is the centre through which the *Adisabdha*, the primordial sound of *'Aum'* which is the conglomeration of the sounds such as *'A'*, *'U'*, and *'M'* have come through. It paves the foundation of being authoritative of all the *karma* getting dissolved into him.[27] It makes him the centre of *yugadharma* and he becomes the authority of *sristi*—creation, *stiti*—sustenance, *samhara*—destruction, and *mukti*—liberation. He saw the significance of the time scale of *Manu* that it includes the traditions *jnana* (*gyana*), *karma* and *mukti*. He came to a deep understanding that *Guru* is *Brahman*. He had no doubt that it is the truth. The trans-age *karmic* power, *yuganthara karma*, of *Manu* that extends to the entire time span of a *Manvantara* revealed him this truth that *Guru*, the *Adiguru* is *Brahman*.

Satyatranan's this realization was followed by a vision that the first *Manu* dissolves into him and everything functions within him. This necessarily led him to the standpoint that he is the absolute authority of all *karma*. He attributed to him the power of all *karma* of the whole *Manvantara* as belonging to him. Hence, he declared: "*Aham Brahmasmi*"[28], "I am the *Brahman*". Navajyothisree Karunakara Guru reveals that out of this self-proclamation Satyatranan derived the other great enunciations too and constituted the four *mahavakyas*: "The present is the seventh *Manvantara*. In the third *Chaturyuga* of the *Manvantara* a great man in the tradition of *Manu* perceived that there is no action in this world that is not *Manu's*. He saw this in both planes, the *sookshmam*, the subtle, and the *sthoolam*, the corporeal, the *kabana*, the cause and the *karyam*, the effect. Out of this experience came the *chaturvakyas*, the four great enunciations. The first one itself is, *Aham Brahmasmi*—I am *Brahman*, the Absolute."[31] According to the Navajyothisree Karunakara Guru, the four *mahavakyas* such as *Aham Brahmasmi* (I am the *Brahman*), *Prajnanam Brahma*, (Consciousness is *Brahman*), *Tattvamasi* (That

Thou art) and *Ayam Atma Brahma* (This *Atman* is *Brahman*) are originated from Satyatranan, a great seer born in the *Kaliyuga* of 3rd *Chaturyuga* of 7th *Manvantara* of Vaivasvata *Manu* lineage.

The Critique of Navajyothisree Karunakara Guru

Navajyothisree Karunakara Guru agrees with Satyatranan's understanding that *Guru* is *Brahman.* Satyatranan came into such a conclusion because he could visualize that everything merges into the nucleus of *Manu* as the centre of the time scale of *Manvantara.* Because of the same reason he could declare himself as the Supreme. He could see in his vision that everything including *Manu* himself as merging into him. Satyatranan's declaration of "*Aham Brahmasmi*" was the necessary culmination of his standpoint that *Guru* is *Brahmn.* But Navajyothisree Karunakara *Guru* asks a most crucial question: How does *Guru* becomes *Brahman*?[29] It is true that everything merges into *Manu* but Satyatranan disregarded the most crucial aspect of wherefrom and how does it emerge. The answer to these questions shows that it is the way that *Guru* becomes *Brahman* as the state of being authorized as the nucleus of the merging point. The actual dissolution takes place into *Brahman* Himself and by Himself. *Guru* is a medium into *Brahman.* It is the creative source of the will of *Brahman* that authorizes *Guru* to be the centre of dissolution into *Brahman.* It is the Will that constitute *dharma* and *karma* and prompts to ask to and know from the very Ultimate itself about the truth and rules that distinguish different ages.[30] Since he somehow missed this crucial aspect he failed to differentiate between the supreme creative will power of *Brahman* and the entitled functional *karmic* centre of *Manu.* The will power is emerged from *Brahman* not from *Manu.*

Though Satyatranan perceived that there is no *karmic* stream that does not belong to *Manu* and he is all authoritative, which made him believe beyond doubt that *Manu* is *Brahman*, by the same way, he came to the consequential mistaken perception that he himself is *Brahman.* Satyatranan failed to know that this supremacy is confined to the temporal *karmic* dimension only. The actual will power for this *karmic* process lies beyond the temporal *karmic* dimension of *Chaturyuga*-s and even *Manvantara*-s. Such is the will of *Brahman* or *Brahmanischayam.* The dissolution of all *karmic* streams is the determination of the Supreme. The error occurred with Satyatranan in interpreting his vision as his ego element got dominated due to the forgetfulness of the trans-temporal dimension of the Will. This ego element is very much present in all of the *chaturvakyas*. Being a *Kalantharaguru*, especially in the twilight between two *Chaturyuga*-s, the purification and transforming process of all the *karmic* streams of previous *yuga*-s into the *Satyayuga* of the next *Chaturyuga* functionally got centred into him and is perceived in vision; but the same got mistaken that Satyatranan himself is the Ultimate.

It is true that *Guru* being the highest evolute has the power of *karma* to perform the will of *Brahman*. According to Navajyothisree Karunakara Guru, even this accumulation of *karmic* power, *sancchitakarma*, itself is due to the will of *Brahman*. Nobody can secure such a *karmic* perfection without the determination of the Will. To perform such a Will, a physical instrumentality is very much necessary. According to Aurobindo, such is the instrumentality of the maximum possibility of human body as the perfect state of evolution. It is the highest state of human existence of receiving the Word from divine Light and act accordingly. It demands the dissolution of ego in its physical as well as mental dimension. It is a state of perfection in supra-mental dimension. *Guru* in the physical form is such perfect instrumentality and functions as an agent of implementing the divine Will. According to Navajyothisree Karunakara Guru, Satyatranan has mistaken this absolute instrumentality as the Absolute himself. It is the instrumental identity of the agent with the will of the Absolute. It is not absolute identity as such. It is instrumental identity of the state of perfection of performance of divine determination. The force to perform such a Will, *icchasakti*, emerges from Brahman Himself. According to Navajyothisree Karunakara Guru, this functional identity is due to the will of *Brahman*. The Supreme authorizes one who is being enabled by Him to perform the Will. It is the supra-mental state of evolution that enables the humanity as whole to evolve to the Absolute being the connecting link between the mental and the Absolute. It is *Brahman* that constitute the creative will power, *icchasakti*, of *Guru*. It emerges from *Brahman*.

It is the state of fullness of oneness with the Absolute. But Satyatranan mistook this fullness of oneness as absolute oneness of himself without the Other. Navajyothisree Karunakara Guru says, "Each one of us, each blade of grass, is full of the *Brahman*. But is the will of the Almighty confined to an individual evolute? One concludes this sage did not have the grace to discriminate between the Absolute and the individual even if the individual has had the realization of the Absolute. Thus was blurred his awareness about the will of the Absolute."[32] It is true that he was full of *Brahman*, but it is also true that each one of us and even each blade of grass is full of *Brahman*. It inevitably shows that *Brahman* is not exhausted by an individual's fullness of *Brahman*. Once he mistook this fullness and oneness with *Brahman* that *Brahman* is exhausted by his oneness as absolute self-fullness he commits the mistake of *'Aham Brahmasmi'*. Navajyothisree Karunakara Guru opines that Satyatranan was not graceful enough to differentiate himself as an individual evolute from the Supreme that causes the evolution. Even if the individual has got the realization of the Absolute it does not mean the absoluteness of the individual. Navajyothisree Karunakara Guru interrogates Satyatranan's standpoint with the question, "Am I only, the *Brahman*?", "Is the will of Almighty confined to an individual evolute?"[33] An individual evolute can never be considered neither by himself nor by others that he or she is the *Brahman*. The Ultimate or His will cannot be confined to individual evolutes.

The Curse from *Brahman* due to the First Error

Satyatranan's error is primarily concerned with his notion of *Brahman* that *Guru* is *Brahman*. His standpoint is rooted on the conception of Brahman as all authoritative of all *karma* that pervaded throughout *Chaturyuga*-s up to the full extent of *Manvantara*. This notion of *Brahman* as *Manu*, the authority of *Manvantara* got shifted to himself when he saw even *Manu* himself as dissolving into himself. First he saw in his vision that everything merging to *Manu* and he considered *Manu* as *Brahman*. Latter he saw that even *Manu* himself with everything else merging into himself. He interpreted his vision with the proclamation of '*Aham Brahmasmi.*'

This declaration was in forgetfulness of the Supreme reality that authorizes *Manu* with a mission. It is the will of *Brahman* that designates and enables *Manu* to function. Satyatranan's egoistic declaration was followed by its necessary consequence that there was a Curse from *Brahman*: "May the very memory of *Manu* is banished from the heart of man."[34] This was the direct consequence from *Brahman* for mistaking *Manu* as *Brahman*. It was this mistake that basically led Satyatranan to the egoistic notion of himself as *Brahman*. Considering *Guru* as *Brahman* includes the projection of one's own ego into *Guru*. Hence this notion is fundamentally faulty and inevitably, given a chance, ends up with or naturally culminates into one's own ego. This egoistic attitude got automatically retaliated as the Curse upon *Manu* tradition and it met with a collapse.

Brahman is the source of creative power behind evolution through numerous births of accumulation of *karmic* power. A *Guru* is not beyond this process of evolution. A designated soul evolves to the state of *Guru* and gets authorized to function as the revealing centre of the word from *Brahman* that is helpful for the evolutionary process of others in the society. *Guru* is authorized as medium of connecting link between the lower domain of the world and higher sphere of *Brahman*. Such a *Guru*, who himself is involved in the evolutionary process and successfully accomplishes evolutionary fulfilment by the determination of *Brahman*, cannot be mistaken as *Brahman*. Navajyothisree Karunakara *Guru* discloses: "This error was akin to the arrogance of knowledge. Nor was this error realized later because a curse ensued from the *Brahman*: *May the very memory of Manu is banished from the heart of man.* All that remained of that memory was *Manu's* time scale, the *manvantaram*. Ancient texts, which might have spoken of the *Manu*, are no longer extant."[36] Thus, the *Manu* tradition met with collapse and *Manusmriti* itself underwent large scale interpolation up to the level that the original text of revelation is no more extant. Now whatever remains as the knowledge about *Manu* and his tradition are completely erroneous? According to Navajyothisree Karunakara Guru, this error happened was not understood by anybody due to the effect of curse. It pushed *Manu* into oblivion. "The name of this author is unknown, as are any details of his life: his date, his geographical location, influences that may have shaped his life and thought, and a host of biographical questions that would shed light on the text itself."[37] Whatever remained after the curse as belonging to *Manu* tradition was only the knowledge of the time scale of *Manvantaras*. The original text and true knowledge about *Manu* tradition was all lost. As the result of the Curse the total forgetfulness of *Manu*, who was mistaken for *Brahman*, took place. The success of the Curse of total forgetfulness of *Manu* is the way to the memories and realization of and revelation from *Brahman*, the Absolute.

Conclusion

According to Navajyothisree Karunakara Guru, this historical incident of declaration is the origin of the well known Upanishadic *chaturvakyas*. This declaration gets repeated in many ways in the renowned texts due to its *karmic* influence from subtle planes of reality. Whosoever reaches to those planes in the process of evolution will get influenced by this *karmic* effect and consequently makes the same mistake or repeats things in more or less the same way. In this case, the source of *Sruti,* what is heard, especially in case of the great *chaturvakyas,* itself is to be interrogated. The influence of this error does not confine to spiritual dimensions only rather pervaded to the whole of human mental domain of attitudes and physical instincts of *karmic* dimension and social consequences of self-privileging social groups to the extent of exclusion of others. "I am the state" can be considered as the political version of this influence. The error pervaded to the entire world by human *karmic* intervention through centuries and centuries with least possibility of rectifying it due to the total ignorance of such an error as ever had happened.

Only with strong determination of *Brahman* one can transcend this error. *Guru* submits his overcoming of this error as solely due to the very will and strong safeguard of *Brahman* Himself. Without such a protection one is only vulnerable to that kind of attitudes. It is the same thing that happened in case of many of the Upanishadic seers, and the prophet of Bhagavat religion called Sree Krishna Paramatma and even in the case of Jesus Christ when he declared that his Father and himself to be one and the same which is the first occasion that prompted a Jew to take a stone to throw at him. It is the same error that eventually leads him to the crucifixion, though it is also true that he got crucified for the sin of the world. The sin of the world is nothing but the same proclamation of "*Aham Brahmasmi*." It all shows that *Manu* tradition had been such an all-flourished tradition but met with a collapse falling out of divine grace due to this error that has been pervading as erroneous influence to the entire humanity. It is revealed to Navajyothisree Karunakara Guru that it is the "First Error" that happened in the history of *Manu* tradition. According to Navajyothisree Karunakara Guru, in Indian tradition it is only Buddha who could save himself from this mistake to a great extent. But when the *karmic* effect of the error started to influence Buddhism through Brahminical intervention, the tradition had to switch over to other countries of better *karmic* atmosphere that is not polluted by this error and consequently got flourished in those countries as a path of enlightenment and liberation. Caste Brahmanism is the direct consequence of this first error. The error of declaration of oneself as *Brahman* evolved to the extent that the leftovers of that tradition as a group of people's self-proclamation as *Brahmins* in the sense of embodiment of *Brahman*. The ego got extended to a self-privileged social class with certain self-acclaimed *karmic* supremacy of worship and scholarship rights for their clannish survival and social ego satisfaction. The same erroneous egoistic attitude forced them to negate the same rights to other social groups in order to egoistically ascertain supremacy over others and it lead to social divisiveness and disintegration into many caste groups. *Brahman*, the Supreme, revealed the truth to *Guru* so that humanity can safeguard itself against this error for proper spiritual evolution at individual level and collective prosperity at social level.

Notes

1. Aurobindo, Sri (1956). *On the Veda*, Pondicherry: Sri Aurobindo Ashram, p. 426.
2. Purani, A.B. (1956). The *Life of Sri Aurobindo*, Sri Aurobindo Ashram, Pondicherry, pp. 214-215.
3. Velassery, Sebastian; *Transcendent Brahman and the Problematic of Ultimate Reality in Vedanta: A Phenomenological Approach*, p. 8.
4. Aurobindo, Sree (1956). *On Himself*, Sri Aurobindo Ashram, Pondicherry, p. 136.
5. Aurobindo, Sree (1960). *The Supramental Manifestation upon Earth*, Sri Aurobindo Ashram, Pondicherry, p. 116.
6. Aurobindo, Sree (1956). *On Himself*, Sri Aurobindo Ashram, Pondicherry, p. 470.
7. Aurobindo, Sree (1960). *The Supramental Manifestation Upon Earth*, Sri Aurobindo Ashram, Pondicherry, pp. 78-79.
8. Karunakara Guru, Navajyothisree (1980). *Dialogue on Human Prospectus*, Santhigiri Ashram, Thiruvananthapuram, p. 22.
9. Karunakara Guru, Navajyothisree (1980). *Dialogue on Human Prospectus*, Santhigiri Ashram, Thiruvananthapuram, p. 23. (Vijayan, O.V., *Introduction*, tr. Usha, O.V.).
10. *Ibid.*, p. 5.
11. *Ibid.*, p. 31.
12. *Ibid.*, p. 33.
13. *Ibid.*
14. *Ibid.*, p. 35.
15. Karunakara Guru, Navajyothisree (1988). *Birthday Messages*, Santhigiri Ashram, Thiruvananthapuram, p. 105.

16. Karunakara Guru, Navajyothisree, (1993). *The Path of Culture*, Santhigiri Ashram, Thiruvananthapuram, p. 35.
17. *Ibid.*, pp. 105, 106.
18. Karunakara Guru, Navajyothisree (1988). *Birthday Messages*, Santhigiri Ashram, Thiruvananthapuram, p. 33.
19. *Ibid.*, p. 81.
20. Karunakara Guru, Navajyothisree (1993). *The Path of Culture*, Santhigiri Ashram, Thiruvananthapuram, p. 34.
21. Karunakara Guru, Navajyothisree (1988). *Birthday Messages*, Santhigiri Ashram, Thiruvananthapuram, p. 75.
22. Karunakara Guru, Navajyothisree (1993). *The Path of Culture*, Santhigiri Ashram, Thiruvananthapuram, p. 34.
23. *Ibid.*, p. 34.
24. Karunakara Guru, Navajyothisree (1980). Dialogue *on Human Prospectus*, Santhigiri Ashram, Thiruvananthapuram, p. 5.
25. Karunakara Guru, Navajyothisree (1988). *Birthday Messages*, Santhigiri Ashram, Thiruvananthapuram, p. 71.
26. *Ibid.*, p. 71.
27. *Ibid.*, p. 81.
28. Karunakara Guru, Navajyothisree (1992). *Gurupooja in Santhigiri*, Santhigiri Ashram, Thiruvananthapuram, p. 13.
29. Karunakara Guru, Navajyothisree (1988). *Birthday Messages*, Santhigiri Ashram, Thiruvananthapuram, p. 75.
30. *Ibid.*, p. 81.
31. Karunakara Guru, Navajyothisree, *Dialogue on Human Prospectus*, Santhigiri Ashram, Thiruvananthapuram, 1980, p. 5.
32. *Ibid.*
33. *Ibid.*
34. *Ibid.*
35. *Ibid.*
36. *Ibid.*
37. Olivelle, Patrick, *Manu's Code of Law*, New Delhi: Oxford University Press, p. 20.

10

A Gandhian imagery of the Civilisation of the World

A Legacy Rooted in *Guru* Tradition

Saji Varghese

Gandhi's life and mission is a grand narrative to be examined and evaluated in the context of the legacy of *Guru* Tradition or wisdom tradition of India. The core of his teaching are rooted in the eternal values of *Sanatana dharma.*

Guru parampara is an age old tradition of India, though of the forgotten past, it lays emphasis on the need of guidance through the medium of an experienced chosen personality who attains highest wisdom in both spiritual and material realms of life. The Sanskrit term "*guru*" has a cluster of meanings with significance beyond that of the English translation, "teacher." *Gu* means "ignorance" and *ru*, "dispeller." The *guru* is a dispeller of ignorance, all kinds of ignorance; thus, there are *gurus* not only for specific spiritual development but also for dancing, music, wrestling, and other skills. The term "*guru*" also means "heavy" or "weighty" and might well illustrate the belief that accomplished or holy persons are characterized by an uncommon weight. Jan Gonda states that "it must primarily have described the man who on account of his special knowledge and function was held to be a bearer of power conspicuous by his prestige, 'weight', and influence." It is also maintained, though not commonly, that "*guru*" is derived from the Sanskrit root girl, meaning "one who calls." Kirpal Singh writes: "Thus he who always hears this (divine) call within himself, and is devotedly attached to the call and can make it manifest in others is described as *Guru*."[1] If the word "*guru*" means many things, it is because the *guru* is many things. He is an entity which in Western culture has no exact counterpart. For the *guru* is a teacher, counsellor, father-image, mature ideal, hero, source of strength, even divinity integrated into one personality. Primarily, however, the *guru* is the personal teacher of spirituality, that is, of the basic, ultimate values perceived within the Hindu tradition. Further, the *guru* possesses experiential knowledge, not only intellectual knowledge, of these values. In a word, the *guru* is indispensable for spiritual development. In early Hinduism he was a vital factor in imparting Vedic knowledge; in later thought the *guru* became the visible embodiment of truth and in some cases he was worshipped as an incarnate deity. Mahatma Gandhi once noted, "There can be no *jnana* without a *guru* is a golden maxim. But it is very difficult to find a *guru*, and it would not be proper to accept any person as a *guru* in the absence of a good one and so drown ourselves right in the middle of our voyage across this ocean of life. A *guru* is one who will help us to swim across. How can a man who knows no swimming save others? Even if such swimmers exist in modern times, they are not a common sight."[2]

There are scattered references of a religious teacher in the Vedas. In the *Rg Veda* (IV, 5, 6) the *guru* is described as the source and inspirer of the knowledge of the Self, or the essence of reality, for the seeker. In the *Yajur Veda* (VII, 27), the *guru* is described as the one who blesses and enhances the seeker's spiritual life. He does this not only through the knowledge he imparts as a teacher but also through the ritual he performs as a priest. The Aryans conceived the world as a realm of powers that affected and controlled their lives. Nature was clearly a main preoccupation as most of the Vedic gods were forces of nature, such as the sun, the moon, fire, and storm. The Aryan priest-teachers could thus bring blessings from this world through their knowledge and performance of the Vedic prayers and rituals. It is the Upanishads, however, that are explicit in insisting on the necessity of a *guru*. It is strikingly clear that education was not an end in itself but a means to the attainment of sacred knowledge or knowledge of the Ultimate Reality. Even the gods and demons must be taught by the *guru* concerning that Ultimate Reality. In the *Chandogya Upanishad* (VII-XII), Indra from the gods and Virochana from the demons go to the renowned teacher Prajapati in order to learn the essence of reality. Only by knowledge received directly from the *guru* does one attain this most beneficent Truth.[3] So also, in the *Katha Upanishad*, the *guru* is represented as indispensable to the acquisition of ultimate knowledge. Mahatma Gandhi writes, "God is one. I do not understand your difficulty in conceiving Him as formless. That which has a form cannot be all pervading, it needs to be the subtlest. It can therefore be only formless. All must admit the need for a *guru* but one may not hastily accept someone as a *guru*. In this age to seek a *guru* is to believe in one, because to acquire a perfect guide one must perfectly qualify oneself."[4]

Talking about the need of a *Guru* in worldly life Swami Sivananda writes "No doubt, the *Guru*'s blessing can do everything."[5] The metaphysical question on the nature of the self and the illusion which covers the eye of the Self directs itself to externality. Here a *guru* is required, who can impart *jnana* to the aspirant, and his internal eye is opened. Without the *guru* you cannot do this.[6] The *guru*, however, is not simply a man of knowledge or a miracle-worker but a man of profound and subtle experience and depth. Mere study of books cannot make one a *Guru*. One who has studied the Vedas, and who has direct knowledge of the *Atman* through *Anubhava* (experience), can alone be enrolled as a *Guru*.[7] The true *guru* is more than a mere man: "The *Guru* is God Himself manifesting in a personal form to guide the aspirant.[8] Concerning the *guru*'s role, he frankly affirms: In the East, the major forms by which you worship the Lord are divided into six sections. The highest of all is the worship of the *guru*. It is very difficult to worship the *guru*. There is ample opportunity to lose faith in him, while there is nothing to make you lose faith in a picture, a form, a statue of a god. When you adore a living person, he is not the same always.[9] Muktananda (1908-), a Contemporary sage particularly well known and venerated in India writes "On the one hand, he [the *guru*] is adept in spiritual matters, and, on the other, he is exceedingly shrewd in his worldly dealings. Those aspirants who live under the protection of such a Master pass through acute crises with ease and meet the most unfavourable circumstances fearlessly."[10] Mahatma Gandhi too cautions about the possibility of a wrong person been selected and guidance be improper, "I am aware, all scriptures and, certainly, the Indian scriptures, hold a *guru* to be absolutely indispensable, but if we cannot get a real *guru*, a sham substitute is not only useless but injurious."[11]

He further writes, "A person in search of a *guru* is vigilant and in the process acquires merit. So I go along unperturbed. It is by God's grace that one is blessed with a *guru*. Therefore, I shall get a *guru* at the time and place that I come to deserve one. In the meanwhile I always pay my obeisance to the *guru* I am yet to see."[12]

In *Bhakti* traditions of India, Sankara did place emphasis on the importance of the *guru*.[13] However, the context and *Advaita Vedanta* in which he situated the *guru* was highly intellectual and did not evoke a response in the popular mind. In reaction to the intellectual thrust of Sankara, other philosophers of the medieval age stressed *bhakti*. An early, prominent exponent of a philosophical basis for the *bhakti* movement was the *Vaisnavite* teacher Ramanuja who lived in the early years of the twelfth century. Educated first in Sankara's *Advaitic* tradition, Ramanuja soon fell out with his teacher Yadavaprakasa, a militant *Advaitin*. In his reaction against *Advaita*, Ramanuja taught that liberation was attained mainly through *bhakti*. He maintained that intense devotion would purify the mind of unbelief, open the individual to divine grace and thereby relieve the individual of sorrow. The individual could thereby reunite with *Brahman* but within that totality retain his own differentiation. Further, Ramanuja democratized this position when he taught that even the *Sudra* and the outcaste could attain salvation by complete surrender to the will of the *guru*.[14] As a metaphysician, Ramanuja achieved a synthesis of the *bhakti* tradition with *Vedanta* and also provided a rational basis for Hindu devotionalism. Ultimately, this development had a great effect on *guru* since the *guru* often became the focus for that intense and saving devotion which Ramanuja prescribed. Nimbarka (eleventh century) was also a philosophical leader of the *bhakti* movement. Nimbarka determined that there are five basic *sadhanas* or paths to salvation: *karma*, *jnana*, *upasana* or meditation, *prapatti* or self-surrender to God, and *gurupasatti* or devotion to the *guru*. In gurupasatti the *guru* leads the devotee to God; and whatever is necessary for salvation is done for the devotee by the *guru*. A follower of Nimbarka, Sundarabhatta, describes *gurupasatti* as the best *sadhana*, uniting *karma*, *jnana*, and *bhakti*: obeying the *guru*'s precepts is *karma yoga*; knowing that the essence of one's self is the *guru* is *jnana yoga*; being devoted to the *guru* is *bhaktiyoga*. In the seventeenth century, Ramadasa wrote in the *Dasabodha* on the absolute necessity of a *guru*, "Without a *Guru* we can never attain real knowledge. Even though one may study the sciences and attain to all kind of powers, both physical and mental, without the grace of the *Guru* one cannot realise the Self. Contemplation and concentration, devotion and worship, would be all useless without the grace of the *Guru*.... Rama and Krishna, and all the Saints and Sages of by-gone times, devoted themselves wholly to the service of their Master".[15] In the same treatise, Ramadasa describes the true *guru* as "He alone can be called a *Guru* who has no desires left in him, and whose determination is as steady as a mountain. He must have extreme dispassion, and his actions should be beyond censure. With him, spiritual discussion must be a constant pastime. He uplifts the world and becomes an exemplar for the various kinds of *Bhakti*. Knowledge, dispassionateness, devotion, rightful conduct, *Sadhana*, spiritual discussion, meditation, morality, justice, and the observation of the mean constitute the chief characteristics of a *Guru*". Ramadasa's admiration for the *guru* was so great that he considered the true *guru* greater than God: He who regards God as superior to the *Guru* is a fool. Before the greatness of the *Guru*, the greatness of God is as nothing. God is made God by men by the power of *Mantras*; but the *Guru* cannot be made even by God. The power of God is the power of illusion; the power of the *Guru* carries everything before it. Thus, these *bhakti* philosophers attempted to provide a rational basis for their devotionalism *vis-a-vis* the challenge of Sankara. In so doing, they gave a pivotal role to the *guru* in spiritual development.

However, in contemporary times under the influence of Western education and culture, the connotation of *guru* has undergone a tremendous transformation. Mandelbaum observes, *Guru* is often a *sannyasi* who is expected to cut-off his secular attachments, to abandon all considerations of kinship, *jati*, and village. Hence he is likely to pass lightly over such matters or to brush them aside entirely as inconsequential and positively harmful to the spirit.[16] By entering the world of the spirit with the *guru* some seek a sense of individual wholeness free from external societal restraints. Richard Lannoy observes "Under the conditions of a caste society, hierarchical interdependence and ritualistic interpersonal relations introduce into every relationship an element of formal and emotional constraint. The only authentic meeting that can still occur between two human beings stripped of their masks, is within the initiatory magic circle of the *guru-sishya* relationship."[17] Thus, the *guru* and his disciples often form an alternative social hierarchy outside caste and class, outside inherited social limits, which provides not an entry into but an exit from traditional Hindu society. On the contemporary scene, however, Hindus in increasing numbers are going to cult centers for religious instruction and corporate worship with fellow devotees of a *guru*. Thus, *guruhood* continues to influence, grow, and adjust to the situations contemporary India.

Thus, though there are myriad ways to preserve traditions which are rational and scientific *Guru Parampara* is an ideal way to sustain and fortify the ethical ideals of a society. The *guru* and the *sampradaya* that is formed around him provide a more meaningful conceptual structure for understanding the core of "living Hinduism", a core that will remain even though ritualistic aspect of Hinduism may recede and become redundant. 'We are also freshly reminded that the study of religions is the study of people and the faith by which they really live."[18] In Indian tradition faith has been and continues to be centred in the *guru* whose appearance is "repeated throughout history as if by historical law." As Renou states: "Philosophy in India involves men; it aims at practical results the type of these founders is repeated throughout history as if by historical law." The dynamic, sacred centre of Hinduism is, in fact, the enlightened *guru*, whose charismatic leadership creates the institution for philosophical, religious, and social change. The rich cultural traditions of India as has been mentioned in the earlier paragraphs grounded on moral ideals can be sustained through *guru sampradaya.*

While Gandhi aimed at fortifying and strengthening the age-old cultural traditions of India as they were founded on moral ideals, the Nehruvian and subsequent period of India with modernist perspective saw almost an opening of the 'doors of India' to the materialist west and its civilisation. The present chapter makes an analysis of rich cultural traditions of India which Gandhi aimed at preserving, to his understanding this would rather be the 'most ideal civilisation of the world' which is best preserved through the enriched imparting at the ancient practice of *Guruparampara.*

The first part of the title though may be considered as an invitation to mind a process of struggle the nation underwent for the attainment of 'self rule', autonomy, in fact, it is used in a different connotation which in due course would find its description adequately clear. The pre-colonised India, more genealogically the ancient India, is romantically, in Gandhi's anti-vanguardist vocabulary, being described as a site of 'innumerable moral values'. However, the advent of materialism which Gandhi claims as the cause for its erosion stands also as an ill effect of colonialism. In the first decade of the last century when he wrote his remarkable work, *Hindswaraj* and substantial, countless editorials in 'Young India' aimed at fortifying the vision he had of India, which stood far distinct from the popular vision of larger section of what modern India would be.

Gandhi envisioned a cultural/moral space that extends beyond the bounds of India and permeating and extending to the entire globe. There are instances that he wanted the rest of the world to learn and practice what India has been spontaneously nurturing for centuries, the age-old traditions of it. Gandhi believes that we can identify a community with a particular moral outlook.[19] Thus, more than physical features what characterises a nation is its identity linked to set of values associated with its cultural traditions. Both Plato and Gandhi are concerned with establishing a moral identity that prevails under any given condition among a people. But in certain sense it is cosmopolitan. The defence of an ancient cultural tradition is cosmopolitan as it aims at extending to the entire humanity. A similar line of argument is perceived in justifying the spread of British/West civilisation being cosmopolitan. However, the apparent paradox here can be removed by viewing which is grounded on morality. Obvious reasons to show the argument favours the former as it is based on moral claims which can be extended well beyond the borders to establish throughout the globe.

Gandhi's thoughts are in a genealogical order, expression of his disgust towards the practice of colonialism and the Western civilisation in general. This is the historical background against which he endeavours to 'reclaim' the glorious tradition of 'ascetic India'. The term 'reclaim' conveys a sense of loss, losing of it which is being claimed again. The erosion of culturally rich tradition is implied here. The ethical ideals that Gandhi wished India to revisit and make their own yet again, are the best, in the entire globe. Gandhi's translation of Tolstoy's 'Letter to a Hindu' contains a view on the loss of freedom of Indians to the British where the responsibility lies with the Indians.[20] The British could not have attained the political and economic control of India without the willing participation and even agreement of Indians. Indians have ceded to a foreign way of life, an ethical outlook that privileges material accumulation as the highest good; this aspect has affected the condition of the mind of the Indians. True freedom, then most fundamentally lies in regaining the ethical outlook based on duty and service to the humanity.

Gandhi was of the opinion that West is based on an ideology that itself is rather false. To quote him 'there is a relentless pursuit of a false ideal conceived as truth'. This refers to the pursuit of materialistic pleasures (occupation, wealth etc. as the greatest).[21] The other aspect which Gandhi in *Hindswaraj* points out is that while the West is more into self-indulgence the practice in India was more of self-restraints and involved in the pursuit of self-knowledge'. Restraints refer to the willingness to keep one free from the objects of undesirable temptations.

Habermas discusses the significance of the life world against the backdrop of the limits of the system world and its threat of colonization. However, the claim that Gandhi makes "Our life with concepts and objects was always complete" was proved ungrounded.[22] The limitation rather lies in continual persistence of a set of beliefs and its application in our lives. This is rather *Sadhana*, the way of life of restraints. Today our life world is colonized by the system worlds of state (administration) and market (economy). The colonisation has extended to the degree of 'cognitive enslavement'. This phenomenon manifests first of all in the way Indians begin to regard concepts as objects, actions and practices as embodiment of beliefs, norms as a necessary horizon of self-understanding. But colonization is neither our fate nor destiny and we can always transform this condition of colonization to one of a post-colonial condition of creative autonomy, intersubjectivity and cosmopolitanism.

Gandhian conceptions of *Swaraj* and *Satyagraha* become relevant in post-colonial struggle too. He writes, "My idea of Village Swaraj is that it is a complete republic, independent of its neighbours for its wants, and yet interdependent for many others in which dependence is a necessity. Thus every village's first concern will be to grow its own food crops and cotton for its cloth. It should have a reserve for its cattle, recreation and playground for adults and children.... this Panchayath will be the legislature, judiciary and executive combined to operate for its year of office. Any village can become such a republic today without much interference, even from the present Government whose sole effective connection with the villages is the exaction of the village revenue. I have not examined here the question of relations with the neighbouring villages and the centre if any. My purpose is to present an outline of village government. Here there is perfect democracy based upon individual freedom. The individual is the architect of his own government. The law of non-violence rules him and his government. He and his village are able to defy the might of a world. For the law governing every villager is that he will suffer death in the defence of his and his village's honour".[23]

This has become more relevant today in order to save us from the various economic, social, ethical and emotional hazards caused by the large scale industrialization and have become silent killers of the human race. The concept of *Swadeshi* that Gandhi included as one of the eleven vows that was stipulated to his followers who lived in his *ashram*. By highlighting this concept, Gandhi wanted to counteract some of the harmful consequences of globalization. The vow of *Swadeshi* means the spirit, which restricts persons to the use of services available in the immediate surroundings to the exclusion of the more remote. In other words, it implies production for neighbours. However, he was quick to add: "A votary of *Swadeshi* will never harbour ill-will towards the foreigner; he will not be actuated by antagonism towards anybody on earth. *Swadeshism* is not a cult of hatred. It is a doctrine of selfless service that has its roots in the purest *Ahimsa*, that is, love".[24] His idea of *Swadeshi*, if applied to the world at large with his theory of *Antyodaya* (the last man), which speaks of providing every individual with the basic necessities, can counteract the undesirable effects of globalization by ensuring that everyone benefits from the fruits of development.

World Development Report 1990 advised the developing countries to adopt labour-intensive technique of production to create job opportunities. "Against the background of achievement, it is all the more staggering, shameful that more than one billion people in the developing world are living in poverty. Progress in raising average incomes, however welcome, must not distract attention from this massive and continuing burden of poverty" (*World Development Report*: 10). For removal of poverty and unemployment, the Report was of the opinion that "rapid and politically sustainable progress on poverty has been achieved by pursuing a strategy that has two equally important elements. The first element is to promote the productive use of the poor's most abundant asset—labour. It calls for policies that harness market incentives, social and political institutions, infrastructure and technology to that end. Switching to an efficient, labour intensive pattern of development and investing more in the human capital of the poor are not only consistent with faster long-term growth; they contribute to it" (*World Development Report*: 3). It was further noted, "Since labour is an abundant resource, encouraging its use is generally consistent with rapid and efficient growth" (*World Development Report*: 56). Indian Planners are not unfamiliar with these views and suggestions as Gandhi discussed them over years ago, initially in *Hind Swaraj* and then in *Young India* and *Harijan* with special focus on Khadi and village industries. He stated: "I have not contemplated, much less advised, the abandonment of a single, healthy, life-giving industrial activity for the sake of hand-spinning. The entire foundation of the spinning wheel rests on the fact that there are crores of semi-unemployment people in India. The spinning wheel is destructive of no enterprise whatever. It is life-giving activity".[25]

Another aspect of Gandhi's criticism towards industrialisation was directed towards the preservation of India's rich natural resources. As globalization has progressed, so has the tendency to try and exploit every possible resource in the country to increase the Gross Domestic Product. Rapid deforestation has occurred throughout the developing world and the most developing countries are facing serious environmental hazards today. Moreover, corporate power has undermined governmental efforts at curbing environmental loss, as seen from the way the United States of America withdrew from the Kyoto Protocol. However, conservation processes led by the United Nations and echoed at the national and even local level, are gradually gathering speed in the second phase of globalization, wherein most of the evils of globalization are now being questioned and checked.

With the rapid progress in science and technology contributed largely by globalization, the contemporary human beings claim that they have conquered the nature. But sadly, the modern globalized world is in the throes of an ecological crisis—a tragedy inflicted by humans themselves when they deviated from nature and began to exploit it to the extent of disturbing its normal functioning. The nature brings forth various factors—sentient and insentient—that cooperate with one another to complete the cycle of life. Unfortunately, human intervention has broken this cycle and so we are in for a great environmental crisis. For Gandhi, the best possible way of restoring the balance in nature is by limiting human wants, which are unlimited in character. His call and example to return to nature has influenced a number of movements that aim at protecting the environment. He could be correctly considered as the precursor of the modern Green Movements in the world. As early as 1970s, the *Chipko Movement*[26] in northern India became popular. It is considered as a Gandhian movement aimed at stopping the mindless felling of trees for industrial purposes. Women too contributed their mite to the success of the Movement.

The development vision that Gandhi envisaged for the emerging Indian nation in the first decades of the twentieth century, despite its several dilemmas and predicaments, must be seen as a radical historicization of the notion of development as modernization, although the hermeneutical background of the Gandhian critique was completely different from that in the works of Heidegger or Foucault. Gandhi was pronouncedly against independent India following the econometric development path of the West for two reasons: (i) the sheer unsustainability of such a way to progress and, more importantly, (ii) the lack of conviction that such a way was indeed "progress". According to *Young India* of 20 December 1928, Gandhi told a capitalist, "God forbid that India should ever take to industrialization after the manner of the West. The economic imperialism of a single tiny island kingdom (England) is today keeping the world in chains. If an entire nation of 300 million took to similar economic exploitation, it would strip the world bare like locusts."[27] According to him, competitive materialism was not the cultural ideal of India. In the *Hind Swaraj's* daring coinage, to ask the English to quit India without India relinquishing modern Western civilization would be to become "Englistan" and not Hindustan (an alternative name for India); that would be to ask for "English rule without the Englishman... the tiger's nature, but not the tiger... [to] make India English."[28] For Gandhi, history is to be lived in the spirit of history's ideals, and not in merely recalling its past glory: "instead of boasting of the glorious past, we [must] express the ancient moral glory in our own lives and let our lives bear witness to our past."[29]

Certainly, Gandhi did not sufficiently historicize Indian cultural ideals but saw them too homogenously, and we might also say today that he had a too essentialist notion of Indian culture. However, in the context of the development narrative, his interrogation of the universal ideals of modernity should be seen as one of the earliest challenges to cultural imperialism. Much of the Gandhian development dream did not hold sway in the Nehruvian independent India. But, one might say, something of the Gandhian political ethos survived too, for example, in the Indian interpretation of secular pluralism, which advocates respect and political provisions for every citizen's religion. In the precariously poised multi-religious modern India, born out of a bloody partition on religious grounds, it is unclear what other alternative would have served every Indian better, given the constraints of a functioning democratic polity. In any case, it would not be right to say that what survived of the Gandhian heritage in India's democratic political ethos was a less historicized account than the economic model India adopted, for the sense of history and context with which Gandhi worked on and literally constructed India's nationhood in the first half of the twentieth century.

In the face of global spread of violence of different types and of varying proportions, Gandhian philosophy of non-violence becomes relevant. Throughout the post-World War II period when globalization was maturing, numerous conflicts took place on the earth among the world powers known as the Cold War. To this day, bitter conflicts exist in numerous parts of the world, notable ones taking place in Africa, Middle East and other parts of the world. After the 11 September terror attack on the US, there is a resurgence of international terrorism in the global arena with new and hideous dedication towards violent means. This spread of violence can be directly linked to the globalization process. In the context of such untold violence being perpetrated, Gandhi stands out as model par excellence in promoting a non-violent world.

Gandhi uses the Sanskrit word *ahimsa* to speak of non-violence. For him, *ahimsa* is much more than physical non-violence; it implies total non-violence avoiding any form of physical violence as well as passive violence. Gandhi translated *ahimsa* as love. When someone loves another person, he/she not only respects that person but also avoids harming that person. For him, non-violence is hurt by every evil thought, by anger, by wishing ill to anybody, by hatred, by fear, by selfishness, by lying, by undue haste and by attachment. Therefore, conditions for non-violence are that one must avoid these evils conscientiously. Non-violence in thought implies that there is no room for harbouring ill will in one's heart even though it is not expressed in acts. Gandhi said: "By non-violence or peace I mean the peace, which comes through inner strength. If I have that peace, that non-violence, I won't have any hate in me... Non-violence works organically, not mechanically".[30]

Gandhi presents to the world the principles of truth and non-violence as natural and sustainable means to fight for the civil rights of the people. In the face of oppressor nations, Gandhi exhorted the people to just withdraw cooperation with the conqueror, and accept the consequences. Though some will be butchered, they remain martyrs in the movement. The jails would be overflowed and become ridiculous, for those jailed would be heroes of the new nation that is emerging. The jails would be the training ground and a classroom for the new leadership. All the time, when the oppressor becomes oppressive, he/she would become weaker and all the time, the oppressed would resist the oppressor with the spirit of non-violence, he/she would become stronger. It would be a losing battle for the oppressor and he/she would have to succumb, be converted or collapse. He was able to organize truth and non-violence into a powerful movement, not based merely on the goodness of the individual but on the goodness organised to withstand evil of hatred and violence. Gandhi named the movement *Satyagraha*. It was a powerful movement, organised by Gandhi as a social weapon to fight evil and injustice as well as a means to inspire the masses with self-confidence in resisting with their own strength against all tyranny. Such a movement inspired a host of world leaders to fight for their rights through non-violent means.

Notes

1. Singh, Kirpal (1967). *Godman*, Delhi: Ruhani Satsang, p. 8.
2. *Navajivan*, 6-2-1921.
3. *Chandogya Upanisad IV*, 4, 3.
4. Letter to Kasamali, June 13, 1926.
5. Sivananda, Swami (1965). *Bliss Divine*, Rishikesh: Yoga-Vedanta Forest Academy, p. 191.
6. Sivananda, Swami (1963). *Necessity for Sannyasa*, Rishikesh: Yoga-Vedanta Forest Academy, p.
7. Sivananda, *Bliss Divine*, p. 182.
8. *Ibid.*, p. 182.
9. Wiener, Sita (1972). *Swami Satchidananda*, New York: Bantam Books, p. 79.
10. *Muktananda, Swami* Guru (1971). New York: Harper and Row, p. 11.
11. Letter to Shevakram Karamchand, March 21, 1924.
12. Letter to Kasamali, June 13, 1926
13. Sankara's *Vivekacudamani*, (1968). trans. Ramana Maharshi in *The Collected Works of Ramana Maharshi*, ed. Arthur Osborne (Tiruvannamalai: Sri Ramanasramam, pp. 198, 200, 201.
14. Srivastava, Ashirbadi Lal (1964). *Medieval Indian Culture*, Jaipur, Shiva Lal Agarwala and Co., Ltd.
15. *Dasabodha V*, 1, 19-43
16. Mandelbaum, *Society in India*, 2:527.
17. Richard, Lannoy. *The Speaking Tree: A Study of Indian Culture and Society*, London: Oxford University.
18. Ghurye, *Indian Sadhus*, 161.

19. Bilgrami, Akheel (2011). *Democratic Culture: Historical and Philosophical Essays*, New Delhi: Routeledge.
20. Murthy, B. Srinivasa (ed.) (1987). *Mahatma Gandhi and Leo Tolstoy Letters*, Long Beach: Long Beach Publications, CA.
21. Letter to Mrs. Maddock 14 March 1924, *Collected Works of Mahatma Gandhi*, 27, pp. 53-56.
22. *Collected Writings of Mahatma Gandhi*, Vol. 10, pp. 256-57.
23. Gandhi, M.K., *Harijan*, 26-7-1942.
24. Gandhi, M.K., *The Selected Works*, Vol. 6, 339.
25. Gandhi, M.K., *Young India*, 27-5-1926.
26. Chipko Movement is an organized resistance against the destruction of forests spread throughout India. The name of the movement comes from the word 'embrace', as the villagers hugged the trees, and prevented the contractors from felling them. Although the Bishnoi community started the original Movement around 260 years back in the early part of the 18th century in Rajasthan, the Movement that began in 1973 is the most famous. The first Chipko action took place spontaneously in April 1973 in the village of Mandal in the upper Alaknanda valley and over the next five years spread to many districts of the Himalayas in Uttar Pradesh. It was sparked off by the government's decision to allot a plot of forest area in the Alaknanda valley to a sports goods company. This angered the villagers because their similar demand to use wood for making agricultural tools had been earlier denied. With encouragement from Dasoli Gram Swarajya Sangh, a local NGO, the women of the area, under the leadership of an activist, Chandi Prasad Bhatt, went into the forest and formed a circle around the trees preventing the men from cutting them down. Mr Sunderlal Bahuguna, a Gandhian activist and philosopher, whose appeal to Mrs Indira Gandhi, the then Prime Minister of India, resulted in the green-felling ban. Mr Bahuguna coined the Chipko slogan: "Ecology is permanent economy." One can notice how the Gandhian philosophy of non-violence had a tremendous influence on this Movement.
29. *Gandhi*, 1960. Vol. 38, 243.
30. *Collected Writings*, 1960. Vol. 10, 15.
31. *Collected Writings*, 1960. Vol. 13, 316.
32. Gandhi, M.K., *Young India*, 20-3-1930: 98. *Sustainable Development and Social Progress*.

11

Sustainable Development and Social Progress Retrieving the Human[1]

Reena Patra

The present chapter is purported to re-look at the concept of sustainable development as a process that goes side by side with social progress which may be understood in more comprehensive terms that go beyond purely economic or materialistic terms; for it is certainly clear that sustainability is more than what the economics that is implied in it. The present chapter is concerned with five main issues. First, I am tracing the genealogies of the concept of sustainable development in philosophy *per se*, comparing those genealogies with two important conceptions of rationality, i.e., metaphysical rationality and instrumental rationality with its previous and contemporaneous developments on other intellectual fronts. Second, I am trying to understand the quality of human life which includes two aspects: its spiritual character and the ability to know and to act. The former consists of ideals which include values, moral consciousness and creativity. The latter consists in knowing ways and means of shaping nature and the capacity to organize and administer socio-economic and cultural development. Third, I am considering the circumstances which are, in contrast, currently encouraging a strong interest in instrumental rationality, which I argue, is the theoretical reason that subordinates nature and use it in an unsustainable way. To this end, I shall be making a distinction between two types of rationalities such as metaphysical rationality and instrumental rationality. One of the distinctive characteristics of metaphysical rationality is that it accords a necessary connection between reason and being and assumed that the world was organized wisely and purposely, because it owed its existence and ordering to the efficient power of a Divine Absolute. Hence, metaphysical rationality rests on the view that reason exists as the definite and potential power not only in human mind but also in the objective world, i.e., in nature (including environment and ecology) and its manifestations, in social institutions, in inter-human relations and in the life of individuals. In the case of instrumental rationality, it lost the transcendent and objective references, e.g., *God, Logos, objective reason, objective order* etc. and, instead, it became exclusively connected with a human subjective reasoning subordinated in the form of instrumental tools to the realization of aims whose reasonableness nobody inquires. Consequently, the scientific and technological changes that we experience, affect institutional stability, individual values and the behaviour patterns of present day human beings. Fourth, I am endeavouring to explicate the metaphysical understanding of the term 'sustainable living' as enhancing the quality of human life and thereby develop social interaction with particular reference to my own thesis that sustainable living implies the unfoldment of the human spirit. Fifth, I am particularly concerned with the application of "the concept of sustainability in the global field and argue that the results and consequences of the transformation of the instrumentalization of reason have resulted to the loss of spiritual roots in human understanding on freedom, justice, equality, happiness, development, tolerance etc." Even if they are being acknowledged as aims for which one strives, there is already no rational instance that would be entitled to giving them value and reconciling them as the objective reality. Consequently, we have lost the 'human' in human settlements, in family relations, in neighbourhood, religion, economy, ecology and polity.

Sustainable development is said to be a pattern of resource use, that aims to meet human needs, while, preserving the environment so that, these needs can be met not only in the present, but also for future generations. The term was used by the Brundtland Commission which coined what has become the most often-quoted definition of sustainable development as development that "meets the needs of the present without compromising the ability of future generations to meet their own needs."[1] Sustainable development ties together concerned for the carrying capacity of natural systems with the social challenges facing humanity. As early as the 1970s "sustainability" was employed to describe an economy "in equilibrium with basic ecological support systems." Ecologists have pointed to the limits to growth and presented the alternative of a "steady state economy" in order to address environmental concerns.

The field of sustainable development can be conceptually broken into different constituent parts such as environmental sustainability, economic sustainability, socio-political sustainability and cultural and spiritual sustainability.

Sustainable Development: In Search of a Definition

More often than not, the concept of sustainability is centred on subjects like economics, ecology and environment. Such an understanding about the concept of sustainability, to my mind, is lopsided, truncated and unsatisfactory. Although, economics is an important aspect of human life, yet it does not mean that this is the only way of understanding and interpreting the concept of sustainability. Nevertheless, one might ask whether this approach in itself is just a supporting tool of the accented intellectualism and commercialism which is characteristic of the modern times. In our modern times, we have somehow lost the deeper metaphysical dimension of sustainability as we have lost the meaning of Sustainable living. Sustainable living is a lifestyle that attempts to reduce an individual's or society's use of the Earth's natural resources and his/her own resources. Proponents of sustainable living aim to conduct their lives in manners that are consistent with sustainability, in natural balance and respectful of humanity's symbolic relationship with the Earth's natural ecology and cycles. In fact, there are two views in terms of human relationship to nature; they are called anthropocentric and holistic respectively. The former sees man as the master of universe with right to treat nature in whatever way he/she chooses. This view has been dominant in history and at times being regarded as a catalyst to technological development. The latter, however, emphasizes man's responsibility toward nature. Man has no dominion over nature; instead he is a steward to serve and manage nature with care. The problem indeed is not economics or technology. Our problem is the contamination of human heart whose insatiable desire and disrespect of nature created the ecological crisis.

Metaphysical Rationality

There are two types of rationality, which stamp our society and culture, the analyses of which can be a good starting point to reveal a very decisive influence upon the occurring processes of technological conditionings of the idea of a new civic cultu... in our societies. The two types of rationality are *metaphysical rationality* and *instrumental rationality.* Metaphysical rationality possessed a number of distinctive features. The most important of them was the conviction of the necessary connection between reason and being and assumed that the world was organized wisely and purposely, because it owed its existence and ordering to the efficient power of a Divine Absolute. This absolute is variously called as the *Being* identical with reason by Parmenides, the *Nous* by Anaxagoras, the *Divine builder—Demiurge* by Plato, the *First substance* by Aristotle, the *God* by Christian philosophers, the *Substance* by Spinoza, or the *Absolute idea* by Hegel. In every case, it was dependent upon the existence of an objective cause that warranted law and order to the temporal world. Despite certain imperfections, the world as a whole appeared as a reflection of the divine Absolute in this philosophy. The metaphysical rationality excluded any accidentality. Everything that exists has a meaning and is purposeful, which can be analyzed into exact logico-mathematical or natural laws originating from the objective reasonableness.

In the metaphysical rationality reasonableness is an attribute of both being and man. The human intellect, *ratio*, is a particle and man is equipped with reason with an end in view of comprehending and disclosing the reasonableness of the whole being. "The reason", wrote Hegel, "is the certitude of the consciousness that it is all-embracing-reality."[2] Rationality belongs to the being itself, where objective rationality, warrants law and order to all that exists; the thinking which takes place in human mind displays the truth of being and in the final account it is a road on which being itself is reached at the true knowledge about himself. From the standpoint of the metaphysical rationality the world is full of meaning; all that exist are endowed with meaning as well the world of nature and human history. In this image of rationality, knowledge is an activity, which mirrors the objective meaning of things and therefore it acquires a positive moral value. The rational behaviour, being compatible with an objective order, is always moral and it directs towards more and more new values. Perhaps one of the most important features of metaphysical rationality is that ideas of truth and goodness are related with themselves.[3]

As explained above, metaphysical rationality rests on the view that reason exists as the definite and potential power not only in human mind but also in the objective world, i.e., in nature and its manifestations, in social institutions, in inter-human relations and in the life of individuals. Such a notion of objective reason has never excluded subjective reason, but the latter has been acknowledged as a partial and special expression of the former. The former was functioning as universal reasonableness from which one deduced all criteria for all things and living creatures. The most important aim of subjective reasoning was bringing to the concordance between objective orders or to use Hegel's words—"everything that is rational", and the human existence, inclusive private affairs of individuals.

Instrumental Rationality

The second type of rationality, which may be called instrumental rationality, is the result of the destruction of classical rationalism on the one hand and as the effect of positivistic phenomenalism on the other; it got eventually combined with the scientific attitude with its cult of techniques together with the widespread technocrat ideologies. In turn, instrumental rationality became the boss in 20th century materialistic and technocrat-ideologies as it steered people's awareness and activity exclusively towards achieving practical, material and consumer aims. It lost the transcendent and objective references, e.g., *God*, *Logos*, *objective reason*, *objective order* etc. and, instead, it became exclusively connected with a human subjective reasoning subordinated in the form of instrumental tools to the realization of aims whose reasonableness nobody inquires. Consequently, the scientific and technological changes that we experience affect institutional stability, individual values and the behaviour patterns of present day human beings. In principle, technology and science are accountable for producing dangerous alterations in the equilibriums sustaining biological diversity and cultural pluralism. But, science and technology, which has unified the world by invading every spiritual or material cubic inch has also acquired the responsibility to run it is a paradigm shift of the consequences of metaphysical rationality to instrumental rationality. In the stereotype of instrumental rationality, the qualification rational has also meant consistency with scientific methods, resting on the knowledge about causality and other laws of nature and thereby in conformity with established aims such as bringing profitable results and to foresee future events optimizing human actions in all forms of life. Hence, instrumental rationality affirms on the model of most efficient instrument for the creation of the conditions of a 'prosperous' society.

An even stranger erosion has taken place in this instrumental conditioning of rationality: while the single-minded pursuit of wealth was first tied to a strong work ethic, this has now been cast aside in favour of creating the impression that one gets his/her things done, the impression that one is a "winner". Rather, science and technology must be looked upon as instruments not only for human development but also as aids in man's interpersonal relations and social progress. It is therefore necessary to take into account the impact of science and technology to cope with the complexities of human nature. This demands a shift of attitude not only in economic or commercial terms but also a sense of the transparency of things, of intimacy with nature as cosmos conveys to man a meaning that concerns him. We have lost such a sense of meaning and contemplation as we have lost the contemplative and symbolist spirit which sees symbols rather than facts. It is a true statement if I say that the West has already forgotten the symbolic view of things. Thus, the modern man of the West live in a de-sacralized world of phenomena whose only meaning is either their quantitative relationships expressed in mathematical formulae that satisfy the scientific mind or their material usefulness. This is to suggest that we have made an extreme effort in emptying the sacred character of the cosmos and made it to become profane. Thus, the symbols in the nature became facts and spiritually meaningless. What I am arguing for is the resurrection of a metaphysics that emphasize on the contemplative and symbolist rather than the passionate and the factual mentality which can revitalize the lost connection between man and nature. As opined by Guenon, the quantitative character of modern science must be pointed out in particular because it exists as a general tendency which seeks the reduction of all quality to quantity and all that is essential in the metaphysical sense to the material and substantial.[4]

Instrumentalization of Reason and the Loss of Spiritual Roots

The results and consequences of the transformation of the instrumentalization of reason have resulted to the loss of spiritual roots in human understanding on freedom, justice, equality, happiness, tolerance etc. Even if they are being acknowledged as aims for which one strives, there is already no rational instance that would be entitled to giving them value and reconciling them as the objective reality. Consequently, we have lost the 'human' in human settlements, in family relations, in neighbourhood, religion, economy, ecology and polity. The shaping of the present rationality within a span of 150 years was able to bring forth a number of negative phenomena in science, techniques, art, concepts of development and sustainability, philosophy, and literature and practically in all spheres of social and cultural life. The criteria of instrumental rationality found its wide application in all spheres of human activity: in science, techniques, economy, organization of collective life, our attitude towards the concepts of development and sustainability etc., and rationality has been universally identified with perfection, splendor, profit and material abundance. As a consequence, one feels obliged to rationalize one's own existence, thinking and acting. In the stereotype of instrumental rationality, the qualification "rational has also meant consistency with scientific methods, resting on the knowledge about causality and other laws of nature" and thereby in conformity with established aims such as bringing profitable results and to foresee future events optimizing human actions in all forms of life. Hence, instrumental rationality affirms on the model of most efficient instrument for the creation of conditions of a 'prosperous' society. Lasch reports that he was "struck by the evidence, presented in several studies of business corporations, to the effect that professional advancement had come to depend less on craftsmanship or loyalty to the firm than "visibility", "momentum", personal charm, and impression management".[5] However, we must also acknowledge that if our modern consciousness is steered to proceed farther in the same direction, then the final consequence of the instrumentalization of reason leads to a situation where we will make ourselves similar to technical mechanisms like our products. All this could mean an erasing of the essence of humanity, and thus in the final accounts it would be inhuman and irrational. All that one can trace the reason for such a state of affairs is the magnificence of instrumental rationality and the loss of metaphysical reasoning.

This attitude is problematic in as much as it means being in control and reducing everything to a matter of technique. The main question is not "what is it", but "how can I get it"? Thus, for the modern person, *Yoga*, for example is not for self-disciplining the human mind but has become a technique for lowering one's blood pressure or for becoming more slimmer and beautiful and maintaining a sense of physical well-being. In fact, the main aim of *Yoga* or for that matter, the martial art of '*Kalaripayattu*' in Kerala was meant to train the mind and brings it into contact with the ultimate reality, in Indian philosophical terms, *Brahman*. As Herrigel says, "if one really wishes to be master of an art, technical knowledge of it is not enough. One has to transcend technique so that the art becomes an "artless art" growing out of the unconscious".[6] In sum, most of our activities have become 'technical' in character and have reduced to mastery, efficiency and neutrality and thereby loosing the authentic selfhood, which I believe is the central pillar of sustainable living. Hence, the characteristic feature of technical thinking is the product, which may be called the loss of meditative thinking in Heidegger's phrase. It is pertinent here to recall the words of Heidegger: "The approaching tide of technological revolution in the atomic age could so captivate, bewitch, dazzle, and beguile man that calculative thinking may someday come to be accepted and practiced as the only way of thinking. What great danger then might move upon us? Then there might go hand and hand with the greatest ingenuity in calculative planning and inventing indifference toward meditative thinking, total thoughtlessness. And then? Then man would have denied and thrown away his own special nature—which he is a meditative being. Therefore, the issue is the saving of man's essential nature. Therefore, the issue is keeping meditative thinking alive".[7]

Human Development and Social Progress

It is often argued in the intellectual circles that quality of human life includes two aspects: its spiritual character and the ability to know and to act. The former consists of ideals, values, moral consciousness and creativity. The latter consists of knowing ways and means of shaping the nature and the capacity to organize and administer socio-economic development. These are intrinsically interrelated.[8] Spiritual qualities play a normative role in guiding knowledge and action. For example, science and technology are fundamental to the abilities to know and act. At the same time, given today's advanced science and technology, the spiritual quality of life depends upon the quality of one's ability to know and act. In other words, the human person is an organic unity of spiritual qualities with knowledge and action. In the process of human civilization and culture, what is lost is the organic unity between man as a spiritual being and his capacities and cravings towards his knowledge and action.

An analysis of human development in relation to social progress can be understood from different perspectives. Usually, the developmental level of the productive social force is taken as the decisive factor and condition of social progress. Though, it is correct, yet, it cannot be considered as the sole criterion or as an integral scale of social progress. I would like to put forward three aspects which are able to work as catalysts to social progress which may be named as productive power, emancipatory power and spiritual power. Productive power is considered to be one of the principles that can govern as well as manage the primary basis for social progress and thereby augment a firm material basis for the mental and physical development of the people. Any society that does not guarantee the development of productive forces cannot possibly vouch for the economic emancipation of a given people. It amounts to saying that the extent to which people are emancipated from poverty is a necessary criterion for social progress or development. Emancipatory power empowers people in their social relations who are reflected mainly in the various developmental stages of the socio-political structure, as for example, the degree of realization of democracy and freedom. Spiritual power is the third aspect of human development in relation to social progress which is independent of its politics, economy, science and culture. What is argued is that we can conceive the improvement of the standard of living and all-round development as a synthetic criterion of social progress because all three aspects are closely correlated with human development.

Metaphysical Thinking and Sustainable Living

Here we are tempted to endeavour to expound the metaphysical understanding of the term 'sustainable living' as enhancing the quality of human life. Thus, the issue is centred on the factors that augment the quality of human life. If metaphysics is called the science of the Real, of the origin and end of things, of the Absolute and in its light, the relative, then sustainable living, metaphysically understood, is the fulfillment towards such a conception of life. It is a theoria of reality whose realization means sanctity and spiritual perfection and therefore can be achieved within a revealed tradition.[9] Understood thus, if I define metaphysics as the manifestation of Being through the medium of human thought and cognition, then we may say that it is the metaphysical thinking by which human cognition first attains its true meaning and man his specific dignity. Thus, breakdown of metaphysical thinking is the breakdown of human existence itself. Accordingly, sustainable living implies the unfoldment of the human spirit from the point of view of metaphysics. The outcome of such an unfoldment of the human spirit is an authentic self-hood. To this end, following the 'capability approach' of Amartya Sen and Martha Nussbaum[10], I argue that sustainable living refers not to a particular component of life, such as pleasure or satisfaction of the basic needs, but to a heterogeneous list of human conditions, inner capacities and external opportunities. Sustainable living is the capability of an individual to function in certain humanly good ways. Hence, physical well-being is merely a necessary condition for the concept of sustainable living and cannot be regarded as a sufficient condition. We must also include in our characterization the mental aspects of sustainable living such as the cognitive capacities and our activities of perceiving, imagining, reasoning, judging and deciding. The latter embraces our being able to choose a conception of the good life. Thus, I argue that a person's conception of good life, *Sreyas* rather than *Preyas*, is the basis upon which the meaning of sustainable living is based.

Metaphysical Rationality and *Guru* Tradition

In accordance with India's culture and philosophical vision, Indian *Rishis* lead a sustainable living by attaining a harmony between man and nature. They were happy with nature because they accepted its norms and its rhythms, so to say, its *Dharma* rather than to seek to dominate and overcome it. Put the same differently, they have not judged nature according to human utility nor have they made earthly man as the measure of all things. They had followed the *dharma* of nature and the *Rta* of the cosmos by accepting and following the nature of things and have not sought to disturb nature by artificial means. That is why Hinduism as an integral tradition has developed diverse cosmological and natural sciences and even spiritual techniques tied intimately to the use of the energy within nature. Thus, man was considered a channel of grace for nature because man only can cast light into the world of nature through his active participation. But only he who has turned toward the inward dimension of his being can see nature as a symbol, as a transparent reality and come to know and understand it in the real sense. This excellence was especially evident in our *Gurus* because *Gurus* visualized in the virgin nature, trees, streams and the sky, in birds and buffaloes, direct symbols of the spiritual world. With the strong symbolist spirit with which *Guru* was endowed, he saw everywhere images of celestial realities. For *Guru*, nature was sacred (not profane) and there was a definite disdain of the artificialities of sedentary life. This may be understood as the visible expression of the implication of metaphysical rationality. We may also add here that from the point of view of metaphysical rationality, the reality of a species is not exhausted by its purely material manifestations. The metaphysical approach undergirds the idea that the species ultimately are the manifold ideas in the Divine Mind which at a particular cosmic moment have become imprinted in the corporeal world and retain their reality on other planes of existence. This is the finest rationality whose embodiment was *Guru Cetana* in Indian culture.

Thus in terms of its own valuation, the Indian (Hindu) tradition must be considered as a tradition based on *Guru Cetana* whose foundations were built on the negation of absolute distinctions as it was rooted in the idea of an underlying unity that sustains all differences. Hence, this tradition was able to postulate and maintain that all realms of existence are continuous—the physical, the vital, the mental and the spiritual—and are perfectly possible for one order of being to be transformed into another. In such a tradition and world-view where the pattern of life events is interdependent, *Guru* is seen as a unitary consciousness and is variously called *Brahma-Jnani, Brahma-Saksatkari,* and *Brahma-Anubhavi* etc. What this tradition undergirds, therefore, is the experiential realization where *Guru Cetana* is the *Brahma Cetana. Guru,* therefore, in this tradition is not merely a person from the Western perspective, but a unitary consciousness who achieves self-expression as the Real in existence. This positive notion of the *Guru* has always had an identical or unchanging meaning in both the Indian Philosophical tradition as well as culture. More than by mere accretion, the notion has managed to incorporate the great achievements of human self-discovery for which, in turn, it has been both the stimulus and the goal.

Accordingly, a philosophical and cultural tradition which is rooted in *Guru* Consciousness as an image of the transcendent principle transforms and sensitizes its culture. *Guru* remains part of nature but rather than being subject thereto as a mere producer or consumer, he is a creative and transforming centre. This is an affirmation of existence as sharing in *Sat*, (existence) *Cit* (Knowledge) and *Ananda* (Bliss) and reflects the meaning of the transcendent for man and of man in the Transcendent. It is embodied personally in a Ramakrishna or a Vivekananda; Aurobindo or a Gandhi, a Sankara or a Ramanuja. Variously termed charismatic personalities, paradigmatic individuals or characters that meld role and personality in providing a cultural, epistemic, political or moral ideal, they supersede mere historical facts. As concrete universals, they express the harmony and fullness of perfection, which is at once classical and historical, ideal and personal, uplifting and dynamizing; in a word, sustainable and liberating.

Sustainable Living and Indian Tradition

The above considerations obviate the necessity to argue that Indian culture and tradition had a unique outlook on the criteria of sustainable living. The criteria of sustainable living that this tradition developed and augmented were not on the lines of the Western conception of life, which is scientific, rationalistic and materialistic. The ancient tradition of Hinduism was not opposed to scientific understanding of anything. But this tradition was opposed to accept science as the divinity to be revered. This tradition, again, was disparate to accept that scientific understanding is the only kind of understanding that we can have about everything, human beings, their lives, ecology or even environment. The ideal of life toward which man strives is dependent upon its spiritual support and the core of man's spiritual force. The word spirituality also may be understood in a different way in this culture. Spiritual search, in this tradition and culture, may be understood as self-integration rather than cosmic or social integration. Indian concept of spirituality undergirds an eternal cosmic order that pervades all of existence, which can be found in the concept of *Rta* in the *Vedas*. The implication is that in the Hindu tradition, there is no absolute barrier between the natural and the supernatural, the sentient and the insentient, the physical and the psychic, the sexual and the spiritual and indeed between God and man. It may be best described as the concomitant relation between reason and being, so to say, a philosophy and a world-view that emphasizes the metaphysical dimension of human existence. Such a life when lived may be called as the sustainable living; like all other Oriental traditions, Hinduism emphasizes on the deliverance from the cosmos which is *Maya*. *Maya* is not mere illusion, nor it is an epistemological category of nescience; rather it is the divine play or art. It is not only capable of concealing the Divine Self, but also gifted to reveal the same Self.

Ethical Implications

The dilemma of our emerging world and its ecological crises are at least in part a matter of values and ideas. What we see is a kind of madness arises from the prevailing nature-conquering, nature-hating self and world-denial. What is obligatory is awareness to the theme of sustainable life in harmony with nature. To implement this awareness, I would like to put forward three themes for consideration:

1. *Man is a creature and thus a part of the ecosystem:* We can be proud of the fact that we are tool-using, thinking animals. Man is said to be the crown of all creation, a homo-sapien as being able to reason. Man indeed is the only creature that survives not only by instinct but also by will and reason. Yet, man is one of the organisms living within a limited world. He shares with all creatures his biological needs for water, air, food and mineral. He will perish once his time is up and dies returning to nature just like any other living things. As such man is a part of ecosphere.

In the distant past, human beings acknowledged that they are a part of natural ecosystems. Hence, humans blended well with their ecosystems, fitting into natural flows of energy and materials in a harmonious way. They were not manipulators but simply taking their places within the universe. All were perfect until man started exploiting nature for his own benefit and since then we live in tension with our supporting ecosystems. In short, we should have the awareness that we are part of this ecosystem; thus let us not take the earth for granted. This is the first *mantra*.

2. *Man is a steward to the earth:* We tend to believe and act that we have a right to subdue the earth. The key word in debate is 'dominion' or 'stewardship'. Lynn White Jr, may be correct when he argued (in his famous article on *"The Historical Roots of Our Ecological Crisis"* published in 1967) that the crisis in ecology is Christianity's fault because Christianity taught that man had dominion over nature and man has treated nature in a destructive way. But let us not forget that the Christian fathers like Origen, Irenaeus, Gregory of Nyassa, and Erigena were able to develop a theology of nature. We also find in the figure of St. Francis of Assisi, a most startling reminder of the possibility

of a reverential attitude towards nature within the aura of Christian saintly life. His life among the birds and beasts that he addressed was a concrete example of the Christian belief that through holiness man can gain a relationship with nature. What I am emphasizing is that only a revival of a spiritual conception of nature which is based on metaphysical outlook can hope to neutralize the havoc brought about by the applications of modern science and integrate this science itself into a more universal perspective.

3. *Man is a finitude:* G.P. Marsh's *Man and Nature*[11] was the first work to describe in detail about man's destructiveness out of his ignorant disregard of the law of nature. Darwin's theory of natural selection that sets the tone of "the survival of the fittest" motivated human kind not only to struggle against nature in order to survive but also to demonstrate his superiority by so doing. Freud[12] even suggested human community to take up the attack on nature, force it to obey human will under the guidance of science.

This awareness must challenge us to develop a new ethics that is not only ecologically but also spiritually based on a value that speaks of man's responsibility toward himself, toward nature, toward other fellowmen and toward God. Thus, M.C. Tai argued that our ecological crisis is derived not only from air pollution, water pollution or the overexploitation of nature, but also from the contamination of human hearts.[13] The devastation and the broken down of a harmonious balance between man and nature are convincing proofs of this spiritual pollution. In order to restore a harmonious relationship between man and environment, a new ethics based on the above-mentioned awareness must be developed.

Developing a New Ethics

There are two views in terms of human relationship to nature, anthropocentric and holistic. The former sees man as the master of universe with right to treat nature in whatever way he chooses. This view has been dominant in history and at times being regarded as a catalyst to technological development. The latter, however, emphasizes man's responsibility toward nature. Man has no dominion over nature, instead he is a steward to serve and manage nature with care. The problem indeed is not economics or technology. The tides of oil that increasingly wash up on miles of beaches near shipping lanes are not the product of technology, they are the result of a complex of decisions which begins with an individual's desire for cars. Our problem is the contamination of human heart whose insatiable desire and disrespect of nature created the ecological crisis.

The new ethics governing human behaviour must emphasize upon a responsible stewardship aiming to develop an appropriate technology which is conducive to decentralization, compatible with the laws of ecology, gentle in its use of resources and designed to serve the human person instead of making him the servant of machines. This model of technology has been reflected in Noah's ark that is used to hold life up in a flood. On the contrary, Babel is an excellent emblem of irresponsible and inappropriate technology for its only purpose is to lift its builders for their own glory. The arks uses human creativity to identity and preserve nature, the tower of Babel uses those same powers to lift human out of nature.

By Way of a Conclusion

Man's relationship to nature has changed from harmony to hostility to man's attempt to re-design nature's formation and order. When man lived in harmony with his environment, everything was regarded as good but when man started manipulating nature, the relationship turned sour. The modern man tries to re-design nature, as for instance, the genome projects which are going on everywhere and the work on cloning to fool natural procreation process, etc. We have witnessed the natural disasters like cyclones and the painful catastrophe in Leh in recent times, it is time that we learn the lesson and confess that we are after all only one of the creatures on earth and take up our duty as stewards to make sure that the harmony which man and nature used to mutually enjoy can be amended. Human life and the ecology are not two separate things. They share the common destiny. A new ethics that is based on accountability and commitment must be revitalized so that life can be preserved and the beauty of natural environment restored.

This new ethics of responsibility emphasizes on accountability and commitment. Responsible persons conscientiously and consciously commit themselves to a task or form of life and readily accept accountability for its success and failure. A responsible person will not destroy or torture other living things under his control, even a tree, a wolf or a cow are not to be ignored. For a sustainable future, this ethics of responsibility cannot be neglected. We have no right unless we are committed to be responsible of what we do. Applying this ethics to our environment emphasizes on three things:

conservation, restoration and preservation. Conservation is to save, restoration to amend what has been broken and devastated and preservation to protect anything from distinction.

Notes

1. Although the concept of sustainability has been around for a long time, it became more widely used in the 1980s. Back in 1983, the Secretary-General of the UN established a commission called the World Commission on the Environment and Development. This commission is frequently referred to as the Brundtland Commission, after Gro Harlem Brundtland, the head of the commission and formerly the Prime Minister of Norway. As a result, the Brundtland Commission came up with this definition of sustainable development which emphasizes meeting needs, not just now, but in the future as well. (Source: *Our Common Future*, p. 8)
2. Hegel, G.W.F. (1965). *The Phenomenology of Mind*, Vol. 2, p. 269.
3. *Ibid.*, 257.
4. "For a profound analysis of this question in all its aspects", see R. Guenon (1953). *The Origin of Quantity and the Signs of the Times* (trans. Lord Northbourne), London.
5. Lasch, Christopher (1991). *The Culture of Narcissism*, New York: W.W. Norton, p. 239.
6. Herrigel, E. Zen. *In the Art of Archery*, R.F.C. Hull, trans. New York: Random. 1953/71, pp. v-vi.
7. Heidegger, M. (1962). *Being and Time*, J. Macquarrie and E. Robinson. Trans; New York: Harper and Row, p. 56.
8. Huajin, Zhang (2006). "Quality of Man and Social Progress", In: "*Chinese Cultural Traditions and Modernization*", (Eds.) Wang Miaoyang, Yu Xuanmeng and G.F. McLean, Council for Research in Values and Philosophy, Washington DC Vol. 4, p. 123.
9. "I am indebted to Professor Seyyed Hossein Nassr's book", *Man and Nature: The Spiritual Crisis of Modern Man*, Unwin Paperbacks, Mandala edition, 1976, chapter 3, *Some Metaphysical Principles Pertaining to Nature*; pp. 81-113.
10. Crocker, David A. (1992). "Functioning and Capability: The Foundations of Sen's and Nussbaum's Development Ethic", *Political Theory*, 20(4), November, pp. 584-612.
11. Marsh, G.P. (1967). *Man and Nature*, Cambridge, MA: Harvard University Press, p. 43.
12. Freud, S. (1984). *Civilization and Its Discontent*, New York: Penguin Modern Classis, p. 11.
13. Tai, M.C. (1985). *Between Ecology and Theology*, Taipei: Yiongwang, p. 98.
14. Holy Bible, *Book of Genesis*, chapter 11, verses 1-9.

Index